The
SILENT
STEPPE

The
SILENT
STEPPE

The Memoir of a Kazakh Nomad under Stalin

MUKHAMET
SHAYAKHMETOV

Translated from the Russian by Jan Butler

Overlook/Rookery
New York, New York

THE SILENT STEPPE

This edition first published in The United States of America in 2007 by
The Rookery Press, Tracy Carns Ltd.
in association with The Overlook Press
141 Wooster Street
New York, NY 10012
www.therookerypress.com

Cataloging-in-Publication Data is on file at the Library of Congress

Printed in the United States of America
FIRST EDITION

ISBN 1-58567-955-0
ISBN-13 978-1-58567-955-3

1 3 5 7 9 8 6 4 2

Maps drawn by Jennifer Skelley

CONTENTS

LIST OF ILLUSTRATIONS

Starting after page 178:
Part of a Kazakh family's train on seasonal migration.
A late 19th century painting of a Kazakh family's horse and camel train.
The last migrations, in 1927.
Construction of a summer yurt in the 1920s.
A Soviet Party official harangues nomadic Kazakhs in 1929.
Certificate recording membership of the 'Kossky' Farm Labourers' Union.
Enforced settlement was accompanied by attempts at mechanisation.
Milk yield from a single cow is delivered in a standard pail.
Feodor Goloshchekin, Stalin's Party chief for the territory.
Families awaiting deportation by rail.
The author in Red Army winter kit in 1941.
The author with a school friend in 1938.
The author with a cousin in 1939.
Mukhamet Shayakhmetov's family.
The author at school *c.* 1937.
The author wearing the medals awarded to him for services to education, together with his military medals.

Maps:

INTRODUCTION

The educated world knows little – if anything at all – of the suffering of the nomadic peoples of central Asia under the rule of Stalin and the policy of collectivisation launched in 1929: least of all, of Kazakhs whose immemorial habitat comprised that vast swathe of steppe-land from the Eastern shores of the Caspian to the great Tien Shan range of mountains which, with the Altai range to the north, forms the frontier of Kazakh territory, and today's Kazakhstan, with China. During that period the population of indigenous Kazakhs fell by approximately 1.2 million from death by starvation. Over the whole of the first decade and a half of effective Soviet Communist rule, from – say – around 1923, some 1.75 million Kazakhs out of a previous population of around 4 million were lost by starvation or execution or, in the case of about a tenth of that number, by flight to other countries in the region, notably China, Afghanistan and Iran. This is a story of willed catastrophe, on a scale of ideological horror unequalled even in the total record of Stalin's tyranny, and only subsequently surpassed by Mao Tse-tung and Pol Pot.

It comprised not only the massacre of people in vast numbers but the destruction of a nomadic culture and way of life of antiquity such as defined in essence the Kazakh nation. In today's terms, it would unquestionably justify the accusation of genocide. It is a matter of joyful irony that it was the Leninist principle of recognising, within the ruthless matrix of his Marxist empire, the factor of ethnic 'nationalities', with their puppet governments of indigenous Soviet toadies and their phoney territorial autonomies, which has resulted today in the Republic of Kazakhstan, the ninth biggest country in the world, no less, and no less than the major economic presence in central Asia with its vast capital of Caspian oil, and with a population of more than 14 million of which over half is of Kazakh blood. Blood carries memories; and today

Kazakhs are, to a man and a woman, the descendants of that remnant who somehow survived the privations of the appalling period this book covers.

The Kazakh people were no strangers to Russian persecution and exploitation. For three quarters of a century prior to the time when Mukhamet Shayakhmetov was born (1922), Russia had been established as colonial authority across all Turkic-speaking central Asia (less the Uighurs of Sinkiang), involving the Kazakhs, Kyrgyz, Turkmens and Uzbeks; and indeed their Farsi-speaking neighbours towards the Afghan border, the Tadjiks. All are of Moslem adherence, converted at various points from the seventh century onwards, albeit some of them quite recently and fairly loosely. They had a sustained if secret allegiance to their shamanistic inheritance, which in turn had coloured that combination of Buddhist, Zoroastrian and Nestorian Christian amalgam comprising what today we term 'tengrism': a faith in the unity of creation with Man at its centre and in communion with it, and of Man as the inheritor of a potential gift of ecstatic enlightenment. All this was mystically exercised among the Kazakhs in the rituals of their immensely ancient nomadic and transhumant existence, based upon their horse- and camel-borne economy of herding sheep and goats across the vast breadth of the steppe, and subject to a climate of extreme conditions, especially in winter. With it came an oral tradition of song and saga and poetry, and a flowering in the written corpus of work of the Kazakh Abai Kunanbaev, who had died in 1904. To all this young Mukhamet Shayakhmetov was a devout heir. His was a way of life traceable down the centuries from the Scythians of Greek mythology and classical times, from the panning of gold by the sacred (and secret) means of the fleece, and indeed from the techniques of domesticating the wild horse for human transportation, first devised on these very steppes some seven thousand years ago.

From early in their colonial intrusion, the Russians had sought to break, or at least override, the traditional Kazakh nomadic life and defiant clan allegiances, its lines of authority descending from its various Khans, and the complex weave of its three *zhuzes* – of the

Senior of the partially settled south and south-east, containing their ancient cities; the Middle *zhuz* of the families and clans of which Mukhamet Shayakhmetov was a part, in the north-east and north of Kazakh territory; and the 'Junior' *zhuz* of the west. In the mid-nineteenth century the Russians had offered to protect the steppeland inhabitants from the ravages of Jungarian invaders from across the Eastern mountain borders of what is today Chinese and Mongolian territory. Their price was an unwanted colonial control and Russian settlement which, by 1854, had become energetic and determined.

From their base in Fort Verny, soon to be renamed Alma Ata (today's Almaty), Tsarist Russia presided over relentless resettlement of Russian peasantry. All Kazakh land serving the nomadic way of life was deemed to belong to the Russian state. The newcomers were invariably and advisedly armed. In 1880, the Russian commander at Fort Verny declared, as he said, in the 'requirement of sincerity' that 'Our business here is a Russian one, first and foremost, and all the land populated by the Kazakhs is not their own… The Russian settled elements must force them off the land or lead them into oblivion.' At the same time, the territory of the Kazakhs (or Kyrgyz, as they were commonly termed, in the absence of distinction from their ethnic neighbours settled in the mountains of the extreme southeast of the territory), was used as a dumping ground or place of exile for those elements or individuals St Petersburg deemed subversive. Those exiled included the novelist Feodor Dostoevsky, dispatched to Semipalatinsk, the main urban centre of the territory covered by the story of this work, and Taras Shevchenko, the Ukrainian writer and poet, to Mangyshlak.

By 1916, six years before Mukhamet Shayakhmetov's birth and two years into the conflict in which Russia was locked with Germany, the Kazakhs rose in steppe-wide revolt against their Russian masters. No fewer than 385,000 Kazakhs, the cream of the entire generation of males, were to be drafted into the Tsarist army, to provide backing for the front line against the Kaiser's armies. In 1914-15 alone, 260,000 head of Kazakh livestock were 'requisitioned' by the Russians without a kopek of compensation. Seizing that moment of evident vulnerability in St Petersburg, a group of Kazakh patriots, headed by the nationalist intellectuals of Alash Orda, raised the flag of Kazakh independence. The rebellion was ruthlessly quelled. Thousands of patriots died, thousands more fled: a few, awaiting execution, were saved by the revolution of February 1917, which ended Romanov Tsarist rule, and led to Russia's withdrawal from the Great War.

For a tumultuous year or two following Lenin's putsch of November 7, 1917 – the 'Great October Socialist Revolution' – it seemed that a renewed surge by the Kazakhs, allied to the Whites, would achieve the people's independence. But slowly the Reds gained the upper hand, and with the arrival of the fifth Red Army under General V Frunze, submission to Marxist-Leninist rule from Moscow became the ineluctable reality for the whole of the former Tsarist central Asia. In 1923, the year before Lenin's death, two of the darkest figures of early Communist rule across the Soviet empire were posted to Kazakhstan. One was Nikolai Yezhov, founder of first Lenin's – and soon afterwards, Stalin's – secret police, OGPU; the other was Feodor Goloshchenkin, who five years earlier had participated in the gratuitous murder of the entire Romanov royal family of Russia at Ekaterinburg. Their brief was to consolidate the grip of the Party on the region. They succeeded. Goloshchenkin remained to develop and sustain the Communist regime in Kazakhstan which in 1928 was instructed to implement the 'collectivisation' and enforced settlement of the entire population of the steppes, exclusively ethnic Kazakhs. This destruction of an ancient way of life and a subtle and successful economy was accompanied by the liquidation of all social distinctions (except in so far as it applied to the new Party hierarchy), the enforced introduction of monetary exchange over against traditional barter, and confiscation of all 'kulak' land or flocks and their 'redistribution'. The winter of 1926-27 had experienced a peculiarly evil *jut*, the climatic phenomenon where a freeze follows a spring-time thaw and the animals' pasturage, while visible, is frozen under an impenetrable film of ice. Herds and flocks were catastrophically diminished when, the next year, collectivisation was promulgated. The policy was imposed under a regime of terror. The grain yield plummeted, animals in their thousands died; hunger was rampant and famine had descended upon the entire rural population. In one year alone (1933) 33,000 Kazakh men and women were convicted and sentenced (sometimes to death) for attempting to hide grain or meat to feed their own families.

Such was the political and social background of the personal story of the boy, so remarkably to survive, who as an old man – now in his eighties – he unfolds here: the record of his own experience kept faithfully throughout those terrible years, and up to his recruitment into the Red Army and his participation in the defence of Stalingrad. It is a document virtually unique, and of unchallengeable honesty and exactitude, first produced in a version in Russian under the title *Sudba* ('Destiny') and printed in Kazakhstan in 2002. Under the deft guidance of his editor, Anthony Gardner, and the skilled translation of Jan Butler, Mukhamet Shayakhmetov has now given access to an English-speaking readership worldwide to the full narrative which seems destined to be treasured as a key resource in the annals of his fellow Kazakhs and their emerging nation.

Kazakhstan was projected, blinking, into independent nationhood in 1991, following the extraordinary events of August that year, and the then virtually powerless Mikhail Gorbachev's 'suspension' of the activities of the Russian Communist Party. Up to as late as December of that year it was widely expected that the USSR's constituent 'Republics' would remain within a Russian-dominated union. Such was not to evolve. It was to be full independence for Kazakhstan and all the constituent republics of equivalent status.

As for the great steppe-land, the eternal Kazakh heartland, collectivised agriculture never succeeded. The yields of animals for meat and milk and wool or hides never recovered. By the death of Stalin, 1953, vast areas of steppe were unproductive and virtually uninhabited. The following year, to great fanfare, Nikita Khrushchev launched the 'virgin lands' scheme – *tselinny kray* – by which vast stretches of northern Kazakhstan were to be settled by 350,000 drafted-in Russian, Belorussian and Ukrainian peasantry, and to grow immense harvests of wheat. The rainfall and soil fertility were not sufficient to sustain the early promise; even so, Kazakhstan remains to this day a significant exporter of wheat. Meanwhile, in the northeast, that same Kazakh territory where the story of *The Silent Steppe* was played out, Stalin had allocated 18,500 square kilometres, the Semipalatinsk Polygon, for the detonation of what – over forty years – was to amount to 470 nuclear bombs, leaving a legacy upon the local population of cancer, leukaemia, stillbirths, and congenital deformity not yet entirely eradicated.

Of the nomadic way of life, a fragment – perhaps some 5 per cent of the stock-rearing population – has to this day still survived, or has resumed something akin to the old way of life. These Kazakh nomads are to be found in the arid far south-west of the country. Farming in Kazakhstan has been formally privatised, and has struggled back to profitable production, albeit patchily, usually as quite large-scale agro-business. The Kazakh nomads of the 'Junior' *zhuz,* of the semi-desert region west and north of the Aral Sea (itself an ecological disaster as a result of the theft of its tributary waters for the sake of Uzbekistan's now defunct cotton plantations), are still to be found erecting their yurts and foregathering in their auls, moving their flocks from one remote region of grazing to another. The herders themselves are vehicle-borne now, not horse-borne. With the freeing of markets they have lately come to flourish, with a high yield per head of animal (often the Karakul sheep), adhering to the remnant structures of family and clan, and benefiting from the long neglect of ancient Kazakh pastures. They are the living relic of a way of life and inheritance of spirit into which Mukhamet Shayakhmetov was born in the far north-east reaches of their homeland territory, some 85 years ago, and which this gallant author so poignantly illuminates and vivifies on behalf of all his nation in his intensely personal, microcosmic account of its devastation.

Tom Stacey

PROLOGUE

The Fugitive

Late Summer, 1930.

It was two days since our aul, or nomadic clan, had migrated from the summer pastures high up in the Altai range's foothills to the natural shelter of the Karagash just east of the Irtysh river where we usually stopped at this time of the year. The dense tussocks of grass were so tall and springy – some of them waist-high to an adult – that they could trip a child up and knock him to the ground. As the cool evening closed in, the summer air grew denser and the gathering darkness blanked nearly everything out; but I was still able to see three silhouettes hurrying through the fading twilight from our yurt to the one next door.

After catching and tethering the lambs of the ewes that were going to be milked, and finishing off the evening chores I was set as an eight-year-old, I returned to our tent and found my mother sitting all alone. Softly, as though fearing we might be overheard, she whispered to me, 'The Chief Aga has arrived.'

Then I realised that the silhouettes had been those of my grandmother and my two elder sisters, on their way to meet my Uncle Toimbai.

He was my father's half-brother, and the head of our clan. His real name was Shayakhmet, but according to an age-old custom of ours, my mother was not allowed to call her husband's male relatives by their real names, but had to invent other ones for them instead. The names, chosen at the time of marriage, were not only terms of endearment, but indicated how closely the person was related to her husband, and his age. In keeping with tradition, we children of Toimbai's younger brother added the Kazakh word for 'grandfather' – 'ata' – to his name and called him Toimbai-ata. The other children in the aul must have copied us because they called him that, too.

Toimbai-ata was the oldest person in our aul, and the wealthiest. He was a naturally taciturn and gentle man, but his opinion and will were accepted unquestioningly by all the members of our clan. Unlike the other elders, he never abused his status by using his authority to override other people's wishes, or interfering unnecessarily in his kinsmen's affairs. In the communal organisation of the aul, he was responsible for all the livestock, making sure that they were properly grazed and calculating the time and duration of each journey between stopping places in summertime. For two years after the Soviet authorities had banned privately hired labour, he had also taken turns with all the other men in grazing the communal flock of sheep in three-day shifts.

It was a whole year since Toimbai-ata had been in our aul. He was very fond of children and always used to spoil me, and as it was very rare for us not to see a relative for such a long time, I had missed him terribly. So I immediately rushed over to my uncle's yurt, dashing across the yard and through the doorway, where I caught sight of Toimbai-ata in the middle of the tent, hugging my grandmother. Although he was sixty years old, he was sobbing convulsively as he quietly repeated two words over and over again: 'Mother! Darling!'

It was the first time I had seen grown-ups crying inconsolably, and it upset and baffled me. Where, I wondered, had my uncle come from? Where had he been for so long that people had grown tired of waiting for him? And now they had seen him, why were they crying so bitterly?

But I also felt embarrassed. I knew that the previous autumn my uncle had been classified as a kulak or class enemy of the Soviet regime, had all his property confiscated, and been sentenced to two years' imprisonment. And now here he was a year later, returning home like a thief in the night, under the cover of darkness.

PART ONE

CLASS ENEMY

Above: *Modern-day Kazakhstan*

Below: *Soviet Central Asia in the Stalin era*

Chapter One

The Life We Lost

For as long as anyone could remember, a stock-breeder's entire life in the steppe had been bound up with his animals. Our people always looked after them with great care, because they were our main livelihood, and we knew just about everything there was to know about rearing them. The death of even one of them was always treated very seriously: a kid accidentally strangling itself on its tether would cause great consternation, and the whole family would mourn the loss of a favourite horse or camel, because they were the main means of transport and work force in a nomadic household. Relatives and friends would solemnly express their condolences, just as if a member of the family had died, and help them to cover their loss. The Kazakh nomads could not imagine an existence without their livestock: they knew of no other kind, and believed that to be left without their animals would mean certain death.

The pattern of our year was dictated by the needs of our herds and flocks. In order to provide enough grazing for them, we were always on the move between pastures, following routes established by our forefathers. In the south and south-west of Kazakhstan, migration to the abundant summer pastures could mean a journey of over a thousand kilometres. For us in the eastern, mountainous part of the country, the distances were smaller: 150 to 200 kilometres, divided into stages of five kilometres upwards. Each move had to take into account the stamina of our animals – particularly the ewes, which could usually cover no more than twenty kilometres in one day.

Each move was like a festival, especially for us children; everyone was happy, and dressed up for the occasion. The caravan was headed by the most respected woman of the aul, who rode on a horse, leading the camels which carried her family's possessions. These animals are very obedient, and quietly followed the leader. The other women came next, also leading pack camels, in a long line accompanied by two men who acted as guides. The rest of the men would drive the flocks separately from the caravan, and the young people would play along the way, racing one another on horses, singing songs, and picking flowers and wild berries.

These moves were made as a rule at warm times of year, and followed the seasons exactly. The first were in early spring from winter camps to places known as 'spring/autumn stopping places of the aul'. These were light dwellings, suitable for habitation in early spring and late autumn – though most of the stock-breeders preferred to put up their yurts and live in those. Here lambing took place; then, after a month or six weeks, when new-born lambs were old enough to travel small distances, there would be a move to new pastures, up to ten kilometres away. In another month – around the middle of June, when the hot summer days came – the nomads headed up into the mountains, or else further north. By the beginning of July they had reached their final destination – cool summer pastures with plenty of grass – and would remain there till mid-August, though they would continue to move their flocks between meadows.

The first part of the return journey would take them down to the lower slopes of the mountains. Then, in early September, with the weather becoming cooler in the lowlands, they would head onto the steppe, staying there until the end of October, with occasional short moves to different pastures: we called one of these a *zhayau kosh*, or 'migration on foot'.

On the eve of the winter, people settled again in the stopping places they had used in the spring. Only when the first snowfall came in mid-November would they move into their winter dwellings, where they would remain until March and the beginning of the next nomadic cycle. This final move was always left as late as possible, in order to conserve the winter pastures.

These moves were easy for us, as they had been developed to a fine art, and the whole business of dismantling the yurt, packing what was needed for summer living and loading it onto a camel could be managed in an hour or an hour and a half.

The yurt was made up of a frustrum-shaped wooden frame consisting of long poles, and panels woven from osiers. The size could be increased simply by adding more panels, if the owner was wealthy enough. The tops of the poles were inserted into a canopy of withies, creating a dome, and the frame was then covered with a large waterproof felt mat. The temperature could be regulated by opening or closing the dome as required.

As for our winter houses, these were simple affairs made from stones, clay bricks or logs. Each had a flat roof and consisted of two or three rooms, or simply one big room for all members of the family. In the one-room houses people would spend the night in different corners, separated by curtains. It was even more hugger-mugger in the yurts.

The floor, whether in a yurt or in a house, would be covered with a felt mat decorated with patterns and thick enough to ensure protection from cold and moisture. Homespun rugs were also used for warmth and decoration. At mealtimes, the whole family would sit at the *dastarkhan* (a low table) in winter, or around a tablecloth spread on the floor in summer.

Nomads had almost no furniture in its present-day meaning, apart from their dinner table, wooden beds, and chests and boxes for storing household things and food. The yurts were even more sparsely furnished than their houses, because they left as much as they could behind in their winter dwellings to minimise the burden on the camels.

Once a week we washed in a bathhouse. There was usually one

of these for each winter or autumn/spring stopping place, though there might be two if there were a lot of yurts based there. They were far from perfect, each heated by a stone fireplace which filled the place with smoke. In the summertime, a temporary bathhouse would be erected wherever we stopped, using a frame covered with floor mats.

Around our winter houses were pens for sheep, camels and oxen – but not for horses, who stayed in their pastures day and night throughout the winter, clearing the snow with their hoofs to reach the grass beneath. The other animals would be let out during the day and brought back to the pens at night. Stopping-places were usually chosen for their light snowfall, or for their situation at the foot of a mountain where frequent winds would blow the snow clear. Nomads did not put aside a stock of fodder for winter, except for the possibility of a couple of horses or animals falling sick. There was always the danger that in severe winters large numbers of animals could die of starvation – a devastating blow to their owners.

On arrival at the spring stopping places, wheat and other crops would be sown in fields some distance away from our pastures. Then, when we returned in the autumn, most of the men and youths would go off to harvest them and make hay. The men generally would not return home at all while they were busy harvesting, and those of them who did come back for a short while would return to the fields the following morning. The older women were left in charge of the aul, along with the old men and children who were unable to manage the heavy field work. The tough, older boys would graze the livestock and look after them under the supervision of the old men. They had a great many duties, such as herding the sheep out to pasture, keeping an eye on the calves, watching the kid goats whose mothers were still being milked and the foals which – unlike in summer – were allowed to run with the herd, attached by a rope to their mothers' necks, and graze in the steppe.

I learnt to ride at the age of five, and my father encouraged me from early on to get used to taking a horse out on my own. He would send me on errands to relatives or friends, and when a regional official came to visit the area and needed to borrow a horse to get to the next aul, I would sit behind him and then ride it home. I used to undertake these journeys with great eagerness and pride, and my father rewarded me with enthusiastic praise.

Every two hours from morning until nightfall, the mares had to be herded back to the aul and milked and then driven out to pasture again – and the boys were expected to do all this work as well as catching the foals every morning. The horses were hard to round up in the chilly mist after the night's rain: when they got near the aul, they suddenly got excited and sometimes spun round and galloped back into the steppe. This caused the old men and women and young boys a lot of extra work: it seemed as though the herd could sense there were no young men around in the aul to chase after them on their fast horses and yell commands at them. This is how our great Kazakh poet, Abai, described the picture in the autumn steppe he had probably seen ever since his childhood:

> Cold storm-clouds spinning darkness,
> Swathe the bare mountain crags in mist,
> And herds of horses in the pasture frolic
> In the frost or drowsy, droning heat.

For us boys, the hardest and most worrying work, apart from grazing the flock of sheep, was looking after the kid goats. Usually born in early spring, the kids would spend the summer grazing with the lambs, which were also separated from their mothers all day during the summer while they were still being milked. In autumn the kids were kept apart from the lambs. They were not as docile as the lambs and harder to graze, because they were always darting about and never stood still. It was difficult to tell whether they were just searching for new grass in the pasture or simply restless by nature and had to keep racing off somewhere.

If you didn't keep your eyes trained on them, they would be gone in a flash and completely disappear. They were particularly hard to manage on windy days. The dry autumn wind was their idea of heaven. They could quickly bunch together in the wind and then, as if something had taken hold of them, dart off all together in the opposite direction to the wind, jostling each other, nibbling at the tops of the grass as they ran. And then before you knew it, they had disappeared from sight and you wouldn't be able to catch up with them on foot. Sometimes they would all wander off far into the steppe and fall prey to wolves – in which case, the boys in charge of them would be sure to get a beating.

These were the jobs all the boys in the aul had to do. But I also had some duties that others didn't. For instance, I used to graze the communal flock two days in row while the other boys only grazed them for one day at a time, since we had twice as many sheep as the others. Even before my father sent me at the age of eight to graze the communal flock, I had already worked as an 'apprentice' shepherd for three years, for I had sometimes been asked by the elders to take charge of the flock for a couple of hours a day.

To begin with, I was really happy to do this work as it seemed so important and made me feel grown-up: I used to stride boldly out into the steppe on my own with the 700 sheep in the flock and drive them back to the aul in good time, proud of myself for managing an adult's job. But as I grew older, the only thing I enjoyed about grazing the sheep was that I could spend the whole day on horseback in the steppe. Pretending you were riding round the flock, you could gallop about as much as you liked, even though it was strictly forbidden for a nomad to gallop and tire his horse out needlessly. If you happened to meet another boy on horseback also grazing a flock, you could have races with him.

While men had overall responsibility for the animals and crops and providing fuel and other necessaries, women were kept busy at home. Contrary to the established Western idea of women in oriental countries, they enjoyed extensive rights, and often became the head not only of the family but of the whole clan. Nevertheless, although they were not expected to do heavy physical work such as building and ploughing, their chores occupied them from early morning until late evening. These included anything to do with dairy produce: they spent three to four hours every day just treating the milk, in addition to milking all the cows and ewes twice a day. They were also in charge of cooking, looking after the children, tanning, felt-making, weaving and sewing.

Meat was the most important part of our diet – though in the summer we tended to eat more dairy produce – and Kazakh women excelled at cooking it. Another staple was millet, which was God's gift to a farmer, since it required comparatively few seeds, was drought-resistant, and stored well. Our traditional millet recipes are rarely used nowadays because they are so difficult and time-consuming. Cooking it in a cauldron and then husking it in a mortar would take several hours, until the grains – known as *tary* – were pearly-white and deliciously crunchy, light and crumbly. They could then be served with butter, cream, milk or simply on their own; they could be made into porridge or added to cream and meat-based soups. A favourite dish was *tary* soaked in warm milk and served with a topping of sour cream; another delicious version of this was to pound it in a mortar with the raw fat of sheep's tail and serve it with tea. It was often flavoured with curd cheese, sugar or honey and then boiled in animal fat and served as a sweet cake to guests at special family celebrations. Sadly, even with all the high-tech expertise available today, no husking machinery has been adapted to process Kazakh millet, so *tary* has fallen out of favour.

Then there were clothes to be made and mended. Most were made from homespun wool, or leather from the skin of our animals (though we also bought factory-made material for things such as underwear and bedding). My winter outfit included a fur coat, wide leather trousers made from ewe skin, and a warm astrakhan hat.

Traditionally, children seldom received much education, since the teachers were mullahs who gave learning the (Arabic) Koran by heart precedence over more practical things. Following the Revolution, the mullahs were banned from teaching, and conventional Soviet schools introduced instead. We nevertheless continued to observe our faith, praying five times a day to Mecca, though the scattered nature of the steppe aul made it impossible to come together regularly in a mosque.

Although we worked hard, there was one free day a week – Friday – and we celebrated various holidays throughout the year, including New Year and the opening and closing day of the farming season. There were also special occasions such as the birth of children, the celebration of a baby's first step, the initiation of a boy as a *dzhigit* or young warrior, and weddings (lasting, as a rule, for several days). Any of these would involve relatives, friends and acquaintances from nearby and more remote aul. In addition, our two-month stay in the mountain meadows was for most men a time of relaxation – and every movement of the aul to a new stopping place was considered a holiday. We would celebrate with folk songs and music, competitions for improvising poetry, and different kinds of sporting contests.

This is how life was while I was growing up in our small aul, with its half-dozen yurts belonging to close relatives. But the Soviet authorities brought it all to an end when they introduced collective farms, and gave the terrible name 'kulak' to my father and Uncle Toimbai.

Chapter Two

My Uncle's Trial

The authorities' drive to dispossess the kulaks – destroying well-off peasant holdings by confiscating their livestock, land and property and deporting the owner and his family from their home – began across the USSR in 1928, and reached the remote regions of Southern Altai and the upper reaches of the River Irtysh in the autumn of 1929. Those of the wealthy people in the aul who recognised the threat set off with their families and possessions in search of safety – some of them crossing the border into China, where the Government not only allowed them to settle but offered them exemption from tax for three years. Others, however, somehow hoped that they would not get caught up in the policy. Yet it hit most of them like a bolt from the blue. In our family, we were caught quite unawares by the alarming news that Uncle Toimbai had been arrested and was likely to be put on trial the very next day.

The men in our aul decided to travel to the local courthouse to see and hear for themselves exactly what was going on there. I asked Mother (as Father was away from home) if I could go as well.

In those days the very notion of a person being convicted by an official court was practically unheard-of among Kazakhs. On this occasion six or seven well-off farmers from our group of villages (officially known as Administrative Aul Number Six of the Kumashinko-Altai rural district, Bukhtarminsk region, Semipalatinsk province) had been put on trial. A large number of people attended the court session, mainly *belsendi* (activists) from local aul who were carrying through the Soviet authorities' policies in the countryside. Relatives of the accused also attended, and so did quite a few people who were there purely for the curiosity value. There were those, too, who had heard that the kulaks' money, property and livestock were going to be confiscated and distributed to the poor, and had come in the hope of receiving a share of the spoils.

At that time there were no particularly rich Kazakhs living in the mountain regions of Southern Altai and the narrow valley of the River Irtysh. The wealthiest among them might own one thousand head of sheep, between one and two hundred horses and several dozen head of large-horned cattle and a few camels. The major landowners (or *bai*, as they were locally known) had been eliminated and deported to other parts of the country back in 1926. Now, three years later, the State set about eliminating and alienating the next group of well-off peasant farmers and nomadic stock-breeders by classifying them as kulaks.

In 1929 – hailed by Stalin and the Communists as 'the year of radical change' on account of the peasants' supposedly voluntary mass transition to collective farms – the Government's efforts to merge small-scale farm holdings into large units had not, in fact, received the support of the population as a whole. The peasants were not joining the collectives. The authorities put all the blame for this on the well-off peasants and decided that the best way of removing this obstacle was to destroy them. A draconian law set out the criteria for classifying an individual peasant as a kulak, defined by the size of the farm holding, by the size of the area under crops, by livestock numbers, the ownership of a single mechanical engine (mill, thresher, harvester, or mowing-machine), and even by the use of a single hired hand. On 1 May, 1929, the farm belonging to my Uncle Toimbai (who, according official calculations, was the most comfortably well-off among us) consisted of 350 head of sheep, three geldings, one stallion, two mares with their offspring from the past two years, five dairy cows, one working ox, four large-horned bullocks and four camels; he had sown no crops.

As an immediate way of eliminating kulak holdings, the authorities devised new taxes and obligatory in-kind deliveries of grain or livestock. The taxes were expressly exorbitant and unrealisable – in many cases they were several times higher than the total harvest or head of livestock on the holding. What is more, the time allowed for delivering the grain and livestock and paying off the tax was impossible to keep to. Failure to pay these taxes on time then resulted in the farmer being convicted of opposing Soviet policy, with draconian consequences.

Well-off nomadic Kazakh farmers who never went in for arable farming were expected to pay tax in the form of grain deliveries to the State, and so were forced to buy in grain from other farms. This meant having cash to pay for it, which was something nomadic farmers never had, since they were used to paying in kind; they were therefore forced to sell off their livestock as quickly as possible to get the cash to purchase the grain with. But inevitably, an increase in the amount of animals for sale caused their value to plummet; and since any livestock belonging to private individuals was being put in collective farms, very few people were interested in buying it.

Even if the livestock was successfully sold off or bartered, it took quite some time to amass sufficient grain to pay off the tax. Delays would occur and the deadline would pass; even if a farmer did manage to meet it, he was then presented with yet more demands, so that in the end some decided that they would never be able to pay everything they owed and simply stopped handing over their grain and livestock to the State. The authorities would respond by instigating criminal proceedings against them. Whether they refused or were simply unable to pay, their actions were categorised as anti-Soviet. Eventually the matter was resolved in court, where the farmer was sentenced to imprisonment and had all his property confiscated, while his family was deported some distance from their permanent home.

The trials of peasants officially classified as kulaks were conducted in a bizarre manner. The proceedings against the group of six or seven men from Administrative Aul Number Six, for instance, were held in a private apartment rather than a courtroom, and could be summarised like this:

Judge to the accused: 'Citizen X, you are accused of malicious failure to pay an obligatory tax to the Soviet State. You have committed the crime of refusing to obey Soviet laws. What do you say to this?'

Accused to the judge: 'I was ordered to pay tax in the form of grain deliveries. I did not sow grain myself. So I have no grain. I didn't have any money either. So I sold off some livestock and got hold of some money and then found some grain and bought it and delivered it to the State, but I didn't manage to do it all in time. I'd paid two taxes before; if I'm given more time and if I can find grain for sale, I'll pay this third tax as well.'

Judge to the second accused: 'You have tried to deceive the Soviet State. You mixed sand and grit in the grain you delivered to the State. Why did you do this?'

Accused: 'The grain I delivered to the State was bought from local people at market. When I was buying it, I carefully checked it for quality and purity. I delivered it myself to the man on duty at the collection point and it was top-quality and totally clean. It is not true that I deceived anyone. I swear it on my children...'

Judge to one of the witnesses for the prosecution: 'Did you receive the grain as an obligatory delivery to the State from the accused kulaks? What can you tell us about the quality of the grain you received from the suppliers?'

Witness to the judge: 'I did not do a quality check on it when it was delivered. Later, when the grain collected in various auls was delivered to the State procurement station it was discovered that the grain had sand and grit in it. These suppliers here, these enemies of the Soviet authorities and working people, had poured sand and grit into the bottom of the sacks of grain.'

Judge to the same witness: 'Give the full names of the accused seated in this courtroom who, with the intent of sabotaging and swindling the Soviet authorities, attempted to deliver grain adulterated with sand to the State.'

Witness: 'All the accused kulaks seated here deliberately did so.'

Those of us who witnessed the proceedings were astonished; some even dared to laugh. It was obvious that everything was designed to speed up the destruction of the well-off holdings in the villages with a total disregard for logic or the law.

The same day 'justice' was administered to the 'most recent enemies of the Soviet authorities, poorest peasants and former farm labourers'. The court's sentence read as follows: 'For malicious failure to fulfil specified deliveries of grain to the State, for sabotaging the State by adding sand and grit to grain delivered to the State, the persons listed by name below are deprived of their freedom and sentenced to two years of imprisonment. All their property – their livestock and domestic property – is to be confiscated. After serving their custodial sentence they will be deported for five years to a remote part of the country. This sentence is final and not subject to appeal and will take immediate effect.'

The convicted were escorted from the 'courtroom' under guard and shortly afterwards their families had all their livestock and domestic property, right down to cups and cutlery, confiscated. Within two days twenty 'class enemies' and 'exploiters' from the various auls had been sent under escort to be imprisoned in the town of Ust-Kamenogorsk (now Oskemen), 250 kilometres away.

Accustomed since time immemorial to a life of freedom and to the fresh air of the vast open spaces, these people of the steppe found it hard enough during the winter months when they were confined to their huts. They regarded life in town – from what they had heard of it – as hell, and were quite sure that incarceration in a prison cell could only mean death. It was therefore only natural for them to seek ways and means of escaping.

The method chosen by the authorities for transferring the

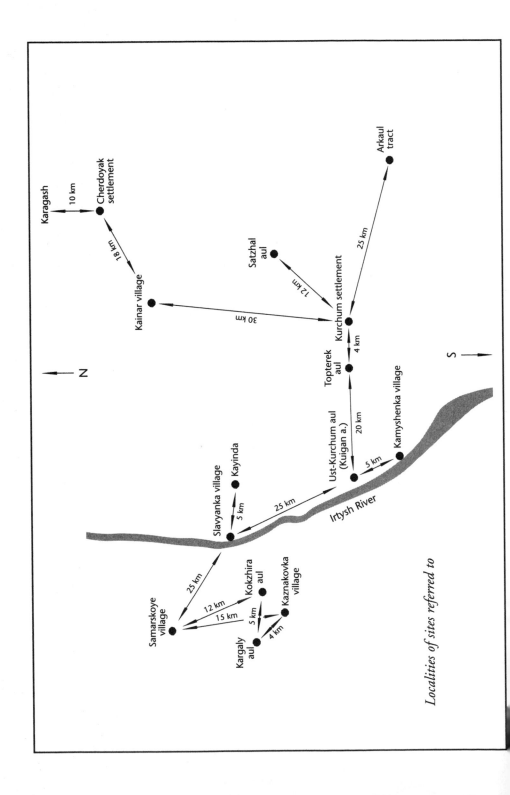

Localities of sites referred to

prisoners to Ust-Kamenogorsk made it easy for them. As they had no organised means of transport at their disposal, the court officials decided to send the group under escort on their own horses. And so, loaded with provisions, the men set off on horseback accompanied by two militia guards. After travelling some 25 or 30 kilometres, the group set up camp for the first night in the aul of Kayinda and were warmly welcomed by the local residents, many of whom were acquaintances and even relatives. The arrested men were put up in small groups in their friends' homes. The people of Kayinda offered them traditional hospitality as well as heartfelt sympathy for their situation.

The morning after their first night in the aul, none of the arrested men was anywhere to be seen and the two militia guards were lying with their hands and feet tied up. But none of the fugitives had any idea what to do now they were on the run: most could think of nothing better than to hide in the homes of friends and relatives in other auls close to home. Some collected their families and fled across the border to safety in China, but these were a small minority. Most did not wish to leave their homeland and hoped in vain to hide from the authorities nearby, with the support of their fellow countrymen and relatives.

Among these fugitives were Toimbai-ata and one of our cousins, Muksiin Nurmukhambetov. That night the two of them crossed over to the left bank of the River Irtysh, and found temporary shelter at the home of some distant relatives. They were convinced they had travelled far enough not to be recognised by any locals, whereas in actual fact they were only about thirty kilometres away from where they had escaped their guards, and seventy to eighty kilometres from their aul and families.

Their hope lay in the covert sympathy and support they were shown by ordinary people. It was no secret that most peasants did not support the Soviet authorities' policy of setting the poor against the well-off. The persecution of the kulaks and the coercion used to turn farms into collectives gave rise to deep discontent, and this led people to harbour fugitives as a form of protest. Nevertheless, within a short time most of the fugitives were recaptured. By staying on the run for a year before the night he reappeared at our aul, Uncle Toimbai-ata proved himself to be much the most resourceful.

He seemed safe among us to begin with. In late summer and early autumn there were few casual visitors to the aul, because most people were busy haymaking and tending to the ripening crops of corn. Only the elderly who were still able to watch over the communal livestock were left in the stopping places dotted across the steppe and lower foothills of the Altai mountains, and though they used to visit our aul to drink *kumys* (mare's milk), they were taciturn men, good at keeping secrets. If they saw Toimbai-ata they would pay their respects to him, and even advise him on how best to hide.

But after he had been with us for a month, his grey horse – which was well-known in the area – was spotted standing by the water hole with the communal herd, and seized by local activists; and though no one came looking for him in the days that followed, Toimbai-ata – discouraged by his loss and convinced of the futility of life as a fugitive – finally decided to give himself up to the authorities. They reaffirmed his sentence, and sent him to prison in the town of Zaisan.

Chapter Three

The Holy Yurt

Toimbai-ata's fellow fugitive Muksiin Nurmukhambetov had given himself up in the spring, but – because he was suffering from a severe lung infection after a winter on the run – the authorities soon released him and allowed him to return home. His presence among us was to cause unexpected problems for our annual migration to the summer pastures in the mountains.

The number of families in each aul had always been determined by the amount of livestock they had between them – the sheep in the flock and horses in the herd. In the summer months, there could be as many as one thousand sheep in the flock (including the new lambs), but only half as many in winter. If this number was exceeded, the grass in the pastures would be eaten too quickly and the weakest sheep in the flock, which ate only what the others left, would fall sick and die.

The need to stick to this size of flock forced the aul members to split the herds of horses and flocks of sheep in two. Consequently, the people who looked after them also had to split up. And so sons were separated from parents and one set of relatives from another, all creating new auls. These could range from two to ten yurts in size, which would be positioned a kilometre or several kilometres apart from the next aul, depending on the time of year and the grazing available.

According to the version of our family tree that had been passed down by word of mouth, our ancestors were descended from the Naiman tribe, once one of the principal tribes of the so-called Middle Zhuz of Kazakhstan. (Zhuzes were originally federations of tribes occupying different parts of the country, which in the sixteenth century took shape as three regions – the other two being the 'Senior' and 'Junior' Zhuz.) Long before, in the twelfth century, the Naiman had their own state – one of the most powerful of the time – extending from the lands of modern-day Mongolia to Southern Altai and the upper reaches of the River Irtysh. For many years the Naiman waged war against the Mongolian Tartar forces of Genghis Khan, but after finally being defeated at the turn of the thirteenth century, they fled to Central Asia, where they remained for 500 years. Their long and peaceful existence there was shattered when they were invaded by the Jungars from Chinese Turkmenistan in the early eighteenth century, and were forced to flee towards the western and northern lands of present-day Kazakhstan. As the Jungars were gradually expelled in the latter half of the eighteenth century, the Naiman chose to settle in the liberated lands of central and eastern Kazakhstan.

The key Kazakh figure at this time was the great leader Abylai Khan, who succeeded in uniting the country's various factions against the Jungars. Among his supporters were two of our ancestors, Barak and Zhandeli, who earned the title of 'batyr' (meaning 'heroic warrior'); both died of wounds received in battle, and after their deaths our family moved for greater safety to a region which was then part of China, on the east bank of the River Kurchum. It was only in 1881, when the State borders between the Russian and Chinese Empires were finally established, that our ancestors – known as the Otei kinsmen – became citizens of Russia.

Zhandeli's eldest son was called Myrzabai, and among his sons was my great-great-grandfather, Nauei. At the turn of the twentieth century Nauei's great-grandsons formed four independent aul with all the administrative and legal attributes of an organised nomadic community; but in 1916 they lost considerable numbers of clan members and livestock when many Kazakhs – aggrieved by the Tsarist regime's policies – emigrated to China. They were further depleted by the cholera epidemics of 1917-1918, and attacks by Jhut invaders in 1911 and 1918, so that at the beginning of the 1920s the four auls were forced to merge into two. Now, because each of these had lost members in the drive against kulaks, it was decided to merge them into one.

Traditionally, the whole aul would move to the summer pastures at the same time, and the families with insufficient saddle horses or pack animals (camels, oxen and sometimes horses as well) would borrow them from the wealthier ones. But now the livestock belonging to the two rich families had been confiscated by the State, there was no longer enough transport to go round. Rather than all remain behind in the stifling summer heat, the families whose kinsmen had been dispossessed decided to move to the summer stopping place in two goes. Part of the aul would move first, and then the necessary transport would go back and pick up the rest.

Among those left behind on the initial journey was Muksiin's yurt, since he was not well enough to complete the journey on horseback. But no one felt at all comfortable about this, because the yurt in question was held in particular reverence, having once belonged to Muksiin's grandfather, the holy Hadji Bayan.

The traditions of steppe Muslims included that of the so-called posthumous 'Hadj by default', whereby arrangements were made for a relative or other person to undertake a pilgrimage to the holy sites in the Arabian cities of Mecca and Medina on behalf of someone who had died. Of my great-great-grandfather Nauei's six sons, the youngest, Bayan, was the most prosperous, and after his death in 1907 his son hired a man who had experience of guiding pilgrims to make the Hadj for him. Unfortunately the man died in Mecca and never returned; but although there was no evidence that he had fulfilled all the conditions of the Hadj, the venerable title of Hadji was still posthumously conferred on Bayan.

In those days it was believed that the relics of such people had considerable power, and it became a custom for everyone in the area to cross the threshold of Hadji Bayan's yurt before starting any important business or embarking on a distant journey: there they would pray to his ashes and eat a meal in the blessed household. This was still the practice when Bayan's grandson became the head of the family. So when this venerated yurt was left behind instead of heading the migrating caravan as it should have done, everything seemed to have been turned upside down.

According to Kazakh custom, it was obligatory for relatives who shared the same great-grandparents to help one another when times were hard. (Even the seventh generation of a family considered one another to be brothers.) So the day after the first section of the aul had settled in its new stopping place, the elders from other aul who were all descended from Nauei and fourth-generation descendants of Myrzabai, gathered together in our yurt at the invitation of my father Shayakhmet, who was now the oldest man left in our clan.

Traditionally, when the elders got together to talk, the young children were expected to remain with them in the yurt. We were encouraged to listen to the adults' conversation, in the hope that we would find it edifying; and anyone with a sensitive ear and curious mind could certainly learn a great deal from their eloquence. I was among the assembled company that day, and I was struck by their brilliant figures of speech, their astute comparisons, their sayings and their proverbs, many of which were in verse and recited from memory.

Pouring fresh mare's milk into the bowl in front of each guest, my father began speaking: 'Honourable elders, older and younger brothers, it is perhaps the will of Allah or perhaps because of our mortal sins that an incomprehensible, grim time is now upon us and some people have started taking away other people's livestock, wealth and happiness. Remember the popular old saying: "God has no wealth. He gives it from one person to another". Well, it now appears to be true. The authorities and aul activists have taken everything away from the rich and handed it over to idlers and made some of us extremely poor overnight. Just such a misfortune has befallen the family of Hadji Bayan. So revered by us all, the blessed yurt belonging to the holy Hadji and all his grandsons and great-grandsons has been left behind on its own in the old stopping place. The Hadji's eldest grandson who now owns this yurt is laid up and seriously ill. In the good old days each and every one of us used to visit this blessed yurt to ask God and the Hadji's spirit for their blessing and assistance. All of you, all of Myrzabai's clan, have more than once received generous help in this yurt, first in Hadji Bayan's lifetime and more recently when it belonged to his son Mukshai and his grandson Muksiin. We have all felt the support and benevolence of the Hadji's spirit. The question now is how to move this yurt which has been left behind on its own, this yurt belonging to the Hadji and his grandsons and great-grandsons and the present head of the family, Muksiin, who is on his death bed, and bring it here to our aul along with the other yurts. I have invited you to hear your advice. What are your thoughts on this and how can you help in this matter which concerns all of Myrzabai's clan?'

It took a short exchange of opinions for the elders to settle the matter. They agreed that it was completely disgraceful for the yurt of the Hadji's grandsons to be moved last when the aul migrated: the other families found this abhorrent and sinful, and believed it might incite the wrath of the Hadji's spirit. And so it was decided to move the Hadji's yurt first whenever the aul migrated. It was also decided to assemble a number of young men the very next day and allocate them pack camels and horses to move the rest of the yurts, and to include several older people in this group – among them the mullah, so that he could appease the Hadji's spirit if need be.

Quite a long time was spent working out how to move the sick man. (In such cases a home-made stretcher was usually strung up between two horses: camels could not be used because they jolted their passengers about so much.) However, the very same evening that the helpers arrived with their carts to pick up the yurt that had been left behind, Muksiin passed away. The funeral arrangements then delayed the move for another few days.

Muksiin was only 33 years old. Either because it was my first experience of death in the aul, or because the adults mourned the death of their kinsman and the Hadji's descendant so profoundly, I have remembered that period of mourning all my life. It was possibly the very last time in an aul that the traditional funeral rite was performed almost in its entirety.

When the funeral procession came within half a kilometre of the aul, the widow of the dead man started weeping loudly and lamenting her loss. Echoing her, everyone else in the aul replied by wailing, 'Oi, baurym! Oh, beloved!' The women of the aul then began lamenting with incredible force. People from neighbouring aul added their voices to the lamentation. So deep were their expressions of grief that I can still hear them today.

When I remember it all now, I cannot fully understand why people subjected themselves to such a harrowing ritual and prolonged period of mourning, involving such heartrending cries and so many tears. The wailing was kept up for more than a day. And over the next few days, relatives, friends and acquaintances of the deceased came to our aul from far and wide. Each visitor to the household in mourning expressed their grief by lamenting bitterly as they embraced each and every member of the family, in keeping with tradition. In addition to all this, the women mourned the dead man with special two-part laments three times a day, just before sunrise and sunset and at midday. On this occasion the ceremony was performed by the widow and daughter-in-law, who extolled the noble and almost sacred descent of the deceased, his forebears' exploits and the exceptional nature of their most recent offspring. This was followed by an account of the deceased's singular merits and noble acts and how he had departed this life prematurely, and how his death was willed by God but caused by the new authorities' evil doings.

It was not, however, the Soviet Government itself, but the *belsendi* who were principally blamed for the tragedy. After all, it was argued, any authority is God-given, and so finding fault with it was a sin; but if it had not been for the activists, Muksiin would never have been persecuted or have contracted his fatal disease. The human emotion of pity was beyond the comprehension of godless people like them. They were wreckers.

The daily two-part laments weighed heavily on everyone's hearts, and the mournful words were hard to listen to – though at least they were never boring, since each was a new and skilfully improvised piece of poetry. For forty days they went on, always being performed exactly at the prescribed times; and whenever they took place, everyone in the aul had to stop what they were doing and listen to them.

Chapter Four

My Sister's Secret Wedding

The activists in every aul comprised a small group of young men from poor families who busily supported the Soviet authorities' class policy and tried to sow discord, even among relatives who had always lived in harmony and relied on mutual assistance in their close-knit community. These were people who sincerely believed all the slogans about the Soviet authorities 'empowering the poor, freeing them all from bondage', and 'granting them the same rights and privileges as everyone else'.

Most of the activists were illiterate. If a very small percentage of them could read and write, it was because some time in the past they had been taught by the poorly educated aul mullah. Some of these young men had learnt to recognise the letters of the alphabet and read words by the syllable at the short-lived schools which were set up to eradicate illiteracy. Only two of our activists had paid jobs: the chairman and secretary of the aul council. The rest worked on a voluntary basis, assisting the aul and rural district chairmen and all the other countless local and regional officials in the hope that if they showed enough enthusiasm, they might possibly land some kind of permanent job. They spent most of their time in the aul alarming the illiterate residents with made-up stories about impending upheavals which the authorities would surely be implementing. At the same time, they tried to impress upon the frightened people that they would intercede for them if need be.

In their daily lives and relations with the locals, they made no particular effort to introduce the Soviet authorities' new policies. They behaved arrogantly towards simple people, just like the officials of tsarist times. They would do deals with the landowners whenever it suited them, so betraying the interests of their political masters, and tried to line their own pockets any way they could. They used to intimidate not only the rich but also the poor and moderately well-off peasants, which was why they were so unpopular and often given derogatory nicknames.

It would be a distortion of the truth to say that all the activists were loathed by people in the aul. Some were serious and thoughtful, and always easy to get on with: they correctly understood the authorities' policies and people's aspirations, and explained the way things were in an intelligent and comprehensible manner. Most, however – because of their lack of education – interpreted the law as they saw fit. They deliberately went to extremes when conducting any campaign, exceeding State targets, and persecuted their fellow Kazakhs in order to impress the authorities. Just one example of their 'assistance' in introducing new laws is enough to illustrate how heavy-handed they were.

The Soviet authorities did quite a lot to give women equal rights with men and elevate their role in society. In particular, they liberated the women of the East from old customs such as polygamy and the obligation of a widowed woman in an aul to marry a relative of her late husband. They also introduced an undeniably progressive law banning so-called 'bride money' – the custom of a man's family paying for his bride.

Originally, this custom probably had a positive function. It was devised as a way of creating comfortable living conditions for a young couple who had just set up home on their own, and – along with the dowry paid by the bride's family – enabled her to be provided with clothing, bed linen, cooking equipment, household goods, somewhere to live, a new yurt and definitely a horse and camel, so that she arrived at her groom's house with the basic essentials for a nomadic way of life and could be independent, at least for the time being. However, with the passing of time, bride money acquired a new significance, and in the hands of certain greedy people often became a commodity and source of easy profit.

No sooner had the new law been introduced than the activists began to abuse it. Every time there was a wedding, they would see to it that it was denounced as a criminal act. They would insist that a payment must have been received for the bride, and ensure that the bride's father was prosecuted; the bridegroom would also face prosecution for buying his bride. And so, to avoid trouble, parents started marrying their daughters off in secret, without weddings. They would announce that their daughter had secretly run away from them; the groom's family, for their part, would then announce that their son had stolen the girl and brought her home and that they now had a daughter-in-law.

Another part of the wedding tradition was that the families marked the couple's betrothal by a verbal agreement sealed with a vow at a *dastarkhan* meal. As it happened, in 1929, our family had concluded just such an agreement concerning my sister Zhamba with a family from the Karauzhasssyk clan who lived on the other side of the River Irtysh. It had been mutually agreed to set the date of the wedding for the autumn of 1930, before the sheep shearing, since nomads usually organised major family celebrations to fit in with farm work and migration schedules. (The best times were after lambing, before the migration to the summer stopping place, or after the migration to the winter stopping place.)

As the time drew near for the groom to come for his bride, the tension started to mount in our family and all over the aul. It was mainly the fear of being accused of receiving bride money, and thus breaking the new marriage and family law; but what also alarmed people was the prospect of a young girl getting married without a wedding ceremony. Unless the customs were observed and rites performed, they believed, neither the bride nor the groom could be happy and prosperous in the future.

It was arranged that the groom would arrive secretly, under cover of darkness, accompanied not by his family or an entourage, but by a single friend. By the time he did so, there was not a single man left at home: they had all officially gone off till the following day to make hay and harvest the ripe cereal crops, so as not to be accused of collusion in the 'sale' of the girl.

The mothers of the aul also tried to get their children to sleep early that night, so that they would not witness the 'crime' about to be committed and perhaps later give away the secret. This included me, on the pretext that I had to go and graze the flock the next morning. Aware of the women's secret plans, I could not get to sleep; but not daring to disobey orders, I peeped over my blanket and watched what was going on. I was aware that I was about to part with my favourite sister and would no longer be able to see her every day.

Zhamba (the name means 'gold ingot' in Kazakh) had only turned eighteen the previous spring. She was the eldest child in our family and not only my parents' but the whole community's favourite. Besides being beautiful, she was skilled at all the duties that would be required of her as a housewife: Mother had taught her how to cut out clothes, sow and embroider and make everything usually found in a nomadic home, such as felt rugs and leather goods. Her graceful manners and the attention and respect she showed older people charmed everyone who knew her, as did her lovely singing. We were all sorry she was leaving.

As she was so young, she was naturally nervous about what the future had in store for her. She had heard of the miserable lives of girls who lost all their freedom once they were married off, and love for her future husband was tinged with fear and uncertainty about the unfamiliar house she would be entering. She felt even more anxious because she was being given away in this secret and seemingly unlawful manner and being deprived of all the usual wedding celebrations and fun and games. She tearfully said goodbye to each of her friends, who were also crying and saying, 'Oh, it's so sad! How shall we manage without you?' And then Zhamba replied sadly, 'Dear God, what sin have I committed against You? Why have you made these cruel laws for me and all the other girls like me, and where have these terrible times come from? Why am I being carried off from my home in secret, like a prisoner?'

Her friends told her, 'Such is the will of Allah! Do we really have a say in anything? We would do all we could to prevent this disgrace and injustice, but all we can do is cry. Instead of tormenting yourself, darling, accept the way things are. You have to leave in total secrecy for your parents' and loved ones' safety.'

After saying goodbye to the women, my sister crept over to where her two younger brothers and little sister were sleeping and started kissing each of us and weeping over us. When she realised that I was not asleep, she started sobbing even more. Kissing me and wetting my face with her tears, she whispered, 'Get Father's permission to come and visit me in a month's time!' I had no idea exactly where she was going or how I would get there, but I silently nodded in reply. Even then I was not allowed to get out of bed and go outside to see her off.

Chapter Five

The Last Autumn of the Nomadic Aul

At the end of 1930, and in the winter of 1931, the Kazakh people's age-old nomadic way of life finally came to an end. The clans were all joined together into collective farms, and each aul settled in one place for good. Many years have gone by since then, and we who experienced the joys and freedom of the wandering way of life tend to remember none of the hardships involved, but only the good things: the green carpet of meadows stretching out before us as we arrived at our summer stopping place, the unforgettable scent of the wild flowers and the blaze of colour they created all around, and the cool, fresh breeze blowing from the snowy peaks.

In autumn, when most of the men were busy with harvesting and haymaking, it was rare for people to come visiting, but once in a while groups of elders would do so for old times' sake, and sit around drinking mare's milk and discussing the issues of the day. Mare's milk was kept chiefly as a drink for guests, and it was very popular: at less busy times men would ride round the aul in groups every morning until midday, visiting the yurts with foals tethered outside to quench their thirst. Fermented in a specially made leather flask called a *saba*, the milk contains much less fat than that of cows and goats, and if well prepared has a sourish-sweet taste.

In 1930, the main topic of conversation was the daily news brought to the steppe by word of mouth (the so-called *uzyn kulak* – 'long ear' – of the steppe telegraph), which was our only source of information. Because we did not have radios or telephones, or even a postal service, it could take up to a year for information about new laws or important events to reach the far-flung regions of the country. The grandiose propaganda campaigns aimed at the masses had yet to get underway, and any news was passed on from one person to the next in the form of stories with a great many embroidered details. But in any case, ordinary people were more interested in local matters, and simply did not have the time or inclination to pay attention to things on a grander scale: all the elders wanted to find out about the new laws and orders issued by the aul council, since this was, as far as they were concerned, the highest authority in the land.

'What we used to call a "region" is now going to be called a "district".' Someone in the know would start the conversation along these lines, having just discovered what had been enacted two years previously.

'An official came to the aul council from this district centre and gathered together our activists and told them that all the people and their livestock and property, wives and servants, children and grandchildren were going to be collectivised and everything would belong to everyone,' another would announce to the alarm of everyone present.

'I've heard that all the people are going to be housed under one roof,' a third would say, 'and everyone's going to go to bed at the same time, and eat and drink together and get up at the same time. Everyone's going to be taken to work in a formation and then brought back in one.' And seeing that he had shocked his companions even more, he would beam with delight.

'It's not like that at all – I heard it with my own ears. They're only going to take away the horses and other working animals to use as transport, and people are going to get together and plough the land and sow wheat all together so that there is more wheat in the country. Maybe, who knows, there's some truth to it somewhere? When a lot of people get together to help someone hard up and work together at haymaking, say, or when a new crop is being harvested, everyone tries to work faster than the person next to them, and the work goes like a dream! You know, you've all done it yourselves. If you've got all sorts of machinery, and horses and oxen, and you get everyone to work together, the results are sure to be very good indeed.'

'I don't know about that: when a lot of people get together to do a job, the result is usually not much good. And when we went and helped out those people who were hard up, there were some slackers who didn't even bother to turn up.'

Yet another of the elders would interrupt, 'This society uniting all peasants has already got a name: it's going to be called a "commune". Before he died, Lenin instructed his aides to get all the peasants to join together. But the people who took over running the country from him forgot all about his instructions. Lenin's widow who, they say, is still alive, went to see Stalin – that's his name, apparently – who was left in charge and said to him: "Why have you comrades-in-arms of Lenin forgotten all about his instructions? Why aren't you joining the peasants together in collective farms and communes? If you don't obey the Leader's orders, you'll anger his spirit!".'

After hearing this story, one of the others would offer a logical conclusion of his own – 'As always, a woman's to blame for the trouble' – before someone else had the last word:

'Everything that's been said here is complete rubbish. And the bit about the collective farms and communes – they've all been thought up by the aul activists. What good is Lenin's wife to us lot here when all the power is in their hands? The power's completely gone to their heads and made them barking mad because they have no idea what to do with it. People who have never managed to run their own affairs are now in charge of people's lives. How can a society be run by people who never obeyed their grandfathers or listened to their wisdom? It reminds me of the old saying, "When there's no lord, a slave with take his place, and when there's no dog, a pig will guard the yard!"'

Such was our community's grasp of the innovations which were to change our lives in ways we could not even remotely imagine.

I still did not understand much about the events taking place in my aul, but I must have heard thousands of lengthy conversations like this one on all sorts of topics. We were always receiving visits from other people, whether neighbours or relatives and guests from other regions. This was partly because all our kinsmen made their mare's milk in our yurt, and partly because people came to pay their respects to my 85-year-old grandmother, who was held in very high regard.

Since we were frequently on the move, our neighbours kept changing as well. The summer pastures and winter stopping places were often far apart, so summer neighbours did not see each other all winter. To make up for it, kinsmen would meet up in their regular spring stopping place, and distant relatives and people from other clans would congregate in camps in the summer months. People would pay each other visits, exchange gifts and eat together – the entire aul would put on a big feast for another aul. In addition, the custom was that any aul recently settled in a new place had to help and support the next aul to arrive by preparing a hot meal and carrying it over to them, since they would be too busy unpacking to cook for themselves.

Our winter stopping place was situated in the territory of a branch of the Karagerei clan named after the 'six fair-haired Naiman', and outside the lands of our Otei clan. My grandmother Aksha was an Aknaiman by birth, from the eminent Konakbayev clan, so as soon as our aul arrived nearly all the most senior members of the Aknaiman family would visit our home to welcome her and wish us happiness and prosperity and rich grazing for our livestock. The village and regional centre of Kumashkino, now renamed Kurchum, was about twenty kilometres away, and members of the Aknaiman family would always stay with us on their way to and from the large market and fair held there every Sunday. And in the spring when our aul was going back to its clan's territory, there would be a similar influx of people wishing to say goodbye. This would continue for nearly a month, until the end of the breeding season.

Similarly, when summer came and we moved up into the hills, relatives and friends who had not seen each other for a whole year would start meeting up again. Communities of different families would live side-by-side during the summer months: the Bur clan would come from the south, descendants of the Zharke and Andagul clans from the west, and the Saryzhomart clan from the east – and they all made special visits to pay their respects to my grandmother. The most important visitors were treated not only to mare's milk, but to special portions of our winter stocks of meat which had been put by.

I remember two guests in particular. One was Mamyr Altybayev, who had governed the Kumashinko region in pre-Soviet days; the other was called Yestaulet Yesberdinov. They were descended from two of our great-grandfather Otei's sons, and Mamyr was the same age as Toimbai-ata, while Yestaulet belonged to my grandfather's generation.

Mamyr was a taciturn, stocky man with a grey-flecked, black beard and swarthy complexion. In his rare visits to different aul he was always accompanied by an entourage, just as he had been in the old days. His countrymen continued to respect him and pay him homage, though as a governor in tsarist times he had apparently kept the province on a tight rein, occasionally losing his temper and cracking his whip, and had not been averse to receiving 'gifts'. He was said to be particularly strict when it came to collecting taxes, and, once, when the members of Administrative Aul Number Seven were late paying, he had begun confiscating livestock and extracting fines despite pleas for clemency from some extremely impoverished families. The local aul poet Meirembai Baspakov had written a poem in response, saying that the governor had amassed quite enough for himself by taking extra taxes from the Taz and Zharylgap clans, and extracting more from a small number of very poor members of the Bur clan would not make him any richer.

Subsequently, in 1926, as a rich landowner, Mamyr Altybayev had all his stock confiscated and was deported to the town of Rubtsovsk, 200 miles north of Ust-Kamenogorsk. After escaping a year later, he secretly gathered together a great many relatives, including his children and grandchildren, and emigrated with them to China. According to people who saw him there, he led a modest life as a poor stock-breeder. One day, on the way to a neighbouring aul on his only horse, which was harnessed to a cart carrying his two daughters-in-law, he accidentally drove over the edge of a local landowner's crop while turning a fork in the road and got badly beaten up. The women burst into floods of tears and wailed, 'How could that filthy Chinaman dare lay a finger on you and injure your noble body?' To which, apparently, Mamyr replied, 'Never mind! It's made me think about the times I used a whip on the backs of my own countrymen.'

My family, and especially we children, always looked forward to seeing the other person we all held in great esteem, Yestaulet Yesberdinov. Every time he visited our yurt, he would bring grandmother a gift of a large lump of sugar shaped like a horse's head. As we hardly ever had sugar or, for that matter, any sweet foods, this was a great treat for us. Tall and lean, Grandfather Yestaulet had a long beard and always wore silver-framed glasses. He used to visit us as soon as our aul settled in the mountain meadows for the summer. As he stepped through the doorway, he would greet my grandmother, whom he had known since childhood, with the words, 'Hello, my ancient friend! Are you fit and well? '

Then they would greet each other in a traditional manner which is hardly remembered any more. My grandmother would silently advance towards her guest with her arms outstretched to the side and palms forward. As they drew near each other somewhere in the middle of the yurt, they would keep their arms outstretched like wings and press the palms of their hands together. Then, their chests touching, they would half-turn their bodies to the right and left before slowly bringing their arms together until they were outstretched between them. They would gently stroke each other's arms with their palms, and finally both touch their own faces with their palms. This was known as a 'greeting in embraces'.

A Kazakh greeting took a long time but few words were exchanged in the process. The greeting consisted of conventional questions and replies from all present. It began with the traditional 'Assalai magaleikum!' and the reply 'Aleikum assalaam!', which mean, 'Peace to your house!' and 'Peace to your house also!' These were followed by enquiries after the health of mostly the eldest in the household: were the person's body and stomach healthy, were the person's arms and legs functioning well, were the people and animals, children, grandchildren and other family members and relatives in good health? Were the corrals and pens for the livestock in good order? Were all the aul in the area fit and well? Were they having trouble with any animals or birds of prey? The host would reply succinctly to these questions: 'Thank God, everything is in order' and then ask about his guest's affairs after each subsequent question. Congratulations would be offered in respect of any joyful celebration that had taken place since they last met, such as the birth of a child, a wedding, or a son's or daughter's engagement party. If a son was getting married, the guest would say he hoped the son's bride entered the household 'light-footed' (happily, in other words), and if a daughter was getting married, he would wish her happiness in her new home and family.

Yestaulet and my grandmother would sometimes spend a whole day sitting next to each other and talking. The rest of the family tried not to interrupt them, and I still recall how emotionally Yestaulet said goodbye at the end of their last meeting. Taking my grandmother's hands and squeezing them tightly, he said, 'Dear Aksha, keep alive and well. I wonder if we'll ever see each other again and have another chance to talk?' Then he held onto her hands for a while.

'That is up to God!' she replied. But he answered slowly and tearfully, 'It's unlikely…'

At the age of 85, he had good grounds for this belief. Six months later, realising he might soon be prosecuted, imprisoned and stripped of his property, he set out with his family to escape to China. But his heart could not bear the pain of leaving his homeland, and he died on the journey to the border.

Chapter Six

The Escape of the Oralman Clans

Yestaulet's family was one of many to head for the border. Nomadic peoples had long ago formulated a simple response to persecution and injustice, and even family quarrels: they would simply up sticks and move away. Within the great expanse of the steppe, it was easy to find new places in which to lead free and independent lives, and when people began being sentenced to prison and having their property confiscated, it was natural that they should react by fleeing en masse into China. This form of protest was widespread in Southern Altai, the upper reaches of the River Irtysh, the Zaisan, Tarbagatai and other regions of Eastern Kazakhstan adjacent to the State border.

Over the past century or so there have been three mass exoduses of Kazakhs to China. The first one took place in 1881-82, when the State border between China and Imperial Russia was finally established. It was voluntary in those days: people living along the border freely chose their citizenship and which side to settle on. Some crossed over to live in Russia, while others moved to China.

The second mass exodus was organised in 1916, to protest against a decree by Tsar Nicolas II conscripting young Kazakhs to the front to construct fortifications in World War I. It is now estimated that one quarter of the border population emigrated at the time. Some of these émigrés went back to their homeland after the Soviet regime had come to power in Russia.

The third and largest exodus took place in 1931. This last escapes into China had in fact begun in 1928-29, after the major landowners' lands had been confiscated: individual families crossed the border, taking a small number of relatives with them. At that time, there seemed little likelihood of peasants with low or middle incomes being collectivised or having their property confiscated; but in 1931, when they too came under threat, the impetus to move became much stronger.

No exact record of émigré numbers was kept in those days, but the State archive contains the minutes of two meetings of the Kumashinko regional committee where escapes abroad were discussed. At the first meeting, on 1 August 1931, it was noted that as many as 108 families had left three of the border aul administrative councils of the Kalgutin, Kustau-Kumashinko and Sarulensk regions alone. A month later, it was stated that the number of families who had left for China had reached 325. When you consider there was an average of four people in each family, it means that over one thousand people emigrated over a two-month period from three aul councils. However, one should not forget that people fled to China not only from auls close to the border but also from places further away. Emigration also continued during 1932. According to data released by the Tarbagatai regional department of the GPU (a precursor of the KGB), 'in 1931, of the 696 families who left en masse for China from just five aul councils of this region, 231 were detained and 464 managed to get away with a large number of livestock'. If these were the official figures, it is fair to assume that the actual numbers were significantly higher.

These émigrés were led by courageous *dzhigit* – prominent young aul members – and experienced older people who had been to China in the past and knew the secret routes. Some were Kazakhs with Chinese citizenship who had slipped over the border to lead their relatives out of the USSR, or who had recently escaped to China on their own and were now returning for their families. People who did not wish to join the collective farms were quite prepared to pack their belongings and follow them.

In those days there were not enough border guards, and large sections of the border remained unmanned. Detachments of local activists were therefore sometimes called upon to help catch the refugees before they reached the border. As soon as information of a planned escape to China reached the regional centre from a remote aul, one or two members of the security service or militiamen armed with rifles would be dispatched there and expected to organise a detachment of activists on the spot. Armed with a few hunting rifles, they would then set out to detain the 'bandits', as they used to call the refugees. If they had no arms, they would simply take more men with them. In fact, they rarely saw any action. In many cases the refugees would make it across the border while the security service personnel or militiamen were still on their way to apprehend them. In others, a detachment would be gaining ground on a group of refugees when the latter spotted them in the distance and lay in wait for them: they usually only had to fire a few random shots from their rifles for their pursuers to call off their search and head home.

One encounter between refugees and border guards became legendary. At the end of 1929, a group of men who had stood trial as kulaks managed to evade arrest and hide from the authorities in the mountains of Tarbagatai. They had planned their escape meticulously, making all the necessary arrangements in advance for spending a long time in the mountains in winter conditions, before secretly collecting their families and heading for China. They had a base set up for them in a narrow gorge in the mountains with supplies of food, ammunition, warm clothing, a yurt and thick felt matting.

In the end, however, the authorities tracked them down, and called in the border guards. Their first assault failed. Unwilling to lose any men, the commander of the border guard detachment decided to seal off the exit from of the gorge and wait until the refugees had run out of patience and supplies. The sporadic exchanges of fire continued. Armed only with three hunting rifles, the refugees returned the armed detachment's fire with considerable tactical shrewdness and expertise, and in this way stuck it out for ten days. Eventually, however, their ammunition did run out, just as the detachment commander had foreseen, and so did most of their food supplies.

They somehow had to find a means of escape. The only way out of the gorge ahead had been sealed off by the armed detachment, and there was a steep rocky precipice cutting off the route to the mountain pass behind them. If they tried to slip round the detachment, they would surely be spotted and shot at, so they decided to escape by finding a way over the precipice. Knowing for sure that the snow in the mountain pass at the foot of the precipice was at least two metres deep, they decided to use it to their advantage. During the night they bandaged their horses' eyes, and led them to the edge of the precipice – which was about ten metres high – and pushed them over the edge. Like soft matting, the thick snow broke their fall while the hobbles on their legs prevented them from floundering about. Next, the refugees hurled all the things they would need over the precipice – whatever was left of their food supplies, matting and other warm things – and then abseiled down after them. Then they spread all the mats out and made a 'pathway' along which they could lead the horses, with all the packs attached to their tails, down through the pass to the Chinese side; the lower they descended, the thinner the snow became until the horses' hooves were finally on firm ground.

Among the escapers was a lame man who was unable to walk through the deep snow. Since the going was too treacherous for a horse to carry him, his companions hit on the idea of rolling him up in one of the mats, then attaching it to a horse's tail so that he was pulled along like a log. When the snow became thin enough, they loaded the packs onto the horses, mounted them and rode on until they crossed the border towards dawn. So confident of success were the border guards that they could hardly believe their eyes when they finally discovered that their quarry had disappeared.

Of course, not all the refugees managed to escape, and it was a terrible tragedy when brothers, spouses, children or parents ended up on opposite sides of the border. Some were tracked down and encircled by border guards and local volunteers: their leaders were arrested and the rest sent back home. Sometimes the same people tried escaping again, and if they were caught once more, they were deported even further from the border. In other cases, they paid for their attempts with their lives.

Take, for instance, this tragic example. In 1932, several families from the Konakbai clan living in an aul in the Kalgutinsk area of the Kumashinko region attempted to slip into China. They got as far as the border without being spotted, and – confident that they would now be able to cross in safety – stopped to rest their exhausted pack animals; whereupon they were surrounded by border guards, who shouted at them to surrender. During the confusion, all the men and adolescents managed to leap onto their horses and hide in the undergrowth of the gorge; but the women and small children were detained with all their belongings and the animals they were riding.

The border guards did not bother going after the men: they simply sent the women and children under armed guard to the regional centre. The men may have intended to return for their families, but whatever the case, they disappeared without trace, leaving all their loved ones and property to the mercy of fate. Instead of being allowed back home, the women and children were sent to live in auls near the regional centre, with no one to look after them. According to official records, at the onset of winter of 1932-33, all of them except for one woman starved to death.

On the whole, the refugees tried to avoid stand-offs and did not shoot to kill. Sometimes, though they kidnapped a few local activists who might inform the authorities about them, and took them with them as far as the border before setting them free. There was only one case we were aware of in which a member of the security forces was killed by a refugee, and it happened near our aul in the summer of 1931.

There was a Kazakh by the name of Zhakitzhan who had previously escaped to China without his family, and decided to come back for them. Having received a dossier on him, the regional GPU ordered one of their security officers, a certain Zhamil Isabekov, to capture him. Isabekov travelled to the aul in question, assembled a detachment of local Communists and Young Communist League members, and set about organising the man's arrest.

Zhakitzhan went into hiding among the reeds on the shore of Lake Zaisan, just outside the aul. Some locals who knew the quarry to be a crack shot warned the security officer to be careful and not to enter into negotiations with him or attempt a shoot-out. Instead, Isabekov should set fire to the reeds at night to force Zhakitzhan out into the open or give him a chance to slip away. Meanwhile, his family should be closely guarded or moved to the regional centre.

However, instead of taking their advice, Isabekov walked right up to the reeds with the detachment of local activists and called out to Zhakitzhan to give himself up. Zhakitzhan emerged from his hiding place and asked Isabekov to leave him alone and return home, but Isabekov responded by taking aim at him. As predicted, Zhakitzhan fired his rifle first, fatally wounding the security officer in the stomach. Once Isabekov had collapsed to the ground, Zhakitzhan stepped out into the open; but the dying security officer mustered enough strength to fire at him from where he was lying, and shot him dead.

Isabekov was brought over to our aul in a cart, and we children were among those who rushed over to have a look at him. After his death, the local authorities honoured him with a hero's burial, and officially invited all the residents of the regional centre and adjacent aul to attend his funeral as a protest against 'fleeing bandits'. However, most people stayed away. Their main reason was that a mullah was not going to officiate at the funeral, so the deceased would not receive a Muslim burial; another was that they had heard that guns were going to be fired over his grave at God. Even witnessing such blasphemy was a great sin for Muslims and might provoke divine retribution. Who would dare do such a thing? Heaven forbid! After rounding up all of us boys who had come together to watch the funeral, our parents kept us locked indoors while the ceremony was going on.

Chapter Seven

School

In the autumn of 1930, I was supposed to start in the third form at school, but Father seemed in no hurry to let me go. Instead, he took me to the fields to learn the art of haymaking and harvesting. One day he taught me to cut wheat with a scythe; as it was my first time, some of our relatives started pestering him in a good-humoured but quite persistent manner, demanding that we observe the special ceremony traditionally held to celebrate this important occasion. They threatened to play some scary tricks on me if we refused, and I remember feeling terribly frightened. However, Father arranged things to everyone's satisfaction, and with all the reapers giving me their blessings, I was ceremoniously handed a scythe. Then various people started showing me the correct way to reap, while others noisily shouted out words of approval and encouragement. An hour later I cut myself badly with the scythe; people who saw me do it exclaimed that the cut was a sign I was going to be a champion reaper – but it simply meant that I had to curtail my session as an apprentice.

Father's anxiety to get me used to work on the soil did not mean that he was unconcerned about my schooling. He deeply regretted being illiterate himself, and wanted me to go on studying until I was properly educated: he used to say, 'If I have it my way, you'll be an old man by the time you've finished.' Being educated, as far as he was concerned, meant learning to read and write letters, composing petitions and requests to official bodies and dealing with other business matters.

He finally took me along in mid-October, having arranged for me to stay with the Akhmetov family, who lived close to the school, three or four kilometres from Kumashkino. They were relatives of ours, since Uncle Toimbai-ata had taken my host's sister as his second wife. Izameddin Akhmetov had until that year been the principal imam at a nearby mosque, and the spiritual teacher of believers in the area; he, his wife Katipa and his mother Granny Maibas all treated me kindly and looked after me as though I was their own son. They let me eat with them, made sure my clothes were clean, and never let me stay out for long without them knowing where I was. Unlike others who had schoolchildren staying with them, they did not make me help around the house or look after the livestock, although I was always ready to help with the chores; and at night Granny Maibas used to check my bedcovers while I slept, and wrap them over me if they had slipped.

A Soviet school for younger children was, I think, first opened in our Administrative Aul Number Six in the winter of 1921-22, but it closed again a year later because of a lack of premises, and the children of the aul did not go back to school until 1928, when the Bukhtarminsk district council (just south of Zyryanovsk) decided to allocate 1000 roubles for a new building. The man behind the scheme was a local education inspector called Murmukhambet Mayakupov, who went to a lot of trouble convincing his fellow aul members of the need and importance of building a proper Soviet school and teaching children by modern methods. Eventually, he managed to get them to contribute transport and manpower to the project. When four classrooms were ready, he was selected to run the school.

I was among the first pupils to join. With its spacious, airy rooms, large windows and high walls, the school seemed to us like a gleaming white palace. Mayakupov was equally impressive: always smartly turned out in a black suit and white shirt, he would stroll around the school and classrooms, asking the pupils – particularly those boarding away from home – about their lives, and finding exactly the right words of encouragement. He devoted a tremendous amount of time and effort to winning round people who did not welcome the new school and wanted their children to continue studying with the mullah; he was also admired for defending ordinary people against the local activists.

Mayakupov played a similar role in his aul to Diushenby in Genghis Aitmatov's novella *The First Teacher*. Sadly, however, he fell ill and died in that autumn of 1930, and during World War II the building he had worked so hard to create was knocked down and dismantled brick by brick.

To my surprise, two weeks after I had begun in the third form, I was moved up a year along with four others: there had obviously not been enough pupils to keep the fourth form going. We found ourselves not only with seventeen- and eighteen-year-olds who had missed out on earlier schooling, but with young men of twenty to 22 who had done little more than learn to read and write with the local mullah; some of them were even married. And though we were placed next to much older classmates so that they could act as mentors, we actually ended up coaching them instead.

The other thing that made our school different from the other few aul schools was that we got taught Russian. It was a real novelty for us Kazakh children to see a Russian member of staff. His name was Ivan Ivanovich Perin; he knew the Kazakh language well, and was always kind and pleasant, and taught the Russian language to us complete beginners with great patience. To begin with, we had a terrible time trying to pronounce Russian words – particularly those containing the letter 'v'. The way we said his name, it sounded like 'Iban Ibanobich'. He finally gave up the struggle and let us call him 'Mugalim', or 'Teacher', as we did the other members of staff.

Chapter Eight

The Kulak's Son

In late 1930, and early 1931, the campaign to eradicate individual farms and collectivise agriculture became more vicious. Lenin (who died in 1924) had said that 'Every minute of every hour, millions of individual peasant farms are engendering exploiter elements and must be destroyed' – and the Government was taking him at his word. Many politicians believed that collectivisation in the countryside would not only eliminate exploitation, but also raise productivity in agriculture and greatly improve the poor peasants' standard of living.

The authorities used all sorts of tactics to push people into the collective farms, from promises of a beautiful life to harassment in the form of taxes and court appearances. Some managed to carry on for a few years as so-called 'individualists', but in the end they had to bow to the inevitable.

According to a Soviet Government decree of 1927, it was envisaged that collectivisation in Kazakhstan would be complete by the end of 1933. However, the officials who were put in charge of running the country – notably Feodor Goloshchekin, the brutal First Secretary of the Kazakhstan Communist Party – were mainly strangers to it, and neither knew nor particularly wanted to find out about the customs and mind-set of the nomadic population. Some of them who originated from Russia, for instance, had no understanding of the differences between stock-breeding in nomadic Kazakhstan and the agricultural districts of their own homeland. They made artificial comparisons between them and resolved to complete collectivisation in Kazakhstan to the same time-scale as in Russia, by the end of 1931; but in so doing, they totally ignored the interests and wishes of the peasants.

The peasantry was not at all keen on joining the collective farms. Those who were of average means or well-off refused to do so, and, as a result, were accused of being enemies of the policy of collectivisation and, by implication, of the Soviet State. Many of these were hardworking peasants who expertly managed their holdings and supplied the country with much-needed agricultural produce; in some cases they had dragged themselves up from poverty by farming land they had actually been given by the authorities. Among them were men who had fought in the Civil War to establish the Soviet regime.

The aul and village councils compiled black lists with the names of well-off kulak peasants, who were then prosecuted as class enemies. This was also a means of intimidating the rest of the peasantry, but it was only partly successful, and so the authorities began searching for class enemies among the poor peasants who were left outside the collective farms and even among those who had already joined them. The pejorative name 'podkulachnik' was devised for these particular class enemies, who were subjected to the same repression as kulaks.

The work of the aul, village and regional councils was now appraised according to the number of 'class enemies' they exposed and convicted. This produced some quite extraordinary results. Whereas, according to official estimates, kulaks made up only 5 per cent of the entire country's peasant population, as many as 15 per cent were exposed and convicted as class enemies.

One thing these officials had given insufficient thought to was what to do with the livestock confiscated from the kulaks. During the winter of 1931, the animals which had been taken in the outlying regions of Eastern Kazakhstan began to be killed for meat and the frozen carcasses transported to the towns of Semipalatinsk and Ust-Kamenogorsk. When, towards the end of winter, the sleigh-roads could no longer be used and the meat stopped being transported to the towns, the local authorities could not decide what to do with the rest of the animals, which then began to die from malnutrition and the cold.

In such a situation it would have been judicious to halt the campaign to dispossess the kulaks, at least until the spring. Instead, the Communists stepped it up.

In the Kumashinko region the decision was taken to keep part of the confiscated livestock for breeding purposes. It was also hurriedly decided to organise a State farm for this purpose which was to be grandly known as a 'model livestock farm'; but when it transpired that the farm was not big enough for all the animals, the authorities decided to keep only the dairy cows, ewes and she-goats and kill off the non-dairy stock. A slaughterhouse was chosen for this purpose on the banks of the River Irtysh. As there were no roads or means of transporting the meat outside the region, the regional authorities planned to freeze the carcasses, stack them on the river bank and cover them with a thick layer of reeds to keep them frozen until the ice on the river melted. When the first river barges arrived in the early spring, the frozen carcasses were to be loaded on board and transported to the towns.

However, as it turned out, the dairy livestock were too weak and malnourished to be driven to the State farm, so they also ended up being driven to the slaughterhouse. This increased the amount of emaciated carcasses stacked in the open air. Nobody thought about the quality of the meat – all that really mattered was that the numbers of prepared carcasses and slaughtered livestock tallied.

But the unusually low snowfall that winter caused the River Irtysh's water level to drop considerably, and greatly delayed the start of the shipping season. By the time the first steamers made it to the upper reaches of the Irtysh, the stacks of meat were stinking to high heaven. The stench was so appalling that the residents of neighbouring aul had to move away. In the end, the authorities had to conscript the local population to bury the rotting meat before an epidemic broke out.

Since the break-up of the Soviet Union, it has been argued that the terrible famine of 1932-34, which engulfed the whole of Kazakhstan and killed a quarter of its ethnic population, was deliberately orchestrated. Whatever the truth of this theory, the overzealous confiscation campaign certainly adds weight to it. The fact is that if it had been delayed only until the end of winter, all the animals would have been saved and could have been collectivised as planned. Instead, 48 per cent of the total livestock in the region was destroyed in one winter. It marked the start of a great catastrophe for the Kazakhs who had no livelihood other than stock-breeding.

ii

To start with, the black lists kept changing, since those who compiled them were easily influenced by personal relationships and grudges. In addition, many changes were made to the instructions from above, as a result of which there was a hiatus between the lists being compiled and the victims being prosecuted. During this period alarming rumours would be spread around the aul about the people who had been classified as kulaks – and it was a rumour which first brought the news to me, away at school, that my family was among them. Before long I found that I was being shunned by some of my schoolmates and – like other children of suspected kulaks – excluded from their games.

At the start of the holidays I arrived home in my aul at its winter stopping place a long way from the school. The first day, before sending me into the steppe with the flock of sheep, my father turned to me and said in a resigned and aggrieved tone, 'We've joined a collective. In spring, while you're at school, all the livestock are going to be taken to the collective farm and you'll never have to graze the flock again.'

To me this was good news, because his acceptance by the collective farm meant that he was no longer blacklisted. I had no idea what a collective farm was like, but I was happy that I would no longer have to bear the shame of being called a kulak's son.

After the holidays I went back to school in a carefree mood; but I soon began to feel uneasy again because of all the rumours and conversations about people who had recently been classified as kulaks and arrested. My fears that we were not yet out of the woods proved well-founded.

Every weekend there was a market at Kumashkino which we children used to walk to. One Sunday, as I arrived there with the other boys from the aul, I spotted the piebald horse Father rode in winter standing by the gates of a house just off the market square. Above the gates was a sign with large letters which said: 'ANIMAL UNION.'

I soon found Father. He said, 'I've just driven in the last stock and turned them over to the State.' On the other side of the fence I could see eleven or twelve animals including our three piebald mares with all their two-year-old and yearling foals, a few other horses and a camel. 'The activists had driven the sheep and cows away straight from the pasture. They said they would turn them over to the State themselves. They told me to bring the horses and camel here. And so they're off my hands now. No other hoofed livestock is left back home. Where the front wheel goes, the back wheel has to follow...Now I know what that saying means.' He was referring to his elder brother Toimbai's dispossession as a kulak in a similar way the year before. After thinking for a few moments, he added gloomily, 'Although I've turned over every single animal to the State apart from my old piebald, I've still got to pay more taxes. Now I suppose they'll start wrangling over our household goods. They're not going to leave me in peace.'

The truth was that his stock was of average size, consisting of 100 sheep, twelve horses, eight large-horned cattle and two camels. As far as the law on these matters was concerned, this was not enough to merit confiscation, and he should not have been prosecuted. He was just another, and by no means the last, victim of an arbitrary selection. The local authorities were plucking figures from the air and deliberately falsifying the number of livestock and size of crops so that they could classify people more or less at random as kulaks: this is what incensed my father most.

He was then 48 years old. By nature an optimist, not inclined to panic, and always sociable and witty, he suddenly seemed totally different. Everything about his demeanour – the slouched shoulders; the hunched body; the eyebrows overhanging sunken eyes filled with despair; the complexion, once so light and clear, turned sallow – reflected the hopelessness of someone who had had his future taken away from him. A man who had spent his entire life as a stock-breeder, and who regarded it as his sole livelihood, had been deprived of everything he had earned, stored up, reared and acquired through honest work all his life, and was now left with nothing except seven mouths to feed. He was totally bereft.

iii

Although he was now officially classified as a kulak, and had had to hand over his last emaciated calf to the State, Father was at least still at liberty for the time being; and I continued going to school, putting up with the hurtful name of 'kulak's son' which the other children called me. Taken in by the temporary lull, I sometimes even forgot about the danger hanging over Father and our family. But then, one ordinary school day in March 1931, when the pupils were starting to leave the classroom after the last lesson, our form teacher – the most popular in the school – Agzam Baitorin asked me to stay behind. Waiting until everyone else had gone, he went up and firmly closed the door, and then returned to his desk. He settled slowly and cautiously down in his chair as though playing for time and, keeping his eyes fixed on the desk, said calmly, without looking up at me, 'My dear child, your father has been sent to prison. As the son of a kulak, you can't come to school any more. That's the law. Don't come back here.'

I stood in silence in front of him, totally speechless. Cold shivers ran through me, and I could feel the tears welling up, but mustering all my self-restraint, I fought them back. Baitorin remained quiet for a while and then said gently, 'Off you go. Keep well. Goodbye!'

When I got outside, there were no children left in the yard. The tears spilled out of my eyes and I let them flow. How I wanted to go to school! I had always been a keen pupil, and now I was barred from lessons for ever. I cried all the way back to my lodgings.

When I got there, I stayed outside until I had pulled myself together and dried my eyes. But the moment I stepped inside, Granny Maibas, seeing the state I was in, rushed over, asking, 'Who's upset you, sweetheart? Why have you been crying?' She started taking off my coat and fussing over me in a way she had never done before, as though she was prepared to go and make the person who had hurt me pay for it. I kept silent for a while, and when I eventually told her what had happened, everyone sitting in the house – the old granny, her son and daughter-in-law – exclaimed in unison, 'Oh Lord! You poor boy!'

Although the Akhmetovs had been extremely kind to me, I was so upset that I hated the idea of spending another night with them, as though they were to blame for my misfortune. However, I had no idea where else to go, or how I might get home, and in any case my host Izameddin refused to let me leave until proper arrangements had been made. He knew that there was no sleigh-road to our home, some 30 kilometres away, and that very few people travelled between the two locations; but the next day he managed to find someone who was travelling in the direction of our aul's winter stopping place, sat me behind him on his horse, and sent me home.

Chapter Nine

Confiscation

When I got home to our isolated aul nestling at the foot of the spurs of the Arkaul Ridge, my mother told me what had happened. The series of court appearances to which my father had been subjected had ended in his conviction for failing to pay tax owed to the State. His sentence was 'to be isolated from society as a public enemy' (that is, sent to prison) for two years, have his household goods confiscated, and then, once released from jail, to be deported with his family to an area far away from his native land.

The scene that awaited me in our house was a dismal one. The floor was bare – stripped of its usual carpet, as it only used to be when it was being cleaned or before we moved away from our winter stopping place. The corner storage area where we kept the spare bed linen and all our clothes was now completely empty. Standing in the space to the left of the entrance which served as my parents' sleeping quarters was a bare wooden bed frame. Outside in the livestock yard, where the sheep pen and cattle shed had been, there was now a silent, empty space. Even the dog which guarded the yard had run off after the requisitioned herd.

The repressive measures against peasants classified as kulaks were, it seemed, being executed more harshly all the time. While in 1929, the procedure had been to leave kulaks with two horses and two heads of horned livestock, and all their household goods, now everything was confiscated, down to the last puny sheep, cups and cutlery.

Not long after my return, two representatives of the aul council turned up at our house. They came straight in and announced sternly like officers of the law, 'Your household is in arrears with its tax payments. To eliminate this debt, we are going to make an inventory and remove the stock and property which you were left with after your other property was confiscated.'

They started taking the mats, blankets and other bits and pieces which they had not bothered with the first time. Then they spotted the bed my sick 86-year-old grandmother was lying on, and her dressing gown hanging on the wall. Seeing their greedy eyes widening, my mother said to one of them, who was called Bozhikov Bolyskhan and was obviously the senior of the two, 'Bolyskhan, you call yourselves activists, but you haven't really lost your human conscience, have you? Are you really not afraid of the spirit of your ancestors, or of God? Fear their anger! Surely you're not going to disturb a sick old person who is closer to the dead than the living?'

However, these officials who were safeguarding the interests of the State lifted my sick old grandmother and laid her out on the floor. They seized everything that was on the bed – the mattress, the covers, and even my grandmother's shawl – and piled it on top of the other articles they had taken. Then my mother again spoke up and said, 'That shawl is very old – 65 years ago Granny was wearing it when she came through the doorway of this yurt as a bride. It's been lying in a trunk ever since and she only wears it on very special festive occasions. It's completely worn and threadbare and of no use whatsoever. At least leave it for its old owner so she can wear it at her funeral, and God will bear in mind your good deed.'

But she was wasting her breath. The senior official responded by cursing all the gods and ancestors' spirits and then turned on my mother, saying, 'You still have some livestock, expensive things and even gold hidden from the authorities. Hand them over! Tell me where you've hidden them!'

Only after they had failed to find anything more did they ride off, taking everything they considered worthwhile. They never bothered to tell us whose authority they acted on, how much tax we were supposed to owe, or how far the confiscations went towards paying it.

As for my grandmother, she remained silent throughout her ordeal, as though she no longer cared what was going on around her. But no sooner had the officials left than she started crying aloud, 'O Almighty Allah! Take me, your slave, to you! Do not leave me to shame and humiliation. Do not make me a living witness to the new sufferings of my children.'

Two days later she died.

While all this was going on, the same officials from the aul council announced to Uncle Toimbai's family – who were now living without their main breadwinner – that they were also in arrears with their tax. They too had to hand over their last miserable bits and pieces and the few heads of livestock that had not been confiscated the previous year, but it was not enough to prevent Toimbai-ata's twenty-year-old son Aiken from being arrested, sentenced and imprisoned like his father.

A week after their second visit, Bozhikov Bolyskhan and his junior colleague showed up yet again. This time they were even more thuggish. With us four children watching, Bozhikov started shouting terrible things at my mother: 'Do you have any undisclosed livestock, valuable household goods such as carpets, mats, sheepskin coats or other rich folks' stuff? Where are they? Confess where you've hidden them! These valuables must be handed over to the Treasury for the building of socialism. If you don't, you'll be put on trial. We'll take you in today and throw you in the clink and start criminal proceedings against you. And your little kulak serpents will be left at home all on their own. Confess!'

My mother replied defiantly, 'You've already fleeced us several times. Do you think anything's still left after that? All our valuables are here in front of you' – and she pointed at our bare walls.

When their attempt to intimidate my mother failed – although they had managed to scare us children very much – the officials gathered together the adults from the neighbouring houses and interviewed each of them separately, using various forms of bribery and threat.

'If you show us where Shayakhmet's valuables and livestock are hidden,' they said, 'you'll get a reward. But if you keep silent and conceal goods that have been hidden by a kulak's family, you'll face prosecution as kulaks' accomplices and enemies of the Soviet authorities.'

These tactics proved equally unproductive. But the officials refused to leave empty-handed, and deemed it lawful and necessary to take away the only things they could think of, an iron cauldron and two zinc buckets.

Those who suffered as we did wept bitterly for their losses and cursed those who had introduced such inhuman laws: for people whose lives revolved around their animals, it was worse than being invaded by Genghis Khan's hordes. Their suffering was shared by their relatives in the aul, and the tears continued for weeks in these communities.

As for the confiscated livestock, farm equipment and household goods, these were supposed to be distributed among poor local peasants and stock-breeders – but as no precise records were kept, it is impossible to know how much was taken and who exactly it went to. In many cases the impoverished peasants did not seem to value these free gifts, and quickly squandered them all. (Some actually refused them, as a protest against the confiscations – though typically the supporters of the new regime attributed their behaviour to underdeveloped class consciousness rather than high moral standards.) One thing is certain: in 1929, the State Treasury received absolutely no income from all the possessions and valuables requisitioned from peasants; and when holdings were collectivised the following year, only a very small proportion of the confiscated livestock actually ended up in the collective farms. The rest had apparently vanished into thin air – hidden, some said, in far-off ravines and gorges.

ii

Simple villagers could not grasp why their neighbours, who were simple workers like themselves, were being classified as enemies of the authorities, and having everything they owned confiscated; nor why the people in question should have to be persecuted and shut away from society. But our administrative aul council did not stop at imprisoning householders it considered to be kulaks: once it had dealt with them, it went on to prosecute their wives, on the same pretext as always – that they had failed to pay the extortionate taxes demanded from them.

Shortly after the confiscations, a messenger from the aul suddenly turned up with a court summons in Mother's name and announced imperiously, 'You must appear in court in 24 hours' time! I have been ordered to escort you there. Get ready this minute!' When asked, however, the messenger could not explain why she had been summonsed. Then she began asking him permission to stay at home for just one more night, explaining that her eldest daughter had come back home earlier that day for the first time since her marriage a year ago; but the messenger would have none of it. So Mother had to set out at nightfall with me to accompany her, leaving behind her other children in the care of a tearful Zhamba, who had only just arrived to visit us.

Next day we arrived at the courtroom, which had been set up in the same building as the school I had recently been expelled from. There were another five or six women there from kulaks' families whose husbands were also in prison; they included mothers with babes in arms. Others had brought along young sons around my age. All the witnesses, prosecutors, local officials and judges were men, and all the defendants women. Everyone sat down at the school desks in the classroom. The officials had either not thought about having children present or decided that they should be made aware of the precise nature of the wicked deeds which their parents had committed, because we children were allowed to listen to the entire proceedings.

The same charge was brought against all the defendants. In each case the judges' questions and defendants' responses were along these lines:

'Why have you failed to pay the tax you owe to the Soviet State?'

'We had nothing left of our property and possessions to pay the taxes with. It's all been confiscated. We've no livestock left. No money either.'

'You are charged as follows: your family and you personally have avoided handing over part of your livestock and valuable household goods, because you want to sabotage and oppose a Soviet policy. Your crime is recorded in this document.' The judge held up some papers.

'We do not have any livestock or valuables hidden at home – I'll be damned if we do. Anyone who thinks we're hiding something can go and find it and keep it for themselves. We have been left without our husbands: you sentenced them yourselves. And what do we women know about the tax levied against our household? Who set it? How much was it? What sort of tax was it? And when did we have to pay it? How much was paid by our husbands and how much was left? Was any left at all? We do not know. Some officials came and asked us to pay the taxes. How are we supposed to pay? Our homes and yards are completely empty. We haven't got a single head of livestock left.'

In addition, the judge laid into my mother on the subject of the bride money which had allegedly been paid for Zhamba the previous autumn; but she kept insisting that she had never made such an agreement with anyone and no matchmaking had taken place.

The court sitting lasted one day. All the defendants, including those with babes in arms, were sentenced to two years' house arrest. Already baffled as to why they had been brought to court, they had no idea what the point of the punishment was.

How could the trial of illiterate, defenceless women help consolidate the collective farm movement? This was a question, to my mind, that neither the defendants nor the prosecutors knew the answer to. As for ordinary Kazakhs, their general response to these events was, 'Whoever heard of women standing trial? It's true what they say: wonders will never cease!'

Chapter Ten

The Silent Steppe

By February 1931, less than half of the peasants in Eastern Kazakhstan had joined collective farms. The campaign to expose 'enemies' of collectivisation gathered such momentum that there were no longer enough prisons to house all the convicted kulaks. (According to the regional court's records, 447 people were convicted as class enemies in the first half of 1931 alone.) Even when all the kulaks of the Kumashinko regional centre were evicted from their houses so that they could be used as prisons for other peasants under arrest, there was still a shortage of places. In addition, the spring thaw made the roads so muddy that it was impossible to deport the arrested peasants to other areas.

Unable to accommodate all the arrested kulaks, the local regional authorities decided to release some of them temporarily on bail. These included Father and my cousin Aiken. As with most actions taken by the Soviet authorities, no explanation was given to the general masses – and in this particular case, the people released on bail were given no information either. Bewildered, they hovered by the gates of the 'prisons' waiting for a passer-by to give them a lift home.

It was time to move from the winter to the spring stopping place, and though our lack of animals made this migration extremely difficult, we managed it with the help of relatives and friends who lent us transport.

Once there, however, we found ourselves terribly isolated, with only three other families (relatives from two other aul, who had also been dispossessed as kulaks) for company. All the rest of our relations in the aul had joined a collective farm and were too busy sowing crops to visit us. In addition, the Government had announced a boycott of all kulaks: the local authority erected black signboards with the word 'boycott' on them next to their dwellings, so that nobody would have dealings with them. This tactic was comparatively unsuccessful in Kazakhstan, where people could not comprehend the idea of being quarantined from their relations merely because someone had told them that the latter were class enemies; but it did not make things easier for us.

Deprived of the way of life we had always been used to, our four families felt desperately unhappy about our new situation. We children could tell how much the grown-ups were suffering by the way they kept sighing deeply and sadly repeating the old Kazakh proverb, 'Poverty is fine as long as there's something in the pot.'

The men were bored because they had no work. Under the terms of their bail, they were not allowed to leave their place of residence for longer than half a day and had to travel once a week to the regional centre to register and prove they had not absconded. Although they managed to sneak off one at a time to see to their affairs, most of their days were spent idly at home, lost in their morose reflexion.

Somehow or other my parents had managed to save a horse and a female camel from being confiscated, and despite all the upheavals the camel gave birth. As her offspring grew bigger and the intervals between its feeds increased in length, the mother camel used to wander further and further away from our settlement (where all the grass had been grazed), longing to roam deep into the steppe and let her instinct lead her to the vast open pastures and herds of camels she knew so well from the past. As she did so, she would plaintively 'sing' and call to her child – which, unable to follow because it was tied up, would tug at its rope and call back to her.

Camels can make a whole range of different sounds, expressing emotions as diverse as anger and pity. They cry out in a particularly mournful way, and the noise made by our camel only served to make us sadder about our own fate.

'Oh poor animal, how she's crying for her old friends freely grazing the wide open pastures,' the grown-ups would say. 'But there isn't anybody or anything waiting for her over the horizon: the herd she's dreaming of getting to isn't there. That's what she and we have in common.'

Life did not continue like this for long. Once the River Irtysh opened to shipping again, some of the imprisoned kulaks were transported further away under escort. This then created more space for others in the makeshift local prisons, and during one of their trips to the regional centre to register, the bailed men in our family were rearrested and slung back into jail.

Our father and cousin Aiken were housed in a kulak's confiscated property, in the winter stopping place of an aul quite near the regional centre. The house had no fence and looked more like a night shelter than a prison. During the day the prisoners were allowed to wander around the aul and visit people they knew, accompanied by the two militiamen responsible for them; and although there was a roll call later on, the militiamen would go off and sleep somewhere else once the prisoners were in bed.

This routine made it possible for the prisoners' relatives who visited them with provisions from far-off aul and villages to spend the night with them – surreptitiously, that is. I once slept there, too, but things did not go as planned. After I had lain down to sleep between my father and uncle, a regional commission turned up to check on the prison's security arrangements, and all the prisoners were ordered to get up and file outside while the sleeping quarters were inspected. Then there was a roll call. I was in such a deep sleep that I only found out what had happened from conversations the following morning: the people carrying out the check had gone through the rooms without noticing me covered with a blanket and a pile of bedding.

After the re-arrest of the men on bail, two of the other families in our aul set off in different directions to seek refuge and a better life with other relatives. That meant that the only people left apart from us were Uncle Toimbai-ata's two wives and two youngest children. We were three or four kilometres from the nearest village, and felt more cut off than ever. According to the women – all of whom, in keeping with tradition, I called 'Mother' – I was now 'the only man in the two families on whom they could totally rely'. I was nine.

Part of my daily duties consisted of looking after the horse which had somehow miraculously not been confiscated: we were so terrified of losing it that we guarded it round the clock and kept it hobbled, whether near the house at night or at pasture during the day. I was also responsible for fetching the mother camel in from the steppe to be milked. Once a week I would ride to the prison, over twenty kilometres away, with provisions for my father and uncle.

During the preparations for one such trip, I overheard the women complaining that they were running short of flour and that some of our dwindling supply of grain would have to be taken to be ground at the mill, which was between 25 and 30 kilometres away. This journey turned out to present a serious problem, since although Kazakh women were fast and confident riders, not all of them knew how to saddle a horse, and it was customary for them to be accompanied by a man on journeys which took half a day or more. After discussing the matter, they decided against going themselves and to send me instead.

When Mother told me of their decision, I gleefully agreed. I considered it to be adult's work and if I was going to do it, I would be treated like an adult as well.

'You know the Karozek Valley,' Mother said as she explained to me how to get to the mill: 'it's where you grazed the sheep last year and rounded up the herd of horses belonging to different aul families and brought the milking cows home from. You also know the first part of the way there. The second half of the journey will take you though the Kaiyndi Gorge, where you haven't been before. If you keep going along the main road, you won't get lost and you'll end up in an aul that runs beside the road. That's where the mill is. Ask the locals where to go. There are always lots of people there. Someone will help you grind the grain if you tell them whose son you are. They'll also help you tie the sack on the horse and remount it.'

This was how firmly Mother believed in other people's kindness.

So the three women got me ready for the journey. After saddling the horse, they managed between them to heave the broad, bulky sack of grain, weighing over 24 kilograms, on top of the saddle and tie it down securely. Before lifting me onto the horse, all three of them went through my instructions yet again. Mother could obviously see I was not paying much attention to the words I had already heard several times before, because she said quite sternly, 'Unplug your ears and pay attention: you must only walk. On no account must you start trotting or even jogging. If you dare to disobey and try trotting, the sack will shift and break the ropes and slip off, dragging you off with it. You won't be able to lift the sack back onto the horse, and if you let go of the horse's reins when you fall, you'll have to make your way in the steppe on foot.' Then she added more warmly, 'Do everything just as you've been told, sweetheart. You've always been good at carrying out instructions.'

I enjoyed riding along at first, all on my own, on adult business. But as I rode further away into the steppe, this feeling of exhilaration gradually faded. On my way to the mill I had to cross a wide valley, some 30 kilometres long and ten kilometres wide, between the small southernmost spurs of the Altai range bordering the Zaisan Basin. Until the previous autumn, the valley had been crammed almost full of the nomadic aul who regularly spent each autumn and spring there, to the extent that there could be arguments over whose livestock had the right to graze where. But now it was completely deserted and eerily silent. The people who used to live here had all joined collective farms, and were mostly living together in centralised winter stopping places or in make-shift camps on the ploughed fields; and as there was now enough pasture near these farm centres for the depleted herds of livestock, it no longer made sense to drive them to deserted pastures such a distance away. Thus the Karozek Valley had turned into empty steppe.

Being all alone in this deserted valley began to unnerve me. What scared me most was wondering what I would do if the sack of grain slid off the horse, even though I was strictly sticking to what I had been told. I was scared, too, that at any moment a grey wolf was going to leap out of a bush and attack me; and every now and then I pictured a bear roaring as it scrambled over the steep river bank which had been eroded by the spring rains. Wild male camels, which went mad at that time of the year because it was the mating season, were another source of anxiety.

Such thoughts were only occasionally dispelled by the smooth sea of aromatic grasses and sweet-smelling flowers, and the sight of familiar places where we children had played games and the adults had competed in sports contests during festive gatherings. Once I had ridden through this valley I knew so well, and got nearer the unknown part of my journey through the Kaiyndi Gorge, I grew more and more anxious. The dense clumps of rose willows, birches, reeds and other shrubs growing alongside the river in the gorge seemed the perfect habitat for bears; and as I drew nearer my destination, I also started worrying about what I would do if nobody else was at the mill.

Just then, to my right, I caught sight of a rider on another road who was going to cross my path. I should probably have been frightened by his sudden appearance in the deserted steppe, but instead I was relieved to see someone I could ask about the journey and danger spots which lay ahead.

We met, as though by prior arrangement, at the junction of the two roads. As luck would have it, he turned out to be originally from our aul, and a cousin four times removed, named Nurkasym Knyazevr. From the conversations of the elders, who were fond of sizing up young people, I knew that Nurkasym was always given preferential treatment as his grandfather's favourite; but he had occasionally done things that had raised eyebrows in the aul, and earlier in the year he had fallen out with his relatives and gone to live somewhere else with his wife's family. Rumour had it that he had joined a collective farm there and was working as a team-leader.

Nurkasym began by enquiring after our family and asking where Father and Aiken were. He asked where we were living and with whom, and how we were coping. When he found out where I was off to and why, he silently turned his horse to the right and started riding alongside. After we had ridden on in silence for a short while, he announced that he would help me grind the grain, for he was sure I would not manage on my own.

When we finally arrived, we found the mill locked up and totally deserted, so Nurkasym went off to find the miller. (The latter was a Russian, as they usually were, since members of this minority – who made up one third of the population in our part of Kazakhstan – tended to be more prosperous than us Kazakhs, thanks to their settled way of life and the fertile lands they had been granted in Tsarist days.) Then Nurkasym quickly ground the grain and put the sack of flour back on my saddle. Finally he accompanied me all the way back to the place where we had first met. By this time it was nearly sunset and slightly less hot. Stopping his horse at the crossroads, he turned to me and said, 'I was going to the regional centre today but it's too late to go there now. I'll go back home instead. You make your way home too: you'll be there by dark. But make sure you only walk: don't dream of trotting even lightly! You'll spill the flour if you do.' Then he added, 'Send my greetings to your mothers.'

When I arrived home that evening, safe and sound and proud of my achievement, the women praised me to the skies. I told them how I had met Nurkasym and how he had helped me, and they began praising and thanking him as well. In view of the hatred whipped up against kulaks in those days, when any offer to help one could result in a charge of aiding and abetting a class enemy, he had taken a real risk by openly going with me to a public place such as the mill – yet he had not been afraid to do so. I realised that I would never have been able to complete my errand without him; and the women, recalling his many scrapes, declared that even a trouble-maker could turn into a decent person.

Chapter Eleven

Leaving Much-Loved Places

With little experience of farming or dealing with the outside world the three women soon realised that it was dangerous – indeed impossible – for our families to remain cut off from other people, and that they would somehow have to move closer to a community.

Kulaks' families were not allowed into the collective farm centre, to which all the able-bodied family members in the nearest small aul had moved with their yurts in the spring. But their elderly relatives had preferred to go on living in their winter stopping place, and it was to these that our women applied for permission to move into their aul, if only on a temporary basis.

This was the first time a move had been organised by women without any men or means of transport. In previous years, we had needed four or five camels, plus oxen, to carry our possessions – and those were just the bare essentials we took with us for the summer. Now all the two families' worldly goods took up less than a quarter of the pack of a single camel. The women felt miserable just looking at its tiny load.

The eldest of my 'mothers', Onal-apa, who had always been at the head of the caravan leading a long chain of loaded camels behind her, now sat mournfully on our one and only horse with her two young children, aged two and six, in front and behind. My mother walked along after her, leading the camel, while the rest of us followed on behind. As we moved towards an uncertain future, the women kept glancing back, weeping as they did so, at the homes they had lived in happily every spring and autumn for so many years. Perhaps they sensed that they were leaving them for ever.

The people of the aul we were moving to were descended from the same great-great-grandfather as us. Myrzabai (1754-1817) had had two sons, the elder of whom, Kultai, was the ancestor of the people of this aul as the younger son, Nauei, was ours. Consisting of nine households in 1931, this aul was named after their ancestors, the two Zholymbet brothers, and also after Anazhan, who was the brothers' mother. (In feudal times, when there were polygamous marriages, prosperous husbands used to keep their wives in separate auls, which then took the names of the women in question.) With the elders' permission, we were given shelter by the people of Anazhan aul, attaching ourselves to it in the same way as a lost lamb will attach itself to another flock.

Like most nomads, the residents of this aul had no spare living space, and we were put up in some sheds used for storing winter supplies such as meat, butter, grain and so on. It seemed as though things could only get better from then on.

Unfortunately this aul turned out to be very close to the main collective farm centre, and as a result we found ourselves under the surveillance of the farm's managers. When they saw that we, a kulak's family, had two heads of working livestock while the other residents no longer had more than one milking cow per family, they decided that something had to be done. So without any warning or warrant, they led the horse and the camel off to the collective farm. When we protested, they simply replied that all previously undisclosed property belonging to kulaks was to be confiscated.

My mother was in despair. But luckily the residents of the aul were well-disposed to us and looked after us, despite the trouble they might have got into for associating with kulaks' families.

The leader of the clan, Toimbai Zholymbetov, was in his late seventies, tall and sedate, with a long white beard. He took it upon himself to ensure that the members of the aul strictly observed all the time-honoured Kazakh traditions, and that the young people showed great respect to their elders. He was also known throughout the district as an expert trainer of birds of prey, and though he had joined a collective farm and given up his horse, he still continued to keep a golden eagle: I remember going into the steppe with his fourteen-year-old son Bilmesbai and killing snakes to feed to it.

Toimbai's other brothers, Tomarbai and Kydyrbai, were also renowned hunters. All the men of the clan were tall and athletically built, and in the past the members of this otherwise average aul had been renowned for their racehorses. Some of them were also improvisers, 'akyn', who took part in singing contests known as 'aitys', and even today people still remember the verses which one of them, Borambai, recited at a contest back in the 1920s.

The aul elders did what they could to help us, taking it in turns, for instance, to provide us with milk. But the most important thing they did was give the three utterly bewildered women moral support. I remember Toimbai Zholymbetov giving my mother the following advice:

'You are not the only ones suffering as a result of this catastrophe: many others today are as well. Misfortune and suffering are easier to bear when shared with many others than all on one's own, as our ancestors used to say. You must not forget about God's mercy. Allah is infinitely merciful to his faithful slave. God willing, all the worst things will pass and be forgotten. Allah definitely knows that your men, Shayakhmet and Toimbai, have done nobody any harm. Those who know them recall how kind they were to everyone and how selflessly they helped others in need. Kind actions are never completely forgotten. He who has a pure and sinless soul has God on his side. What you must also bear in mind is that other convicted kulaks were transported far away from home long ago, while your husband is still in the area; and the prison he's in, I've heard, isn't like a normal one – the prisoners are apparently free to walk around during the day and are only locked up at night. That's also through Allah's mercy.'

Subsequently, my mother fondly recalled this clan on numerous occasions. 'In those days, Father's closest relatives were afraid of being prosecuted for associating with us,' she used to say, 'but the Zholymbetov clan never were.'

The demography of this kind-hearted clan – and, indeed of the whole Kazakh people – during the Soviet period reflects the tragedy that occurred. In 1931 it had twenty male members (including fathers and their children); of these, one emigrated to China soon afterwards, while those who remained produced only seven male descendants between them by the end of the twentieth century. If one considers that the natural average annual population growth rate is 3 per cent, the number of male descendants over 60 years (1930-91) should be 36. The actual figure was only a fifth of that.

This was typical of nearly every clan: not until 1970 was the Kazakh population restored to the same level as it had been in 1920. The table below shows the development of our own clan, which in 1900 had 53 members altogether.

NUMBERS OF CLAN MEMBERS 1900-1990

Year	Men	Women	Total
1900	25	28	53
1910	28	27	55
1920	24	35	59
1930	31	38	69
1940	9	17	26
1945	11	12	23
1950	13	18	31
1960	21	29	50
1970	24	26	50
1980	33	28	61
1990	34	36	70

The founder of our clan, Nauei, was the progenitor of 25 male descendants in the course of one century (1820-1920). If each of them had emulated him, one would have expected the total increase in the number of males over the next 100 years to be 625. Instead, by 1990, it was seven. Such was the tragic fate of our entire nation in the twentieth century.

ii

With the arrival of the summer of 1931, the local authorities decided to make use of the convicted kulaks' unpaid labour 'for the good of socialism in the region'. The prisoners were organised into groups to do building work in the town of Ust-Kurchum (now Kuigan), which was then a regional centre. Arrangements were also made for their families to be reunited with them.

Our family – but not my uncle's – was among the first group of kulaks to be settled there under surveillance. It was twenty kilometres away, which at the time seemed very far indeed; and though we were very glad that Father was now living with us instead of being in prison, being forced to move to a strange area and leave the relatives with whom we had always lived was deeply depressing. My mother and two aunts wept bitterly as we parted.

We were among 27 deported kulak families, who expected to find houses awaiting them near the brick factory where the prisoners would be working. As it turned out, though, the factory was not yet in existence, while each deported family had to search for a roof over their heads themselves.

The prisoners had to build the 'factory' from scratch, which involved digging into the steep, high clay bank of a gully and installing a kiln there for firing the bricks. Then two large holes for mixing the clay and sand were dug nearby, and the sides of the hole lined with planks; finally, a tall shelter was erected to dry the bricks in – and that was the brick factory ready.

All the work was done by hand without the use of modern

machinery. The clay, sand and water were transported on two four-wheeled horse-drawn carts and then mixed with a wheel which was pulled round by a pair of oxen. The clay and sand were loaded and unloaded using spades. Then the prepared clay and sand mixture was manually transported again and poured into moulds, dried, and loaded into the firing kiln.

Working at this 'factory' were twenty convicted kulaks, mostly aged 50 and under. They included a father and son by the name of Keshubayev, who at just under 70 and 32 respectively were the oldest and youngest of the group. Slim and handsome, the son, whose name was Alkhan, always looked clean in his work clothes. He had an attractive pale face with large dark eyes and a neatly trimmed black beard and moustache. He was widely known in the region for having been the chairman of the rural consumers' society for several years; but he was even more famous for his bay racehorse, which had never lost a race. He also managed his holding superbly well, and that was why he had been classified as a kulak. After he had served his time of two years' sentence, he moved to Zyryanovsk, where he worked in the local food industry. Later, however, he was declared an 'enemy of the people' (the label devised for anyone who fell foul of Stalin's regime) and disappeared without trace.

Another remarkable kulak in the group was Abish Baskarbayev, formerly an aul mullah, who was the type of person Kazakhs would refer to as a 'one-horse pauper'. Unfortunately for him, several related aul decided to build a mosque for their clan, raised sufficient funds, and put him in charge of its construction. This was enough for local activists to classify him as an enemy of the Soviet authorities: he was put on trial and had his one and only horse confiscated. Other workers at the factory were peasants of average means who in one way or another had fallen victim to the class struggle.

The prisoners were issued with a ration of flour once a month, but it could not have been very much, because I remember Father talking about the need to get more food. Even so, like his work-mates, he never forgot to express his gratitude to God for giving him food and letting him stay with his family, even though he was forbidden to travel anywhere. Generally speaking, Kazakhs were taught obedience and humility from an early age, especially where their relations with the Almighty were concerned, and were afraid to criticise His actions. They zealously proclaimed their submission to their fate and to Allah, particularly when news came about even more unfortunate relatives who had already been transported to centres far away from home.

One letter told of a group that had been sent to Pakhtaral, on the border with Uzbekistan. 'It's so baking hot there that everything's shrivelling up,' the letter said. 'People can't stand the heat because they're unused to such temperatures, and they're getting sunstroke and falling dangerously sick.'

'Another group from our area,' someone wrote in another letter, 'was taken to a small place called Karaganda, where there is apparently just bare steppe and no buildings or other people except convicts. The convicts are kept outside in the open and made to dig underground dug-outs. The water is very salty there and it's caused a mass epidemic.'

Perversely, with all these terrible things going on, that summer of 1931 was for me and the other kulaks' children of my age the most wonderful time of our childhood. There were no animals to be rounded up or milked: we were totally free. We could play to our hearts' content, making up games, having fun and letting our imaginations run riot. A whole gang of us used to go swimming all day long. We had two rivers to choose from: the Kurchum, a cool, fast-flowing mountain river, and the broad expanses of the Irtysh with its gently flowing, deep and relatively warm waters. We could splash about and dive as much as we liked. Along the banks of the Kurchum there were tons of wild berries such as blackcurrants, blackberries and bird cherries for us to pick and eat till we were bursting. What more could children ask for? Our parents were nearby, we had no jobs to do and total freedom. We did not even think about the future. Bliss!

iii

The grown-ups, however, found it very hard to adapt to a totally unfamiliar area where they were no longer close to their relatives. They loathed their new surroundings which, though only about twenty kilometres from their beloved aul, seemed terribly far away, and they spent a lot of time reminiscing about the places and people they had left behind. Just the word 'deportees' made them feel depressed.

Compared to others, our family was definitely – if only slightly – better off, since the locals around Ust-Kurchum were from the Bur clan, to which my mother also belonged. Although two of my mother's brothers had also been dispossessed as kulaks and their families were living in extreme poverty, her more distant relatives did all they could to help. For instance, although they had to make do with the milk of a single cow in their holding, they got together five goats and gave them to our family to milk for the whole summer. At a time when people were being forced to turn all their livestock over to the collective farms, this was a considerable show of support for us. My father was delighted, but also dismayed by the contrast with his own first and second cousins, who had not visited us during the whole summer.

Father's close relatives from the aul might have forgotten about him, but the officials certainly had not. We received a visit from two of them, from the Topterek collective farm, which Father had been a member of for a short while: the chairman, Zhumakhozha Abishtayev, and the accounts clerk, Sydykbai Molymbetov. They both knew us, and indeed the latter was a distant cousin. Nevertheless, they announced that my father – despite having had his possessions confiscated on four separate occasions – still had some unpaid tax on his holding, and that the local authority had instructed them to confiscate any property and livestock he might have remaining to pay this off. They then started rummaging through our household possessions, searching for anything out of the ordinary. After listening to what they had to say, Father stood by the doorway and replied, 'Take all you consider necessary from here, right down to the last cup, so that you don't have anything to come back for!' Then he strode off.

The officials picked out two blankets and the last rug we had. It was not until many years later that we found out what the law actually was in those days: apparently, after property had been confiscated once in lieu of unpaid tax, and the head of the holding had received a prison sentence, no more property was to be seized and any outstanding tax was to be written off. So in fact these characters had simply been lining their own pockets, taking advantage of their victims' ignorance. Later, however, many of them overreached themselves by trying to take property from collective farms, and ended up being prosecuted as a result.

Chapter Twelve

My Perilous Journey

At the end of that summer of 1931, with the crops in the fields ripe, the farms started bringing in their first collectively grown harvest.

Meanwhile, cut off from everyday life back home and forced to stay put under the surveillance of militiamen, the brick-factory workers were only too aware of their lack of rights and uncertain future, and they spent much time pondering it. They made no secret of how much they missed and longed to see their close relatives, but the rule forbidding them from being absent from their place of work for more than half a day made it impossible. So one day Father said to me, 'I've arranged with some people staying overnight with our neighbours on their way back over the River Irtysh to take you with them so that you can visit Zhamba. And then her husband will bring you back.'

My journey of 50 kilometres would take a whole day, which, by the standards of those times, was a long and hard expedition: no one living in the steppe would tackle such a distance unless it was absolutely essential.

People nowadays find it difficult to believe that a parent could send his nine-year-old son off on a journey with travellers he had only just met and knew nothing about. It seems odd, too, that the travellers should have agreed to take me along without even having an address to deliver me to: they were simply given the name of an aul, where they were to drop me off. Father explained to me that when I arrived I could ask the first person I met where the Bokyshs' house was, and they would point it out to me and that would be that. That is how different things were in those days, when people believed in mutual trust and respect, and did their best to help out those in need.

So off I went. It was not only the first time I had ever been on such a long journey, but also the first time I had travelled in a light cart drawn by a pair of horses. Five adults sat alongside me, and I was given the place between the two back wheels: I only squeezed into it by sitting back to front with my legs dangling over the side of the cart. And I travelled like this all day with one short stop during the ferry crossing over the Irtysh. The dust kept flying in my face off the wheels as the horses trotted lightly along, and whenever they increased their speed, I was pelted with clods of crumbly earth. I found it a long and tedious journey. The adults killed time by telling various stories and exchanging opinions on what they had seen and heard at some regional meeting; from their conversations I gathered that they were teachers. They also told all sorts of funny anecdotes and jokes which I tried to commit to memory. I noticed that not once during the whole day did they use bad language or swear: that was the way people usually behaved in company in those days. Towards evening, when we had reached yet another aul, the oldest person among them said to me, 'The Bokysh-Tokysh live here,' and helped me out of the cart. Then they continued on their journey.

The yurt I was looking for belonged to my father's elder sister Batish and her husband, Zhantursyn Zhanybekov, who would take me the rest of the way to my sister's aul. When I was taken to my Aunt Batish's house, she greeted me as though I were an adult, performing the entire ritual reserved for such occasions. First she embraced me solemnly and began weeping and reciting rhyming lamentations in a suitably sombre musical key. She bemoaned the scattered clan and the fate of her brothers who had had everything taken away from them. She was deeply anxious about their futures, and it took her quite some time to regain her composure.

Her parents' only daughter, the second of three children and darling of the family who was used to being pampered and spoiled, Aunt Batish now held a respected position in the aul. Her husband was, by Soviet standards, a typical poor peasant who owned a single horse and was therefore entitled to all manner of privileges and benefits from the Soviet authorities However, he, too, had run away from a collective farm. Instead of going abroad, he had moved to his married daughter's aul in a neighbouring region. Here, in his new home, he had managed to retain his own smallholding and stay outside the collective farm. What's more, as a poor peasant, he had been entitled to a mare that had been among the livestock confiscated from local kulaks, and so now he was the owner of two horses. In keeping with the law, he had been allocated a parcel of land on a temporary basis and had sown it in the spring. Just then, he was busy bringing in his first harvest on his private land and sleeping overnight out in the fields along with other farming folk: that is why the onward journey to my sister's house was indefinitely delayed.

My sister evidently grew tired of waiting for me, because one day her elderly mother-in-law turned up and took me back home on the back of her horse. Zhamba regarded my first visit to her one year after her marriage as a dramatic, distressing, and almost shameful affair, and she greeted me with a melancholy song about the troubles that had befallen Father. She lamented the fate of the whole family who had been left destitute, and sang about how, according to age-old traditions, her brother should have come to see her with a large number of adults and not all alone, like some totally destitute peasant, on the back of someone else's horse. Usually in such instances, the other people present, who were mainly women, would comfort the singers and not let them weep for long. On this occasion, however, people went on listening to the words of Zhamba's lament without interrupting her: they were obviously extremely moved, because they also started weeping.

We Kazakhs have always treated anyone related to us through marriage with great reverence. As a popular saying put it: 'In-laws should be venerated like God.' But I had always imagined that this treatment was reserved for adults, so I was astonished when these people of the Karaulzhasak clan in the aul of Kalmakbai all started addressing me as 'boy-in-law' and treating me with enormous respect. I suspect that it had something to do with the esteem in which my sister was held.

Even as a child, I could spot several distinct differences between this aul and those in our Kurchum region, in terms both of prosperity and of the treatment of kulaks. The log huts used in winter here were more solidly built, taller and more attractive-looking than those in our area. Moreover, some of the people owned a one- or two-horse open carriage, known as a *britzka*, which in those days was for us Kazakhs a sign of considerable wealth and something none of the people of Kumashinko had; and although Zhamba's father-in-law was among those who had been persecuted as kulaks, her husband Manap was able to keep a britzka with impunity. Kulaks' families had not been deported like those in our area, and no one had even heard of the boycott; nor had the collective farm workers from the various aul been made to live all together in one place.

I felt happy and free at my sister's. Manap spoiled me, and his mother and grandmother looked after me just like one of their own children. There were several boys of my age in the aul whom I quickly made friends with, and we all spent time playing together. And so I lived there like a happy, carefree child for nearly a month.

But this came to an abrupt end when the news filtered through to us that Father had been put behind bars again. Someone had to go to Ust-Kurchum and verify the rumour as quickly as possible. But the collective farm would not let Manap off work because of the harvest, and he could not find anyone else for me to go with. In the end he said, 'I'll saddle up the young chestnut for you: he's a quiet ride. You'll be able to ride home alone on him, find out all about your father and family, and then ride back again, won't you?'

This chestnut had caught my eye quite a while ago – he always behaved very sedately in the herd, which was unusual for such a young animal – and I had been longing to ride him. I failed to fully appreciate what it would be like for an eleven-year-old to undertake such a long journey alone on horseback, and eagerly agreed to Manap's suggestion. But I still cannot understand how the adults came up with the idea of sending me off on this long journey alone.

'You know the way home as you've recently done it with the people who brought you here,' Manap told me. 'I'll go with you as far as the main road, and then you'll keep going until you reach the ferry across the Irtysh. Once you get to the other side, you'll keep going along the same road you know well, all the way home. But don't ride the chestnut fast: he's only two years old and he'll tire. Only walk or trot gently, or you won't make it there.'

So off I rode. I reached the riverbank without a hitch, and joined several other people on horseback and the drivers of two pair-horse carriages waiting to cross.

The ferry was the kind that had to be paddled, and was powered by the passengers themselves: the ferryman shouted out instructions and steered. The passengers took tremendous care to follow all his directions precisely: whenever the ferry started drifting, they had to paddle faster, like barge haulers, to keep it in line with the jetty. For safety's sake, the ferryman had all the saddled horses bunched together in the middle of the ferry and told me to keep them still. After reaching the right bank of the Irtysh, I recalled Manap's instructions and rode on slowly, lagging far behind the other riders.

Towards evening I reached the lodgings where I had left my family a month before, only to find that they had moved to another hut nearby. The owner had returned from the collective farm's centre, where he had spent the summer living in a yurt. This set the pattern for many years to come, in which we never had a place we could call our own, and sometimes did not even a roof over our heads. Our new hut belonged to a man who had gone off somewhere faraway; Mother had arranged with his relatives to spend the winter there at a very low rent.

The next day I rode over to the prison to visit my father. Over the summer a low, flat-roofed prison building had been erected in Ust-Kurchum and surrounded by an adobe wall much higher than the building. As the prisoners were not allowed visitors, three or four of them would take turns to climb onto the building's flat roof when nobody was looking, while the visitors crowded round the back and called out to them the name of the prisoner they had come to see. He would then climb onto the roof. Conversation was impossible, since if the prisoners were caught the ban on them seeing visitors would be made permanent, and their food rations suspended for a certain length of time. So they would scribble a note on a scrap of paper, tie it to a small stone and toss it down to the group of visitors on the other side of the wall, who then handed it over to the person it was intended for.

When my turn came, I received the following message written in clear Arabic script: 'Go back to my son-in-law as soon as possible. Get him to bring me some food supplies. We're leaving here soon.' I noted that he specified 'supplies', not just 'parcel'.

I was about to set off for home when a Kazakh militiaman suddenly rode up to our group with a young Russian striding along beside him with a briefcase in his hand. The Russian started telling us in a hotchpotch of Kazakh and Russian that there was a public holiday to mark the autonomy of Kazakhstan. The whole region was celebrating. All the residents of the regional centre and visitors were getting together and going on a march along the streets with a banner to celebrate the occasion – and our group was to join the march as well. When people started muttering about urgent business and getting home before nightfall, the militiaman bellowed, 'Never mind that! Your business can wait! If you don't get home today, you will tomorrow!'

So we found ourselves being led towards a large waiting crowd. Then we were arranged in columns; some of us were handed red flags, and off we set, with the people on foot ahead and us riders bringing up the rear. Our column was flanked by mounted militiamen who kept yelling and chasing people back in line every time any of us attempted to sneak off.

Ust-Kurchum consisted of four two-storey buildings housing the regional authorities' offices and officials' apartments, and about a dozen aul log huts dotted randomly about. The column of pedestrians and riders press-ganged into taking part in the march now headed across a piece of wasteland. People kept shouting out things like 'What a nuisance this is! I've got business to see to!' and 'If only I'd left when I had the chance!'

There was something extraordinarily alien about it all. The people taking part could not understand the idea behind the march, or why it had been organised like this. I, on the other hand, thoroughly enjoyed riding along in the column of horsemen, because I had never done anything like it before.

We were led to the front of a two-storey wooden house. A man then stepped out of the second-floor window onto what to me looked like a calf manger, but was apparently a 'balcony', and started saying something in Kazakh. From what he was saying I gathered that besides our Altai region which I knew so well, with its cool, clean air, splendid grasses, flowers and berries, there were other wonderful and even more beautiful places such as Zhezkazgan, Karsakbai, Karaganda and Ridder. I now realise that the speaker was proudly listing the names of places that were to become Kazakhstan's key industrial centres; but at the time I could make no sense whatsoever of all I had heard and seen. Nevertheless, I was so fascinated and delighted by the novelty of it all that for a while I forgot all about my father's message.

As soon as the celebrations were over, I recalled Father's request and hurried home to Mother. I tried to tell her what I had seen of the festivities, but she listened with only half an ear as she started getting me ready for the journey the next day.

'You're the only man we have in the family now. Who else can we rely on besides you? Get to your sister and brother-in-law's as quickly as you can tomorrow, and pass on your father's greetings and request. Get them to deliver the food supplies to Father as soon as possible. Any delay could be dangerous. The prisoners are apparently soon going to be transferred somewhere far away. If that happens, your father will go off without any food supplies and he'll be hungry.' Then she added, 'Make sure you don't push your horse too hard on the journey tomorrow. Be sensible and keep alert while you're riding. Give him a rest on the way, otherwise he won't make it.'

Neither she nor I imagined at the time the obstacles that lay in wait for a lone eleven year-old traveller.

Next morning, after an early start, I reached the ferry across the Irtysh near the village of Slavyanka. All the passengers had boarded and the ferry was ready to depart. I rode straight on board. No sooner had I dismounted than the elderly ferryman said a couple of words to me often used by Russians who did not speak much Kazakh, 'Akcha davai!' ('Give money'). Baffled, I asked him to repeat what he had just said. In broken Kazakh he again asked me to pay him for the crossing. So I said, 'Akcha zhok' ('I've no money'), to which he replied, 'Akcha zhok – parom zhok' ('No money – no crossing'); and taking my horse's reins off me, he led him onto the bank with me trailing behind. Then he stepped back onto the ferry and cast off, leaving me standing all alone with my horse.

I was completely bewildered. On my two previous crossings I had not even noticed other people paying. The first time, with the adults in the cart, I had been more interested in the ferry itself and the riverbank than in what people had been doing. On the second occasion, the ferryman must have overlooked me because I was surrounded by the other travellers' horses.

There was nothing else for me to do but go back home to Mother, weeping with frustration. I was cross with myself for my stupidity, and miserable about all my family's bad luck, and upset with all the adults in the family, who should have known that the ferry crossing had to be paid for. Why had they forgotten to give me money for the journey? Then my thoughts turned to Father: this setback would delay the delivery of food supplies to him by at least two days. I grew more and more anxious about what was going to happen to him.

I had covered five or six kilometres when a group of riders appeared in the distance, coming towards me. I immediately started trying to wipe the tears away so as not to look like a cry-baby; but the riders were approaching at a fast trot and soon came alongside. They were young Kazakhs who did not look like collective farm workers, and one of them immediately asked, 'Why have you been crying, lad? Has someone hurt you? Has something happened?' I briefly explained why I was so desperately sad. As I replied to his questions and looked at him, I realised he was one of the people I had travelled with in the cart along this route a month previously. After thinking for a moment or two, the man said, 'You can ride with us to the ferry and we'll help you get across.'

We reached the ferry and boarded all together, leading our horses by the reins, one after the other. All the horses were bunched together again in the middle of the ferry and just like last time, I stood among them, holding onto their bridles. This time the ferryman did not ask for my fare. Possibly, he did not notice me again because of the horses: I have no idea.

After reaching the other bank, we set off again on our journey all together. The man who had helped me said, 'Don't try and keep up with us, lad. We're going to ride fast. You won't manage to on your young horse. Ride slowly or you'll never make it out of the steppe with him.' And with that they galloped off.

I eventually arrived at my sister's aul and recounted all my adventures and Father's news. After much head-shaking and sighing over my mishaps and telling me how anxious they were about my father, all the members of my brother-in-law's family spent the whole of next day assembling the food supplies for him. They slaughtered a sheep, chopped it up and salted all the cuts of meat in preparation for drying it, which was essential if it was to keep for a long period. This would take another week, after which it had to be delivered to Ust-Kurchum. The collective farm again refused to let my brother-in-law off work, as he was a 'key operative' responsible for delivering its grain to the State procurement station on a daily basis; so, once again, it was decided to send me.

'You already know the route well,' said Manap. 'I'll saddle a good, quiet and strong mare for you this time instead of the young chestnut. She's fast and strides out well and never stumbles. I'll tie the load on so tightly it won't budge an inch. You ride her slowly and she'll get you home within the day.'

I jumped at the idea without giving it any serious thought; I even recounted how I had ridden over to the mill in the spring, to show that I was up to the task.

So I was got ready for the return journey, despite the doubts and objections raised by the women, and my sister Zhamba in particular. Manap slung the massive homespun woollen sack containing the dried cuts of mutton and thirty or so kilograms of wheat grain over the saddle. After carefully packing the foodstuffs into the sack and making sure the whole load was evenly balanced, he secured it tightly to the saddle. Then he hoisted me on top of the sack, walked with me to the road leading straight to the ferry and gave me the customary instructions to take it slowly: 'Only walk. Whatever you do, don't let her trot: if you do, the load will get jolted and shift to one side, dragging the saddle and you with it. You'll be on the ground before you know it, and the load will stay there on the road if you don't meet a good person to help you. Be really careful.'

The mare I was riding was a large chestnut with a white blaze down her face. She had a light, fast walk, covering the same distance as another horse at a light trot. Taking great care, as I had been told, I reached the ferry across the Irtysh without a hitch. A group of riders and two or three loaded carts were waiting on the bank to cross. One of the drivers turned out to be an acquaintance of our family and resident of Ust-Kurchum, by the name of Toktagan Yensebayev. It turned out that he was working as a groom in the regional department of the NKVD (another precursor of the KGB) and was on his way home in his pair-horse *britzka* with a load of oats from the village of Baty's grain depot. After finding out where I had come from and what I was carrying, he said to me, 'Dear lad, you're too late. The day before yesterday your father and a group of other ex-kulaks were sent off on a boat God knows where. So poor Shakye [as he called my father] left without any food supplies. He'll find it tough without them in a strange place.'

We crossed the Irtysh and then rode on together. (Toktagan's *britzka* was moving very slowly, because the horses could hardly manage to pull the heavy load.) Toktagan told me all the news from his aul and I described my most recent adventures. An hour passed in this way. It was late afternoon when Toktagan said solicitously, 'Bala [boy], at this rate we aren't going to get to Ust-Kurchum today. I'm going to spend the night at an aul on the way and get there tomorrow. But you can go a bit faster and not wait for me.'

When I pointed out the danger of riding faster, he replied, 'Don't worry, you can go at a light trot. Then you'll reach home today before dark.'

Somehow he convinced me. I pushed the mare into a light trot and shot forwards, breaking my promise to my brother-in-law. The next thing I knew I was lying on the road with the sack and saddle on top of me, and the mare – whose reins I had dropped as I fell – was galloping off in the direction of the Irtysh, two kilometres away to the right of the road. The jolting motion of the trot had been sufficient to shift the sack and break the fastenings on the saddle, causing the sack to crash to the ground, dragging the saddle and me with it.

While I was pulling my legs out from under the sack and saddle, Toktagan drove up in his *britzka*. After making sure I was in one piece, he quickly unharnessed one of his horses, mounted it and galloped after the runaway mare. Both soon disappeared over the ridge down to the river and out of sight. They were gone for a long time. It was already nearly evening. There I was alone on the road in the middle of the steppe with a *britzka* loaded with sacks of oats and one horse harnessed to it. I started to get anxious. 'What if Toktagan can't catch up with her?' I thought. 'What shall I do?'

After what seemed like an eternity, Toktagan suddenly appeared leading the loose mare. He rode up to the *britzka* in a leisurely manner and tied her up; then, harnessing his horse to the *britzka*, he grumbled good-humouredly at the mare, 'You're an old nag and that's why you're crafty. She just wouldn't be caught, kept weaving this way and that. Trying to get to the river, she was, to swim across. The winter stopping place of her aul, you see, is just over the other side and she knew it all right! Clever beast!'

He silently lifted my sack and saddle into his *britzka*, then placed me on the mare's back and lifted me onto her and told me to ride in front. He explained to me that he was going to tie my mare's tail to the front beam of the *britzka* to help pull the load, since – he assured me – any horse could pull as much weight with its tail as it could with its neck in a harness. So I had to ride ahead, making sure the mare's tail and the rope attaching her tail to the beam were kept taut. Every now and then Toktagan would still shout out, 'Don't let it go slack! Whack her with the whip! We'll get to the aul that much quicker.' Sure enough, we soon reached the aul and stopped for the night.

At his acquaintances' house where we were to sleep over, Toktagan continued to look after me. When he was invited to sit down at the table by his hosts, whom I had never met before, he sat me down beside him and made sure I got plenty to eat. Before he went to bed, he sat by the dim light of a paraffin lamp and mended my girths so that I could saddle my horse in the morning.

Next day we continued our journey in the same way. Half a kilometre from the regional centre, he stopped the *britzka* and said, 'We mustn't ride any further together. If we appear in the aul like this, some Communist activist or other will spot us and accuse me of carrying a load for a kulak's family on horses belonging not just to the State but the militia as well. Better to be on the safe side. Ride on alone now.'

He hoisted the sack onto my mare, secured it tightly, checked it over and then added, 'Go ahead and keep to a walk. Don't worry, it won't come loose again. While you're riding into the aul, I'll hang on here so nobody sees us together.'

When I told Mother how and why I had been sent off on such an important journey on my own, what had happened to me on the way, and how Toktagan – with whom we were only slightly acquainted – had helped me out and ensured that I did not spend the night in the steppe, my startled mother started listing all the things that might have happened after my accident with the horse. Then she began praising my rescuer: 'It takes a good upbringing for someone to behave in such a noble and kind way. May God grant him good health and a long life. May he see his children happy.'

Her prayer was granted. Although we were never to see much of each other in later life, I used to hear about Toktagan Yensebayev from other people. He lived to be 90, and while he himself was never more than a simple collective farm worker, his two sons and two daughters became leaders of industry, and all his needs were well catered for during his many years of retirement by his children and grandchildren. No wonder it is said that God is good to good people.

During my first evening home, Mother told me how worried she was about Father setting off on his arduous journey without any food supplies or warm clothing for the winter. She also complained to me, as though to an adult, about having very little wheat grain left for ourselves. We had no kerosene at home, and ate supper by the light of the hearth fire. How desperate she must have felt!

There remained the matter of returning the chestnut mare to her owner. Although Mother did not want to send me off on another journey by myself after all that had happened to me, she decided she had no choice. What scared me most was remembering my accident the day before: the mere thought of how I had nearly been left alone in the steppe overnight sent shivers down my spine.

The journey ahead seemed just as difficult, since this time I would have to lead another horse to ride back again. Manap had given us a bay mare when Father was sent to do hard labour at the brick factory, saying she would be useful in an emergency, and since then she had lived at our place – but nobody had ever ridden her. Now I was going to have to control both her and the borrowed chestnut.

It requires a special knack to lead a spare horse so that it does not slow your journey up, and in everyday life nomads rarely did so. A traveller might use one if he had to cover a long distance fast over several days: he would then ride each of his horses in turn.

Sometimes, too, a spare horse was sent over to collect a particularly honoured guest, or (if someone had a dangerous illness) the healer. But in all these cases adults were put in charge.

In our community, nine-year-old boys like me would think nothing of bringing in the hobbled work horses grazing in the pastures nearby, riding one and leading the rest on ropes; and ten- and eleven-year-olds could ride out to the herd grazing freely in the steppe, catch the horse they needed, and lead it to the aul. It was quite another thing, however, for a boy of my age to take a second horse with him on a journey that was to last a whole day. I was afraid I would not manage; in the end, however, the journey passed without incident.

ii

After returning the chestnut mare to my brother-in-law, I rode back on the bay, only to find that my family had again moved in my absence. A woman I had never seen before greeted me in the yard and asked me if I was Shayakmet's son: when I nodded, she told me that my family had gone to stay with my mother's younger brother, Uncle Kozhakhmet. This was the third move my family had made in as many months since being forced to leave home. Whether the owner of the hut we had vacated had been after more rent, or someone had objected to a kulak's family living there, the woman didn't say, but my family had been asked to go and another family had moved in.

Uncle Kozhakhmet was a kind, straightforward sort of person: naïve and placid, but a terrifically hard worker and very generous, he was highly respected in his community. Everyone at the collective farm, both young and old, affectionately called him 'Adem' – 'Charmer'. But he had suffered dreadfully when his older brother Mukatai, whom he had always worked with, was dispossessed as a kulak and had his smallholding confiscated; he himself then became virtually destitute, and was scared stiff every time the local activists menacingly reminded him of his family connections with a class enemy. So he tried to keep his head down as much as possible, and this submissiveness was taken advantage of by the local collective farm managers: he was always being sent off to do the most laborious jobs, and during the first years of collectivisation he apparently spent over a month sowing seeds manually for the entire workforce. Later, in the autumn of 1944, an article in the Kumashinko regional newspaper would record that 'Kozhakhmet Zhambazov, a thin, slightly built, elderly man of 60, threshed 7,000 kilograms of wheat grain daily, by hand, using a spade, and sent wagon-loads of grain to the State's procurement station'.

Like the other members of the farm, Uncle had relinquished all his own property and relied entirely on whatever he got for his labour. But the collective, which had promised to feed and support its workers, had announced that it was unable to pay them until the end of the year: in the meantime they were fobbed off with so-called 'work-day tokens'. Somehow, he had to find a way of feeding us as well as the four members of his own family.

He must have worried about it a lot, because he often spoke of the coming winter and not having the usual quantity of food put by. It was a measure of his desperation that he decided to rent out half of his house to the collective farm as its office – even though it consisted of only one room, which now had to accommodate all of us.

Close to the wall and windows on the sunny side of the room stood a desk that squeaked terribly every time anyone touched it. Alongside was a chair for the collective farm chairman, and an old rickety bench that looked as if it was about to collapse. In the other half of the room there was a single bed and a raised wooden platform, on which all our two families' possessions were heaped together. There was also a stove and separate range with a cauldron for cooking on. The earthen floor was completely bare – not that there was any point in putting rugs down, because the constant stream of visitors left huge amounts of mud behind them. We managed to get a rest once in a while by taking it in turns to sit on the bed or the pile of soft clothing and bedding alongside it. The farm managers can hardly have found it ideal either, since they had to wrestle with complex State plans and targets while household chores such as bringing in firewood, heating the stove, fetching water, cooking food and carrying out rubbish were going on around them.

The rental brought one bonus, in the form of a young bull which was loaned to my uncle by the collective farm for the whole winter, supposedly to help carry the firewood used to heat the office. With it, Uncle hoped to earn something extra on the side to feed us all. He could not put the bull to work himself, as he was constantly being sent off on various urgent jobs, so he delegated the work of chopping and bringing home the firewood to his sixteen-year-old adopted son Bazar, and asked me to go along and help.

Every day we had to fetch enough wood to heat the house, and every other day take a load to Ust-Kurchum to sell to its residents. First thing in the morning we used to ride the short distance over to the River Kurchum with its thickets of rose willow, dogwood, bird cherry and stunted birches growing along its bank; Bazar would chop branches down with his axe, and my job was to pick them up and carry them back to the sledge. He would work non-stop, and move so far away from the sledge that I sometimes had difficulty picking up all the firewood.

By our competitors' standards, however, our load was not particularly large, because our bull was only two years old and not very strong. We would accept whatever we were offered for the wood, usually in the form of food, and I'm afraid we did not do very well. So one day Uncle Kozhakhmet found another source of income for us.

'There's a depot at the regional centre which employs people to sort spuds,' he told us. 'Once you've sorted ten bucketfuls and handed them in, the eleventh is yours to keep. If you two manage to earn one bucketful each a day, you'll be doing well. Work there for a few days while we've got enough firewood put by. Then we'll have spuds to eat as well.'

But we earned next to nothing there either. Most of the potatoes were rotten and our job was to find the very few good ones among them. There was a huge slimy mess all over the depot floor, and practically nothing worth picking out of it. It took us both a whole day to win less than a bucketful. We never went back there again, preferring to persevere with our firewood instead.

As the hard December frosts set in, life became increasingly tough for our two families. Although, with the colder weather, the number of buyers increased together with the price of the firewood, our work also grew much more laborious. When it was bitterly cold, it was unbearable to go out every day, so we started going out every other day instead – which made the adults even more worried about how little food we had put by.

The other cause for anxiety was that we had received no news from Father and Uncle Mukatai since they had been transported under armed guard somewhere unknown several months ago. In those days there was no postal service in rural areas, and the lack of news from people sent far away to prison – who were often unable to write anyway, because they were illiterate – caused deep distress to their loved ones. However, after three months of waiting, a letter arrived from another of the men who had been deported in the autumn, called Kabyl Kilybayev. He wrote that the whole group from the Kumashinko region had been taken to the town of Ridder, where they were living in wooden barracks and working underground in a mine. He listed all his fellow countrymen with him, and my father and Uncle Mukatai were among them. Of my father he wrote: 'Shayakhmet is fit and well. He sends greetings to his family and is worried about them and about not getting letters from them. He asks them to write.'

After studying for three winters at school, I still could not read other people's notes, but I managed to write a letter to Father that Mother dictated to me, telling him that we were all well, where we were living, how things were going and how we were all missing him. As far as she and the other adults were concerned, I might have been one of the venerable scribes who undertook writing for members of the aul in tsarist times.

iii

Flowing in a northerly direction through the south-west of the Altai region, the River Irtysh freezes first in its northern lower reaches and then gradually further up river. Once the first ground frosts arrive, a film forms on Lake Zaisan, the river's source in the south, and then slowly solidifies into a thin crust of ice. The ice is then carried down-river by the current, gradually forming massive, thick blocks, the further north and colder it gets. Every time they strike an obstacle in their way, these blocks fracture and then mass together again as they speed down-river. Further north, they thicken and spread outwards until their outer edges reach the opposite banks, forming a solid sheet of ice. Once thick and strong enough, the blocks of ice no longer fracture upon impact with the stationary sheet of ice but come to a standstill and freeze onto it.

Residents on both banks of the river eagerly waited for it to freeze over, because the distances between villages would instantly become shorter and communication much easier than in the warmer months of the year. The day after it froze, locals would start attempting to cross the ice to the other side, and a short while later would make the first journeys across in horse-drawn carts.

It was at this time, when the river had only just frozen over, that Aunt Batish's husband Zhantursyn Zhanybekov unexpectedly paid us a visit. Arriving on two sledges, he announced that he intended taking us back home with him. We had never previously discussed our situation with him or asked him for help, nor had he ever said anything about wanting to take care of us; but it must have been clear to him what dire straits we were in.

Uncle Zhantursyn was in a great hurry because he had to attend to some urgent matters, and intended setting off the very next day. Mother wanted to collect a few things that had been hidden at relatives' houses the previous winter, but he refused to delay his departure. So they decided that Uncle Zhantursyn should take all of them except me with him, while I was given the job of fetching the hidden things from the aul where father's relatives were living. I really did not want to stay behind and make the long journey on my own in the winter frost, but I remembered what my mother had said to me that autumn: 'You're the only man in the family now. We depend on you.'

Once my family had left, I set off for the aul where Father's cousins – Yeskendyr and Zhakyp Makazhanov and Rakhimzhan and Alzhan Mukazhanov – were now permanently living in the huts that used to be their temporary winter stopping-places. There I collected our few possessions – two new felt rugs and two strips of white felt.

Uncle Alzhan would not let me set off back to Uncle Kozhakhmet's in daylight, in case one of the activists came across me on the way and confiscated the felt rugs and the horse on the spot. Worse still, he himself might be accused of concealing kulak's property and hauled up before the courts as an accomplice. So he made me wait until nightfall. He even hid my mare in a closed pen so that it did not attract unwanted attention: now that all the local residents' livestock had been collectivised, you hardly ever saw a tethered riding horse or anyone riding about the aul.

Confined indoors all day, I had to listen to my 'uncles' and their neighbours chatting about their daily lives on the collective farm. The main topic of conversation that day was how their last head of livestock – their one and only cow – was supposedly about to be taken away to the collective farm. The men were arguing that the rumour must be true because people in neighbouring auls were already slaughtering their cows for meat. They decided that they had better slaughter their cow that very night, and started to sharpen their knives while I was still there.

At nightfall, Alzhan put our 'valuables' behind my horse's saddle, helped me mount and get comfortable in the saddle, and then accompanied me to the ring road where nobody would be travelling at such a late hour. I had to ride nearly twenty kilometres along this road on my own. I still cannot fathom out how these adults, who had taken such care to store things of no particular value, gave no thought to how dangerous it might be for a nine-year-old boy to travel alone at night and how he must be feeling.

The winter night sky was overcast and the deserted white steppe stretched out all around me. Visibility was poor: I could hardly make out the tracks in front of me because of the fresh sprinkling of snow. I rode slowly, afraid of straying from the road and a bit scared. What really frightened me were the pictures that kept flashing before my eyes: first I saw the black outline of a bear, and then some other terrifying creatures. I kept going just as cautiously, my sense of alarm increasing all the time. After I had come out onto the main road leading to the regional centre, all of a sudden I noticed two bright specks of light ahead, glittering like eyes. I immediately pulled on the reins and stopped the horse in its tracks. The terrible idea flashed through my mind that it was a devil lying in wait for me.

I decided to turn back and escape; but then I remembered grown-ups' stories of devils and the horrible tricks they played on people. I also remembered you could not escape from a devil by running away as it would catch you anyway. If you encountered one, you had to remember that the best way to defend yourself was to attack it, especially on horseback, calling out the words of the Koran, 'There is no god but God, and Mohammed is his prophet!'

So I whipped my mare as hard as I could. The blow must have hurt, because she shot forwards and started galloping towards the glittering lights. A small gully appeared ahead. As soon as we had galloped into it, the lights disappeared. After racing along the night steppe for a while, we reached a piece of high ground from where I could see the lights of Ust-Kurchum shining in the distance. It slowly began to dawn on me that this was what those two scary eyes had actually been.

I must have strayed off the road when I was trying to attack the devil, so I set my bearings by the lights of the town, turned left, and rode across a trackless stretch of ground towards the aul I had left that morning. I then rode carefully across the steppe. My mare kept stubbornly pulling me to the left but, following the lights, I kept heading towards the right. All of a sudden my horse stopped sharply and stood stock still. Leaning forward slightly, I stared ahead and gasped in horror: we were standing on the very edge of a ravine, some fifteen to twenty feet deep. I started gently pulling on the reins and getting my mare to back. Just as terrified as me, she willingly did as she was asked.

After moving a safe distance away, I had a good look around. As the ravine was not far from my aul, I easily found my bearings and soon reached the ford across the River Kurchum. The ice on the river there was only two days old. I had managed to cross over that morning, but now, just to make matters even worse, I could distinctly hear the sound of rushing water.

Sometimes deep, fast-flowing sections of mountain rivers freeze over during the first hard frosts. Then, if the sun appears and there is a sharp change in temperature, all the springs with their relatively warm underground waters start rushing onto the ice and along the main riverbed in torrents. If the thaw continues for several days, this water may erode the thin crust of ice on the surface, making it extremely perilous to cross. Not only is there a danger of going through the ice, but the blocks floating by the banks make it harder for you to step down into the ford and then out onto the bank the other side, especially if your horse is unshod. The idea of crossing the ford now on an unshod horse – and, what's more, in the dark – absolutely petrified me.

I stood still, pondering what to do next. I knew I could not retrace my steps, and I had nowhere else to spend the night nearby. It would also be dangerous to linger on the bank in the freezing cold until daylight.

One thing, however, encouraged me: I was having a job to hold back my mare as she kept sniffing the edge of the noisy torrent of water, straining forwards and asking to be allowed to start crossing the ford, which she knew well and had crossed that morning. I remembered ages ago hearing adults say that horses always had a keen sense of danger, and the fact that my bay mare was unworried by the water made me feel braver. I had also had the notion drummed into my head since I was very young that every person has his or her own destiny which has been charted out in advance by the Almighty, and you can do nothing to change it. If I was destined to drown that day, I definitely would; if not, I would make it safely to the other side.

So, naïvely relying on predestination, I slackened the reins and the mare stepped confidently into the water. I, meanwhile, was shivering with fear, imagining the thin crust of ice cracking under my horse's weight and plunging us both into a black abyss. But my mare continued walking, even though her unshod hooves kept losing their grip on the slippery ice awash with water, sometimes splaying and nearly collapsing under her and jolting me out of the saddle. At moments like these my heart missed a couple of beats; however, she miraculously managed to draw herself back up and right herself and keep going.

Eventually, she made it to the other bank and I breathed a huge sigh of relief. It was hard to tell what had played the most important part: the horse's instinct, or predestination.

Next morning, when I told Uncle Kozhakhmet about the ride, he gave me the following advice: 'Once you'd seen the lights and reckoned they were a devil's eyes, you did the right thing to head straight for them – that's what people generally advise you to do in such cases. But lights at night don't always have to do with evil spirits: they also tell you there are people living or travelling nearby, and can help you find your way in the dark. Remember, though, that – especially in the steppe – a light may seem close in the dark when it is really a long way off. If you ride straight towards it, it may take you the whole night and even longer.

'As for you being scared at the ford, it was through not knowing about such things. A fresh crust of ice on the river at the start of winter, no matter how thin it is, will never get worn through by the torrents of water in just one day. In your case, the slippery ice under the water was more of a danger to your mare: in such conditions, unshod horses keep slipping and sliding all over the place and usually fall. It was lucky for you that your mare was used to fords like this.'

Another journey, longer and even more difficult, now lay ahead of me: I had to ride over to the other side of the Irtysh with the load of felt rugs and our other belongings to Zhantursyn

Zhanybekov's home. In the frost and snow the journey would take all day, and I would have to cross the new ice on the Irtysh and make the second half of journey along an unfamiliar route. I was dreading it: I was fed up with these journeys I was having to make through sheer necessity, and no longer hankered after adventure.

However, I had to rejoin my family somehow. By today's standards, I did not have to travel far: at the most, 40 kilometres by the shortest route from Uncle Kozhakhmet's home. But at the last minute he decided to send me round the ring road, making the journey half as long again. He explained his decision thus: 'The short, straight route you're familiar with goes right through the regional centre. You might bump into people there who know whose son you are; you might also run across them on the steppe road, as it's always very busy. The activists are always after easy money, and they might just take the rugs and mare off you as kulak's property that should have been confiscated. That's why you need to avoid places like that. If you go along the ring road, you won't meet a soul and you'll be safe.'

Then he gave his son Bazar instructions to accompany me on the first part of the journey and show me the way: 'The Irtysh is frozen over near the village of Kamyshenka and people started crossing over today. See Mukhamet over to the other side. Follow the cart tracks over the ice across the river. Keep in single file: whatever you do, don't ride side by side or trot. The ice may not be strong enough to stand the weight of two horses or pounding hooves. Once you've crossed, lead him to the road by the sand dunes.'

Then he turned to me and continued, 'There won't be any tracks but the snow's thin enough for you to be able to follow the road. Keep going along the edge of the sands and the river valley. On the way you'll come to three lakes that you have to go round, keeping to the sand. These lakes are joined to the Irtysh by a marshy strip of land with a narrow stream running through the middle.

'This marshy strip may be covered with ice, but it takes a long time to freeze over properly. It's dangerous to take the shortest route through the marsh, because if your horse falls in, you'll never get it out again. That's why you need to go round the west side of each lake, along the sands. Just remember this: you must keep to the sandy track. The sand will be frozen hard just along the surface and it can just about bear the weight of a horse if you go at a careful and slow pace. At a fast trot or canter her hooves will sink through the sand. This will slow your horse down: without a firm surface under her hooves, she'll have to work harder and tire more quickly, and get sore feet; then she'll go lame and you'll be stranded in the deserted steppe and freeze to death. If you follow all my advice, the journey won't be that hard for a saddled horse. Follow the outline of the road which you'll make out through the thin layer of snow, along the edge of the sand dunes as far as a daub and wattle cottage with a wooden roof by the roadside, where there is another road leading off to the left towards the sands. Go along it over the dunes and you'll reach the aul of Kokzhira where your family's now staying.'

So, following my uncle's instructions, I took the longer route to be safe and – after parting company from Bazar – found myself once again all alone in the deserted steppe. There were no tracks at all. I followed the outline of the road that I could just make out under the snow. A short while later I came across the hoof prints of two saddled horses that must have passed this way about two days previously. They ran along side by side all the way, which meant the riders must have been chatting as they rode along. I couldn't help feeling envious that they'd had each other for company.

There were no people or animals anywhere to be seen. Since having their livestock taken away from them earlier that year, the locals had stayed closer to their collective farm in their spring and autumn stopping-places instead of moving to their usual winter homes. I kept coming across abandoned homes and livestock pens, and there was something eerie about the gaping narrow windows and doors. I felt even more scared when I remembered some of the adults' stories I had heard about deserted houses and yards being haunted by devils and demons which were always trying to harm people, especially if they were on their own and did not know the right words to chase them away – just like me, I thought to myself. Then I started wondering anxiously if there were any wolves about. I recalled the adults' stories about packs of wolves surrounding a rider out alone in the deserted steppe and – just like me, I thought again.

Terrified by all these imaginings, I finally reached my destination at dusk when the frost was beginning to bite. A man from next door spotted me first and rushed towards me, exclaiming, 'O, Lord, the boy's frozen stiff!' The stranger then helped me off my horse and into the wooden house. The moment they set eyes on me, my family started fussing around me: I really had come close to freezing to death.

Chapter Thirteen

At Kalmakbai Aul

The year 1932 began without many falls of snow, but the frosts were bitterly cold. The aul we were now living in consisted of three family homes set apart from the other aul along the River Laila, in what was then the Kokzhira area and is now part of the Samara region. In the absence of any means of communication such as telephones or a postal service, it was totally cut off from the outside world: collectivisation meant that there was a severe lack of transport at people's disposal, and no sledges had established the usual tracks on the winter routes between remote villages. We had heard not a word from Father since his last letter in the autumn, and nobody knew for sure where he was. We had not heard from any of our other relatives either.

Our kind hosts, Zhantursyn Zhanybekov and Aunt Batish, were both around 50. Uncle Zhantursyn, having managed to hold onto his individual holding and even acquire the use of some additional land on a temporary basis, had sown a variety of cereals, including a high percentage of millet, and they had all grown and produced quite good crops. After delivering the statutory amount of cereals to the State (by way of tax paid in kind), he still had a year's supply of grain for his own consumption. Although these supplies were not vast, he and his wife, as was traditionally expected of them, felt a deep-seated sense of duty towards their relatives, and decided to take care of the mother and four children whose breadwinner had been taken away from them.

Apparently, Uncle Zhantursyn had once owned a prosperous holding with a large number of livestock. Back in 1916, however, he and Aunt Batish had emigrated to China, and lost everything there within the year: they had just made it home alive, with nothing more than the clothes they were standing in. They chose to return to her parents and brothers rather than his relatives, and were welcomed with open arms. Within a few years they had received enough help to start a home of their own and erect a yurt, and every family in the aul donated a head of livestock to them. So here was Uncle Zhantursyn, who had once rebuilt his own life with the help and support of his wife's relatives, helping the destitute family of his imprisoned brother-in-law.

People's perception of living standards varies strangely, depending on their own circumstances at the time. Only a year ago, Uncle Zhantursyn had been looked upon as an impoverished peasant with only one horse to his name; now his neighbours, who were all collective farmers, reckoned he was 'wealthy'. What it was really about, however, was the extreme poverty of the collective farmers.

While they had only a week's supply of food put by and were waiting for the end of the agricultural year to be remunerated for the number of days they had worked, Zhantursyn, who worked for himself, had a full year's supply of grain stored up. While the collective farmers toiled in the freezing cold, either looking after the small herd or doing unwaged work in State enterprises by way of paying off the collective farm's taxes, the individual peasant farmer was resting at home in the warm. In his yard he kept a horse which he could ride wherever he liked, while the farmers had no horses of their own and were not allowed to go anywhere without the collective farm management's permission.

Still, it could not be said that we lived in great comfort: our diet consisted of millet and the meat of an old gelding Uncle

Zhantursyn had recently slaughtered. As for his house, it was a ramshackle hovel belonging to someone else who had run away from his collective farm. Zhantursyn had arranged with the owner's relatives to rent it until the end of the winter.

But 1932 had barely begun, and we were still in the coldest part of the winter, when we were told that the house's owner was returning to the aul and wanted his property back. Zhantursyn looked so dejected when he came back home with this news that we guessed something was wrong at once. The three adults kept asking each other questions like, 'Where are we going to find somewhere vacant to live at this time of the year?' and 'Who's going to agree to having seven people, even for a short time?' We could sense how desperate they were.

Failing to find a solution to their dilemma, they tried to tell themselves that the reports about the owner's return were just a rumour. This state of uncertainty did not last long, however, as sure enough the owner turned up and demanded that the house be vacated within the week. Adhering to the traditional custom of honouring our host, we were forced to obey. As we were unable to find a temporary refuge in the neighbouring aul, we all had to move eight kilometres away to a house belonging to our young in-law, Manap, that had stood empty all winter.

Moving all our household goods, lock, stock and barrel, to another place in the freezing cold was dreadfully hard, and nothing like the festive migrations to the summer pastures we used to enjoy so much. It was hardest of all for Uncle Zhantursyn, who had to travel over to the new house three days in a row and gradually heat it up enough to make it habitable. On the fourth day he at last moved all the members of the family over except for me, as I had to stay behind to guard all the belongings in the old house. He then spent the next week transporting the winter supplies of logs, hay, grain and seeds. I accompanied him every day on another sleigh loaded with our belongings, helping him as much as I could.

The most difficult part of the journey was making the first sleigh tracks along the route between the two aul, as it usually took until midwinter for them to become established by frequent use. This must have been what made the journey so exhausting and laborious that I still remember it clearly. Our horses struggled very hard to pull the sleighs along the trackless route; there were times when they came to complete standstill, overwhelmed by the weight of their load. Then Uncle had to take off some of the things and leave them on the wayside. It was a good thing that nobody else was travelling that way and none of the things we left behind got stolen.

All these hitches put Uncle Zhantursyn in a foul mood, and he began cursing the horses for refusing to pull the half-empty sleighs, and the Soviet authorities for leaving people without a means of transport so that there were no tracks through the snow that winter, and the house's owner for foolishly deciding to return to his aul in the depths of winter, and, finally, God for not giving him his fair share of happiness and a normal life. Nevertheless, he still went on giving me useful tips on how to deal with each situation as it cropped up during those few days. He obviously enjoyed giving instructions whenever he could, repeating over and over again, 'When you do a job, you're doing someone else a favour, and when you learn something new, you're doing yourself a favour.'

Certainly, this move of ours taught me a lot – and not just that being evicted in midwinter is a most demoralising and harrowing experience. Perhaps the most useful thing was that horses fed only on hay during the winter tire quickly and cannot pull heavy loads for several days in a row. As a popular saying puts it, 'If you want your horses to go faster, use oats and not a whip' – though I did not hear this until later on.

ii

Our new house was in an aul named Kalmakbai after its founder, the great-grandfather of the people living there in the 1930s. It consisted of five or six fairly prosperous-looking households: three smallholdings had already been classified as kulak, and their property and livestock had been confiscated and the heads of family repressed, but the kinsmen who were still there went on supporting and helping one another just as before. There were several Russian villages nearby and the people of this aul had adopted some of their farming methods and learnt a smattering of Russian, which was unusual for Kazakhs in our area.

The people of Kalmakbai strictly observed their time-honoured traditions, and treated us newcomers with great kindness and consideration. It was here that I first heard people cite the popular saying, 'Your duty to your neighbour is as sacred as it is to God,' and I think I understood what it meant when I saw how attentive our neighbours were to us. 'Friendly and just how an aul should be,' was how Mother summed up the reception we were given by our new neighbours, who were all Manap's relatives, and therefore our in-laws as well.

I do not know how the adults in our families felt in their new surroundings, but I had a marvellous time. I had several friends of my own age whom I had first met the previous autumn while I had been staying with my sister. As this aul had no livestock except ours and no school, the children were not required to do any work, and could play games and have fun all day long. My only duty was to give water to the two mares twice a day and muck out their stalls. My friends used to come over and help me, and between us we used to finish the chores quickly and then go off to play. The aul stood directly beneath the eastern spurs of the Kalpinsky Ridge, and it was really good fun sledging down the foothills: I was enjoying myself so much that I even forgot to think about Father, where he was and what might have happened to him.

And yet, without our neighbours' livestock, an eerie silence hung over the aul: there was no mooing, bleating or neighing. 'People are missing the sounds of their animals,' the aul elders would remark. This had been an aul devoted to stockbreeding, but everyone had either surrendered their animals to the collective farms or slaughtered them before they were forced to do so.

But those who had turned over all their livestock still regarded it as theirs, and believed that it would eventually be returned to them. When someone was doing a job on the collective farm or borrowing a cart for his personal use, he used to try to borrow a horse, camel or ox he had once owned. There were cases when a former owner would see someone mishandling his horse and tell him off, and sometimes fists would fly. It was even known for ex-owners to slaughter animals to provide their families with meat. I once saw some neighbours of ours doing this, and nothing at all happened to them afterwards. A huge number of livestock must have gone missing from the collective farms, however, because the local authorities started organising commissions made up of activists and getting them to travel round the aul, on the pretext of checking if there was any livestock still to be collectivised.

One such commission   g of three of the most trusted
officials from   rned up in Kalmakbai and
im   h the houses and yards. They
                           r house, peering in all the
                           tock pen, trying to sniff
                           itly searching for was the
                           collective farm. None of
                           hey had to conduct the
                           to do so. None of the
                           on the contrary, they
                           irch, pointing out all
                           not thieves.
                           mmission spotted
                           e hay store and
                           e and tail.
                           kbayev that he's
                           e should have
                           there today.'
                           commission
                           sation, way
l   his father-
ir   ngs to the
he   n, Manap's mother-
in-l   r keeping going. Have pity on
these   been left without a father and let them
keep   mare.'

But the custodians of the collective farm's property had already made up their minds to confiscate the mare. Then Zhantursyn said to the commission head, 'One old mare isn't going to make your collective farm any richer. Why don't you take what else you like from us but leave the bay mare be?'

'What have you got? What can you give us?' asked the commission head, his eyes lighting up.

'I've got a bottle of vodka I've set aside to exchange for tea. You can take that.'

'All right, we'll leave your mare. Only you'll have to get rid of her tonight,' the commission head told my uncle, 'or else someone else will spot her tomorrow. Then you, Zhantursyn, will be accused of stealing and concealing a collective farm mare and have to suffer the consequences.'

Uncle Zhantursyn brought him out the litre bottle of vodka with a factory stamp on its side. The official went on his way delighted with his perk. Later the same day we slaughtered the bay mare for meat rather than let her be taken away for good. It was a sad moment, even though we were accustomed to killing and eating the animals we reared.

In the collectivised aul, the very foundations of the tribal system began to be destroyed. Since time immemorial blood relatives had lived together in the same aul, and anyone who left it brought shame upon the entire clan. People now started moving away from their close relatives, either to flee the collective farms or to spend the winter working for the State in distant places to fulfil their tax obligations, often never to be seen again.

The Soviet State always made extensive use of the collective farmers' unpaid labour, particularly during the first few years when the farms were being set up. It relied heavily on these fledgling enterprises to finance many of the projects that should have been paid for out of State funds. There were always plenty of projects on the go, be it the construction of roads, the introduction of a postal service, or timber felling and transportation. (This became a key industry when the regions acquired a telephone network and vast quantities of telegraph poles were suddenly needed. It was the collective farms that provided the manpower to deliver these poles, dig the holes for them and secure them.) Auxiliary workers from different regions were also sent to help in the mines in the Altai and Kalba mountains. These endless contributions of manpower seriously damaged the collectives' fledgling economies, since they never had enough for their own needs.

There was always a shortage of accommodation and food at these places. Far away from their homes and families, collective farmers often lived at the timber-processing sites in makeshift shelters. Those of them who were sent to work in the mines used to leave their aul with their entire family, often to find on their arrival that they had not been allocated any accommodation: such families would end up in a small hut with fifteen to twenty people sharing the same living space.

It has to be said that collective farmers willingly went off to work in the mines, because they were issued with ration cards there which they could exchange for food and horse fodder. Generally speaking, however, the position these people were in was appalling: nobody at their temporary work places took responsibility for their welfare, while the management of the collective farms washed their hands of them once they were no longer living there. Although they were supposed to return to the farms the following spring, some of them decided never to go back.

Why did people put up with all this? Mainly through fear. Not only did the law forbid them to leave the collective farms without permission, but unemployment was so widespread that they knew they had little hope of finding work anywhere else.

iii

The crisis gripping Kazakh society was made even worse in the winter of 1932 by an appalling smallpox epidemic. Although this disease had generally been eradicated in European countries, many people in the vast expanses of Kazakhstan had yet to benefit from vaccination programmes, especially those living in remote aul. In our community that winter, the seven families lost a total of eight infants. Four children ranging in age from two and a half to eight died in Manap's family alone, while three of my friends aged between ten and eleven, who only a short while before had been full of life and playing boisterous games with me, also fell victim to the dreadful disease.

My youngest sister Sharizhamal, aged two and a half, was the one member of the family to fall sick with it, and I witnessed its progress from start to finish. The first signs of a child having contracted the smallpox virus are frequent bouts of sneezing; 24 hours on, the sick child develops a high fever and his body breaks out in a red rash. These spots gradually increase in size and form blisters all over his body. Then his body starts swelling, his face begins to droop, his eyes also lose their shape and there is now a thin line between his swollen lips where his mouth used to be, and two holes in place of his nose. The disease peaks between the fifth and the seventh day. This is also the time when it becomes possible to predict whether the sick child is going to pull through. If, on the seventh day, the large, light reddish blisters full of fluid suddenly start shrinking rapidly and becoming darker, and the swelling begins to go down all over the body, you know that the disease has overwhelmed the sick child and he cannot fight it any longer; he dies shortly afterwards.

On the other hand, if a crust begins to form on the surface of the shrinking blisters on the seventh day, you know that the child is starting to recover: you just have to be careful that he does not catch a chill and there are no complications or relapses. At the next stage of recovery, the scabs that have formed on the blisters become extremely itchy and the sick child starts furiously scratching them. It is now up to the adults not to let him scratch his face, because if the scabs come off, others form with even thicker crusts and leave pockmarks when they eventually clear up, sometimes causing serious facial disfigurement. More appalling than these pockmarks, it can leave a person deaf or take his sight away. Superstitious people were so terrified of its terrible after-effects that they never dared refer to the disease by name, and tried to appease it by calling it the 'holy illness' instead. Thanks to God and science, there has never been another smallpox epidemic in Kazakhstan since that terrible year of 1932.

But only two months after the epidemic there was an outbreak of another virulent children's disease – measles – which proved fatal for quite a number of children still recovering from smallpox. Poor parents who could expect no help from any source except their Creator had to suffer the heartbreak of losing a child. Despite the slogans to the contrary, the Soviet State offered them no support or medicine whatsoever.

My mother was just such a parent. Already weakened by smallpox, Sharizhamal, my little sister and everyone's darling, could not cope with another illness in such a short space of time. She died, and was buried in the aul cemetery.

iv

Among those living in the aul was a 37-year-old man by the name of Koramsak Yentibayev, who was on the run from the authorities after refusing to join a collective farm and being denounced as a kulak. He had left his family, smallholding and livestock to the mercy of fate, taken his favourite bay horse – which was much admired throughout the area – and just headed off.

The fugitive had spent the whole summer of 1931 hiding from the authorities at relatives' and friends' homes; then, just before winter, he had come back to live with his family at home. His aul where my family was then staying was five kilometres from the aul council's centre and the villages of Kaznakovka and Moskovka. By then nobody seemed to be searching for him any more, and although wary of strangers, he lived more or less openly among us. When an outsider visited the aul, he would take a furtive look to see what the visitor looked like, and then go out and say hello. 'I haven't got a sign on me,' he would say, 'so how is he to know who I am?' If he recognised the visitor, he would sometimes go out and greet him with the words, 'Here's someone who knows how to keep their mouth shut.'

He lived like this for most of the winter. Many of the people in the surrounding aul knew where he was hiding, but nobody betrayed him to the authorities.

The month of March arrived and the sun grew warmer with every passing day. The children in the aul who had survived the smallpox epidemic were already playing on the sunny southern slopes of the foothills above their homes. Meanwhile, livestock continued to vanish from the collective farm. Our aul received a visit from yet another commission created by the local aul council to track down the stolen animals, and any other livestock that had been concealed by the local residents to avoid being collectivised.

The commission members again started rummaging through everything – peering into all the dark corners of the old livestock pens, digging in the piles of straw, firewood and snow in the yard, and poking in trunks of clothes and under beds. Although they failed to find anything when they came to Koramsak's house, their suspicions were aroused by a fresh haystack standing in a yard with no animals in it. They decided that it was being used to hide the meat of stolen livestock – but after pulling the whole haystack apart, what should they find there but the fugitive's famous bay horse. So delighted were they that they looked no further for its owner, who was actually hiding in one of the houses, in a pit that had been made under a bed for this purpose.

We children were fascinated by all the goings-on and eagerly watched events unfolding, taking in every detail. The haystack had been made against the wall of the livestock shed, with the hay carefully piled around the outside in a semi-circle right to the top of the wall, leaving a hollow space inside. Poles had then been laid across the top and covered with more hay, and the bay horse hidden inside. A small opening had been made in the shed's wall through which the horse could be watered and fed. In the daytime, the opening in the wall was covered so neatly with adobe bricks that in the shadowy light you could not tell it was there.

When the horse was led out into the light after standing in the dark for so long, it started prancing joyfully on the spot and trying to lunge forwards. The two burly young commission members holding onto its reins on either side just managed to hold it back. Its large rolling eyes flashed in the bright sunlight, and its fine shiny coat quivered every time it moved. It kept snorting like a wild mule and neighing in a fierce but delighted manner. It must have been kept in hiding for a long time, because its front hooves in particular had grown so long that they looked like upturned round trays or saucers.

In the end, though, the horse was not led away to join the collective farm herd. In full view of us and all the other people present, Koramsak's brother – known, in honour of his advanced age, as Elder Mambet – emerged from the house carrying a folded length of black cloth, and handed it to the commission member in charge, who was sitting on his own horse. The man took the bribe and, without dismounting, shoved the whole thing down his baggy jodhpurs. A secret deal had obviously been struck. The only details still a mystery were the length of the cloth and how much the man's baggy jodhpurs could hold, if a bulky 'gift' could easily fit down one side of them. Satisfied, the commission members went on their way.

They evidently kept quiet about having found signs of the 'fugitive bandit', as they called Koramsak. But after this, he no longer walked around the aul in the daytime. Now that the ground on the southern slopes of the foothills was clear of snow, he would ride out into the mountains during the hours of daylight and hide in the gullies.

After a while, though, the authorities found out where he was living. The newly appointed chairman of the aul council (and in those days they were appointed and dismissed nearly every month), wanting to show his mettle in the service of the Soviet authorities, determined to catch the fugitive and hand him over to the courts. So he organised a detachment of local activists. After arming them with three rifles, he set off with them in search of Koramsak.

However, Koramsak was used to being constantly on the lookout. As soon as he heard the riders' loud voices as they rode toward him between the snowy hills, he galloped into his aul to warn his family that the activists were after him, and then raced off into the mountains again so that he was well out of the reach. The activists followed his tracks to the aul. Reluctant to pursue him further, they stopped there and the chairman of the aul council called out Koramsak's brother and began swearing and shouting at him in the street, in front of other people. Then, still sitting on his horse, he started pointing his rifle at him:

'Where's the bandit Koramsak? Find him and hand him over! I'll arrest you if you don't.'

Elder Mambet replied, 'If you're searching for the bandit, look – here are his tracks and they'll lead you to where he's hiding. Go and catch him. But it does not become the chairman of the aul council to frighten people with a gun with children around.'

All the chairman's companions kept silent, not wanting to interrupt his conversation with the elder. The chairman, however, responded instantly by striking him a sharp blow on his head with the butt of his rifle. The old man slumped to the ground. Beside himself with anger, the chairman leaned over his horse and went on striking him while he lay motionless.

At first, nobody reacted to the chairman's brutal conduct by saying or doing anything. Then the injured man's wife went rushing over to the chairman, seized hold of his rifle, and started shrieking, 'Murderer! Go on then, kill me too!'

The chairman tried to pull the rifle out of the woman's hands, but she would not let go or let him strike her poor husband any more. Embarrassed, he eventually gave up and stopped shouting. Just then one of the activists piped up, 'It's nearly evening. The bandit Koramsak might take a pot-shot at us from the hills and hit someone. We'd better get going fast before anything happens. We can start searching again tomorrow morning.'

The others agreed with him, and they all galloped out of the aul.

For some reason, they did not return the next day, and nobody bothered him the following days either. But after the new chairman's savage attack on Mambet, it became clear to everyone concerned that the fugitive could not go on living in the same manner as before. His relatives started pleading with him. 'The way you're living now,' they said, 'you'll end up one day falling into the hands of some brute of an activist and being shot dead. It's getting even harder to hide from strangers and the authorities. The aul aren't going to be in remote places in the future like the ones you've been used to hiding in: they're all going to be brought together in a special yurt settlement for the summer. You've got to stop living like a fugitive: you should turn yourself over to the regional authorities and hand them a confession. That's the best answer.'

In the end they talked Koramsak round. 'If you want to run away from the Soviet authorities,' he said with a sigh, 'you have to escape across the border to China. I don't want to leave my homeland. If I can't live as a fugitive in my own area any more, I'd better turn myself in and pay the penalty just like all the others who've been persecuted for being hard-working, thrifty farmers, good at raising livestock and producing plenty of wheat.'

His mind made up, Koramsak rode his horse to the regional centre and turned himself over to the security police. But initial questioning and checks established that there was no official record of him being a bandit on the run. Nor had he committed any anti-Soviet acts: his only indictable crime was the civil offence of not registering himself or his horse. It was also established that neither he nor his smallholding figured in any documents concerning kulaks and their dispossession: he was considered a peasant of average means, and therefore not liable to be dispossessed. In short, the man had spent an entire year on the run quite unnecessarily.

But just when it seemed that fair play would triumph at last, the reason for his problems became clear. The whole situation had arisen because of his splendid and much-coveted bay horse. The activists' main motive for pressuring him to join the collective farm had been not to swell the labour force, but to get his horse there so that they could ride it.

Now that he had been proved innocent, the horse became the subject of heated arguments between the leaders of the regional authorities. The head of the regional security police, Semionov, wanted to requisition the horse so that he could keep it in his department, while the regional executive committee chairman, Omirzhanov, got the regional prosecutor to help him bring charges against Koramsak for failing to register himself and his animal. Then, while he was being held in custody, the prosecutor offered him a deal.

'Look here, Yentibayev,' he said, 'of course you're not a class enemy, but you've broken Soviet law. You didn't register your horse or yourself, and you went on the run from the authorities, so you're liable to be prosecuted. But there may just be a way of getting you out of this fix. The regional executive committee chairman has taken a liking to your horse. If you were to present your horse to the regional executive committee in exchange for another, you might be let off and set free. You can choose any horse you like from the collective farm in exchange for yours.'

So Koramsak agreed, and the 'bandit on the run' was set free.

v

The spring of 1932 arrived. It was the time for nurturing new-born animals, and for ploughing and sowing for the next harvest. That year, however, the residents of the aul did none of these things, because they no longer had any land to sow crops on or livestock to breed from. Only on the collective farms were preparations underway for the spring sowing. Detailed instructions on the types of crops, quantities to be sown and dates for the sowing had been issued from above. We found out about this just as the thaw began and there was slush everywhere. The farmers who had been sent off by the collective farm to fulfil its obligations by doing unpaid labour on State enterprises started returning to their aul.

Among them was my sister Zhamba's husband Manap, who had been sent off by his collective farm to work at the Kuludzhin mine after the autumn harvest and whose house my family had been staying in since midwinter. Three families with thirteen people between them now had to live together in one large room. As the

Kazakh saying goes, 'By spring, fat stock grows thin, and by spring thin stock's nothing.' Two of the families – Manap's and mine – had very little food put by, and the adults kept discussing ways of increasing our supplies. None of our three families had any money to buy food with; nor did we have any spare things of any value to sell – and even if we had had, there was nowhere and nobody to sell it to. We knew because we had tried.

In our house we had two saddles specially designed for women riders which had somehow escaped the confiscations. Gilt- and silver-edged, they had once been worth as much as a good-quality horse or camel. The adults decided to take them to the nearest Russian villages of Kaznakovka, Orazbai, and Moskovka to sell or exchange for grain, forgetting that the people there had also been collectivised. The Russian villagers they showed the saddles to looked them over admiringly and then asked good-humouredly, 'But why would we want them? What would we put them on – our women? Bet they wouldn't let us!' And then, sighing, they added wistfully, 'We ain't even got pigs left in our yards. Not even a hen!'

So we remained broke. The days grew warmer and the snow melted away. The earth became steamy and the roads between the aul dried out. Beggars appeared from other auls, asking for help. As far as I can remember, I had hardly ever seen people begging like this in Kazakh auls before. Now, in the spring of 1932, several turned up every week.

To start with, our adults greeted them sympathetically and hurriedly gave them something or other, anxiously asking them about themselves and their clans and relatives, and how their circumstances had changed so drastically. They were genuinely concerned and anxious for them. The growing number of beggars testified to the national catastrophe that was getting ever nearer. Although in the spring of 1932 the famine was not yet widespread in the Altai region of Eastern Kazakhstan, you could still sense it was not far away.

As soon as it was time to sow the spring crops, Uncle Zhantursyn went off with Aunt Batish to prepare the soil on the plot of land he had been allocated as an individual farmer. The three families left behind consisted of ten people, none of whom worked except Manap, who was getting a very low wage at the collective farm. In my family there were now just three of us – my mother, my six-year-old younger brother Mukhametrakhim and me – as my second sister, Altynzhan, had got married that winter.

When work began in the fields again, Manap got Mother's permission to take me along as a driver, reckoning that I would at least be fed there by the collective farm.

That spring, after the merger of several small collective farms, teams of labourers known as 'brigades' were set up for the first time to work the land. Another innovation was that all the farmers working on the land ate food from the collective farm field kitchen, so all those whose food supplies were running low moved to a field camp with their families. Any who still had yurts took them along to live in, while the rest lived in shelters and very basic makeshift tents. There was no reason for the members of the collective farm to stay in their winter stopping-places, as they had no livestock any more or – unlike Russian villagers – even vegetable gardens to tend to.

It was wonderfully novel for us Kazakhs to live and work together in a field camp with the twenty other members of the work brigade and all their family members, including children. Each family or single man was given a hot meal prepared by the collective farm cooks three times a day, with portions for everyone taking part in the field work and all their family members entitled not to work. Then they all went back to their yurts and tents to eat their food.

From the very start, communal cooking provoked amazement and derision, sarcastic remarks and criticism. People were forever grumbling about the poor quality of the meals and the unfair way the food was shared between members of the brigade, with some getting bigger, better portions than others. After the first ten days these conversations turned into arguments and nasty slanging matches, and the brigade members refused to eat the same prepared meals. All the families and single men in the brigade decided to get food raw from the collective farm in whatever quantities they were entitled to, and cook it themselves and eat in separate family groups. This was mainly how meals were provided on Kazakh collective farms until they became State farms at the end of the 1950s.

Work in the brigade began at sunrise. After two or three hours, the brigade would return for breakfast and to rest and feed the horses. The ploughing would then continue until lunchtime, when the horses were rested for a couple of hours. After lunch work would resume until it grew too dark to see the furrows.

The ploughmen worked in pairs, or teams as they were called. Manap and one of his relatives were issued with a double-blade ploughshare, a brand-new piece of farm machinery which kept steady without the ploughmen constantly having to steer it. Instead of walking behind it all day as they had done with the single-blade model, they waited at the edges of the field while we drivers guided the horses from the front, and then, when we reached them, helped us to turn round and head in the opposite direction. As for us, each in charge of five horses, we spent the whole day in the saddle, and always managed to exceed our daily target of one and a half hectares. (We were also responsible for harrowing the ploughed area after it had been sown – by hand, of course.) Our work in the fields continued like this for nearly two months.

It is important to stress here that in the spring of 1932 all forms of work on Kazakh collective farms were still done using draught horses and camels. Bulls were seldom kept on Kazakh farms, as they were not recognised working animals. Later on, as the years went by and there were fewer horses, oxen became the principal draught animal and means of transport on collective farms. There came a time when there was only one horse left on the whole collective farm, which was ridden by the chairman while all his assistants rode bulls.

It seems to me that, compared to later on, the farmers in those early years of collectivisation had a more responsible approach to their work: they still had the natural instincts of honest workers and landowners, and had not yet learnt ways of shirking their duties. There was not a single case of even a tiny patch of land being left unploughed or unharrowed – the brigade-leader and ploughmen made quite sure this never happened. However, there were already some signs of things to come.

During the long sowing process, I spent the whole day working beside the men, listening to all their stories, anecdotes and arguments, and watching rows flare up. I noticed that some of the collective farmers in the brigade used to steal a proportion of the seeds that had been brought over for them to sow – as much as a quarter of them. However, nobody except the brigade-leader considered it to be theft or did anything to prevent it. I gathered from comments passed by the adults that it was not wrong to take something for oneself if it did not belong to anyone in particular in the first place – and if it was public property, it belonged to nobody in particular. As a child, I instinctively felt that this attitude was wrong; but unfortunately for our society, a great many people were subsequently to adopt it.

Chapter Fourteen

Deportation

Since the letter in autumn informing us that Father was alive and due to be sent to the town of Ridder along with others from the same area, we had heard nothing more about him. It was a whole year since we had left our home and relatives in the aul, but none of them had tried to find us; nor was there any chance of us going to see them, though we would have dearly loved to. The Soviet authorities, however, had not forgotten about us.

After the sowing was over, Manap went on working at various jobs on the collective farm, while I stayed at home. When he got home from work one evening, he announced with downcast eyes that the aul council had received a letter from the regional authorities informing them that my family was being deported to Ridder. The actual instructions read as follows:

'Shayakhmet Aitlembetov's family members are to be delivered within 48 hours to the quay at Baty village for deportation to the place where the head of the family is being detained. They are then to be handed over to the Baty village council, together with documents containing a certified list of the deported family members, in exchange for a signed receipt. Kokzhirinsk aul council is to be responsible for transporting the Aitlembetov family to Baty village.' The local collective was to make a cart available and enlist Manap to drive us.

Ridder was, in fact, a very much sought-after destination in those days. Thousands of hungry Kazakhs were simply longing to get there because you could actually find work where you were given proper food rations. But we, thanks to our isolated life in the aul, had no idea about this.

We reached Baty village after dark, and discovered that we were the first deportees to arrive. The local village council had turned the village hall into temporary accommodation for families like us. That night, without any supper, we lay down to sleep just inside the entrance to the hall in the dark. Manap went off into the steppe on the other side of the village to graze his horses until morning. Trembling with fear in this horrible empty building that used to be a church, the three of us could hardly wait for morning to come. We had plenty of reasons to be scared. Baty was a Russian village, and we had never stayed in one of those before. You see, we had heard stories more than once in the past about Russians supposedly killing Kazakhs in cold blood just because they had strayed into the village on their own. In addition, empty rooms, especially those belonging to Christian infidels who did not know the divine word of Islam, could quite easily shelter all sorts of evil spirits. These terrifying fancies played havoc with our imaginations.

In the morning Manap came to the hall with a Russian woman and helped us move our things over to the far corner of the hall's stage. Once he had settled us in, Manap said his goodbyes, wished us a safe journey, and set off home.

For a week we lived in this hall on our own. We could not chat to anyone because we hardly knew any Russian; we had no idea when we were going to be taken to Ridder, and in this state of uncertainty the time we spent there seemed like an eternity. It was only during the second week that other deportees began arriving, and they all turned out to be Russian. A week later there were as many as ten families, mostly women and children.

Their arrival made our life much more interesting. Although we could not speak Russian at all well, my brother and I had great fun playing with the boys of our age. Far from shying away from us, they eagerly accepted us into their group of friends. In the evenings the Russian women used to dance to the sounds of an accordion, sing songs together and see who could make up the funniest rhyming verses as they danced. Mother used to call these contests 'aitys', after the improvised singing contests Kazakh nomads used to hold in their aul. The Russian women used to have a really wild time, as though they were waiting to go to a party instead of to be deported. Amazed, Mother used to enjoy watching the dancing and listening to the songs, and stop brooding for a while; however, as soon as they stopped, she would become lost in reverie again. Part of the problem was that she could only communicate with the other women using sign language: it was a great relief to her when two Kazakh families arrived.

Along with all the other families, we stayed in this hall for nearly a month. Nobody properly explained the reason for the delay. We were simply told that the steamers could not take us yet, that we would be informed of our departure on the actual day, and that we had to wait.

Living in such makeshift accommodation for a long time was very difficult for families with young children and elderly relatives, and only women in charge. We had no equipment to cook hot meals, no beds to sleep in or even washing facilities, let alone a bathhouse to get properly clean in. The authorities showed no concern whatsoever for our living conditions or food supplies, and some families went hungry: even those who had money were unable to buy food from the locals.

The long-awaited day of our departure finally arrived. That morning the chairman of the local village council announced that all the deported families heading for Ridder were to board the steamer that would be arriving from the upper reaches of the Irtysh. A horse and cart was provided for the families to take turns in conveying their belongings from the hall to the quay and the steamers' moorings. And then we sat all day in the baking heat on the banks of the Irtysh waiting for the steamer.

The women whiled the time away chatting and exchanging views on what was happening. As each family's belongings were loaded into the cart and then unloaded and placed in a separate pile on the riverbank, the Kazakh women noticed that the Russian families had large bundles of belongings and huge, heavy, trunks – quite different from their own tiny bundles and small cases, which even a small child could lift and carry. They eventually decided that the Russian families had such a lot of valuables with them because the Russian activists were not such determined robbers as the Kazakh officials: they might be infidels, but they were still more sympathetic and kind-hearted.

We finally boarded the passenger steamer in the evening. As we had never set eyes on a steamer before, all of us, adults and children alike, found the whole experience very frightening: the narrow wooden plank between the quay and steamer, the unusual roar of the steam and the ship's engine, and even the hollow sound as you walked about the steamer's metal floor. And its hooter made us jump in fright. We were also scared because some villagers had warned us that there might be petty criminals on board, as the steamers had called in at various towns on the way.

My family did not have long to worry. It turned out that the authorities in our region had assembled all the families of the kulaks who had been dispatched to Ridder the year before, and decided to send them on the same steamer – so travelling with us were families we knew from aul and villages in the upper reaches of the Irtysh, including families of Father's workmates from the brick factory. Among them was Uncle Mukatai's wife, Aunt Atish, and her children, whom we were overjoyed to see for the first time in a year.

The steamer carried us down-river at what seemed like a terrific speed. The scenery began changing fast. Accustomed since early childhood to the rolling hills of Southern Altai, I found the more dramatic landscape along the Irtysh spellbinding. The thick reed beds on both sides gave way to hills and steep cliffs, which looked as though they were touching the sky, and made me gasp in amazement and delight. Seeing the river on the bends ahead growing narrower and narrower, I could not help wondering if the steamer was going to get stuck between the two steep banks; gazing at the huge rocks and cliffs our steamer was speeding between, I could not help imagining how wild it must all have looked in prehistoric times. This stretch of the river seemed totally unpopulated, even though the steamer made stops at settlements on the way; and when we did happen to catch sight of the small villages carved into the hillsides, I was baffled as to how their residents could live there, so cut off from other people.

No matter how fast I imagined the steamer to be speeding down the river, it actually took no fewer than 24 hours to reach Ust-Kamenogorsk. After the ship had let us all off, it resumed its passage down river. Having never been far outside our villages and aul, we all found the town utterly fascinating and, at the same time, disquieting. Once on dry land, we instinctively huddled together like wild animals sensing danger.

Our alarm grew even more acute when we caught sight of the railway track and a steam engine pulling several goods wagons towards us. Once it had drawn up to the quay, we were all ordered on board. We crammed as tightly as possible into the small wagons standing on the narrow-gauged track, and each family sat down on our pile of belongings. It gradually grew dark as we were getting on. When someone outside closed the wagon door, it became so dark inside that you could not even see the person sitting next to you.

As the wagons began jolting forwards, we became even more scared.

'God, God! The train's moving!' 'Allah, save us! Lord!' 'Holy Mother of God, save us!' the passengers started praying in their different languages. The families travelling in our wagon turned out to be mostly Russian. There were only three Kazakh families – our two related ones and another one with children. The terrified Kazakh women kept quietly praying and begging their Creator to save them. Gradually getting used to the train's motion, the Russian women started talking to each other about being afraid of the train. From their conversation in the darkness I understood the following: 'The train's started and it's getting faster and faster. I hope to God it doesn't go off the rails! My father-in-law told me last year about a train going so fast that its wheels came off the track and all its wagons rolled over and all the people in them got killed. It's going a bit too fast, isn't it?'

After hearing about this dreadful accident, I was overwhelmed by a sense of helplessness. I want to tell my mother and aunt about the accident, but I checked myself, realising that I ought not frighten them, although I was still shivering with fear myself.

When I woke up, the door of the wagon was wide open and the sunlight was streaming inside. The wagon was standing on a siding carved out of the rock. To the left of the track, far below, you could hear the sound of a mountain river. People were staring out of the wagon doors at the rails, their heads all in a row like a string of beads. Like us, they were afraid of getting out of the wagons in case the train chose that very moment to leave without them. With difficulty I managed to decipher and read out the letters of the word 'Ulbostroi' on a sign over the one and only building not far from the train. However, I had no idea what the word meant. How was I to know that it was the station's name? The train remained standing for some time.

Since the start of our journey I had been in charge of carrying the lighter knapsacks, and keeping an eye on my six-year-old younger brother. Once in a while Mother got me to fetch and carry things; on ordinary days I was allowed to go off on my own and play out of her sight. She did not particularly mind, perhaps because she trusted me not to go too far or do anything stupid or perhaps, like all mothers, she was worried about her child but did not let it show. She behaved in the same way during our journey to Ridder.

While our train was standing at Ulbostroi station I had an attack of malaria. I had caught it at the very start of spring that year, and got attacks of it at exactly the same time, every other day.

To begin with, you usually start feeling terribly cold as though you're standing out in the frost with no clothes on. You shake all over and your teeth begin chattering uncontrollably. You cannot get them to stop, no matter how hard you try. There is no way to warm up either, until the time comes when your temperature soars and you start running a very high fever. Feeling wretchedly cold in the wagon, I decided to try and warm up in the sun. So I went and lay down in the open wagon hitched to ours, carrying Father's warm coat with me. I do not remember how long I lay there. I managed to cope with several recurring attacks of the shivers before falling fast asleep.

When I awoke, my open wagon was rumbling along after the wagon the rest of my family had been travelling in, rocking from side to side and being blasted by the winds. I was lying there alone. I had no idea where my mother or the other passengers were. The malaria attack had sapped all my strength and left my whole body feeling limp and even, I think, affected my memory and thinking processes. I could hardly work out where I was.

As our fellow-passengers told me later, when the train left Ulbostroi station and Mother saw I was not in the wagon, she became so distraught that she could not take in a word of what people were saying to reassure her about her son being in the open wagon next-door. While I was coming to my senses in my open wagon, Mother was going through hell, unable to see me from her wagon, doubting people's words of comfort and powerless to stop the train. We were both hugely relieved to see each other again.

Speeding through several stations without stopping, the train finally took us to our destination. Instead of going all the way to the town of Ridder, it stopped eight kilometres away by the Kirpichnaya mine. As the railway line at this point cut deep into the hillside, the train stopped in an open-topped tunnel whose walls were much higher than the wagons. After spending the entire journey in a state of heightened anxiety, the deep pit we found ourselves in as we emerged from our wagons completely terrified us. At once, people began scrambling up the side of the cutting towards the open, and in their panic and confusion failed to notice the narrow wooden steps running all the way up. Instead, they started scrambling up the steep wall, losing their foothold and skidding back down before scrambling up again, trying to carry their bundles, sacks and trunks with them. Once they had seen the steps, they charged up them in a panic with their belongings on their backs, getting stuck and bumping into other people on their way down to fetch the rest of their things from the wagons, afraid that the train might leave with their belongings still on board.

Meeting Father again after a whole year was extraordinary. After lifting the first bundle of things on her back, Mother took me by the hand because I was feverish and weak, helped me to climb the steps and led us out of the cutting. Leaving my brother and me sitting on the bundle of things to 'guard' them from 'thieves', Mother went back down again. A short while later a gaunt man with an earthy complexion and a grey beard came up to us, saying, 'My children! My darlings!' Then he wrapped us in his arms and started kissing us. I realised it must be Father.

No wonder I had not recognised him. This was not the handsome father we had known, with ruddy cheeks, a light complexion and raven-black beard. He was 49, but he now seemed old; his large eyes seemed to have sunk back into their sockets. Something else had changed, too. In the past, he had never spoilt us, and we had thought him severe; but the loving way in which he now kissed and hugged my brother and me made us inwardly glow with happiness.

Other heads of families started coming up. Children stretched out their arms to hug, kiss and hang on their fathers' necks; husbands and wives embraced each other; and the air was filled with joyful clamour, laughter and tears as families were reunited at last.

ii

We began life in this new place by being locked up in a local clubhouse. There were lots of us in very little space and stifling conditions: it was so overcrowded that people could only sleep lying on their sides. The stuffiness and lack of fresh air were particularly unbearable for the little children, who cried continuously either all together or one at a time, preventing their mothers and everyone else from getting any rest.

The authorities kept the deportees in these cramped conditions for three days under the pretext that we were in 'quarantine'. However, as the adults later explained, the real reason was that they had nowhere else to put us.

Evidently, our arrival came as a complete surprise to the management of the Ridder coal-mining complex and local authorities. With no other option to choose from, they decided to accommodate us in the barrack the heads of our families were living in. The single men without families were moved into other accommodation, and then all the new arrivals were squeezed in.

The barrack consisted of a room measuring thirty metres by ten with a few small windows along the half-metre of wall above ground level. There were single-tier plank benches lining three of the walls, and a row of two-tier benches down the middle.

The authorities in charge of the deported families must have had to write reports on their 'living arrangements'. But how could they possibly have used this phrase to describe the provision they had made for these families – large numbers of children, grandfathers and grandmothers lying on plank benches?

Each family was allocated a certain amount of space, depending on their numbers. There were no screens or partitions between the beds. There was so little room that people again had to sleep huddled together on their sides. They took turns to eat food, since there were not enough places for them all to sit at the trestle table together. Nor had any thought been given to compatibility: for instance, opposite my family on the benches in the middle of the room was a young couple with children, a grandfather, grandmother and an adolescent brother; on our left was a family with two adult daughters, and behind them another family with adult sons.

Inmates had to contend not only with these unbearably cramped conditions, but also with the humidity. The semi-underground barrack was very badly ventilated, and with too many people in it, it was always stifling inside. This proved disastrous for people used to the wide, open spaces of the countryside, and especially for young children: several infants died soon after their arrival, including Uncle Mukatai and Aunt Atish's youngest son.

Deportees such as us made up most of the population of Kirpichnaya Station. A passenger train stopped there once a day on its way to or from Ust-Kamenogorsk, but the freight trains went straight through. Apart from the barrack I have just described, there was a wooden house known as 'the office', which was empty most of the time, and a shop where you could get nothing with your ration cards except your strict quota of bread. Half a kilometre away on a hillside you could clearly make out the entrance to the mine where the deportees had to work.

Although people in the 1930s used to say, just as they say now in post-Communist times, that the Soviet authorities always ignored people's interests and wishes, not everything they did was bad. Despite the financial restraints they were under, they still took the trouble to build a bathhouse and dispensary for the deportees, even though there were no other people living there on a permanent basis. (This has a particular resonance for those of us living in Kazakhstan at the beginning of the twenty-first century, when, following the disintegration of the Soviet Union and declaration of independence, many hospitals and medical centres have been closed and bathhouses left in abeyance.) The other positive action taken by the local town authorities and management of the coal-mining complex was to provide the deportees' families with work whenever possible. Given the high unemployment levels throughout the Soviet Union in those days, it was not an easy task. In this respect, officials were not merely doing their job but displaying genuine concern for these destitute people.

In those days the official daily food ration was 200 grams of bread per non-working member of the family, and 600 grams per working member. The main work place for women and children was a smallholding belonging to the Ridder group of mines where quite a few people were needed to look after the market gardens. This gave them an extra 400 grams of bread on top of a wage, which, though meagre, made a lot of difference.

The women and children were divided into brigades. At ten, I was the smallest and youngest of the fourteen lads in the children's brigade; the oldest was a fifteen-year-old boy called Trofimov, who was appointed our leader. Our job was to weed the potato crop. A lanky man whom the boys nicknamed 'The Camel' was our work foreman, and he used to visit the plot we were working on in the mornings and mark out the area we had to cover; then he would come back towards evening and check how much work we had done and how good it was.

Our brigade worked conscientiously, without any supervision, meeting its targets every day. Every now and then Trofimov would announce a break during which we used to play games, but all the members of the brigade pulled their weight and there was no slacking: he would not allow anyone to mess about. We all finished work at the same time, and if someone was not managing to keep up and do his fair share, the rest of the brigade would give him some help. What I find astonishing now is how obedient, hardworking, disciplined and responsible we children were.

Trofimov made quite sure we were all good friends. If scuffles broke out, he would defuse them at once. I was the only Kazakh in the brigade and all the rest were Russians, but to my surprise they accepted me as one of their own and never bullied me. In fact, because I was the youngest, they looked after me particularly well. Spending all my time with them also helped me to learn Russian fast, and within a month I spoke it better than I had done back at school. So I learnt that shared experiences – particularly unexpected traumas – put all those involved on an equal footing, and give them an awareness of the need to help each other. In such circumstances, people quickly become close friends, regardless of nationality and religion.

iii

It was only natural that after work the people living in the makeshift shelters in Kirpichnaya should want to forget about their misfortunes and make merry. Man does not live by bread alone, and no matter how harsh a person's life might be, he will find ways of distracting himself from his misery, if only for a short while: conversation, music, poetry and song help us to heal ourselves and renew our energy.

The deportees were of quite a few different nationalities, and each group would entertain themselves in traditional ways. The Russians were not just the largest group but also the liveliest. One of them used to play the accordion while the others took turns to perform songs and dances, and often they would sing all together. They used to laugh loudly and spend longer having fun than anyone else. We Kazakhs used to marvel at the way they could have such a hilarious time, though some of those among us used to mock them and say things like: 'Just look at them singing all together like a flock of sheep! And there they go, stamping their feet like bad-tempered devils!'

The Kazakh deportees also used to get together in the evenings after work, but they did not play music. They spent most of the time talking to each other, retelling epic tales and legends about warriors and good and evil rulers, and lyrical epic poems about people in love. The men used to recite them from memory. Whenever the conversation turned to everyday topics, the women would improvise songs and sing sorrowfully about the deportees' misfortunes, nostalgically recalling their idyllic past life. Touching upon the reasons that brought them to Ridder, they would mostly blame the aul activists who were responsible for carrying out Soviet policies.

What I still remember of these evenings when Kazakhs got together are the various fairy-tales and epic poems that were recited, not people singing at the top of their voices, laughing raucously or dancing wildly like the Russians. In those days Kazakh people did not feel like having fun: life under Socialism was just too grim.

PART TWO

FAMINE

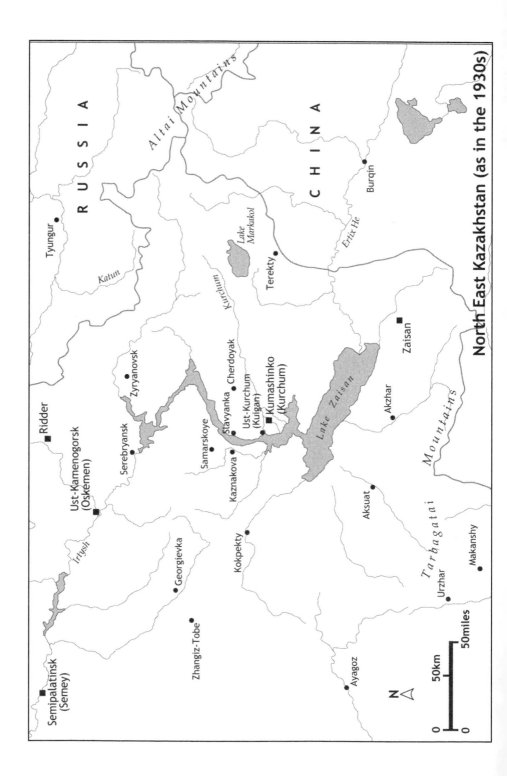

North East Kazakhstan (as in the 1930s)

Chapter Fifteen

The Refugees

1932 was a year of terrible famine in many regions of the USSR. The immediate cause was a bad harvest following a period of drought – but collectivisation made the consequences many times worse for the Kazakh people. Transferred hastily and without any preparation to a settled way of life and method of farming, the nomadic livestock breeders simply did not have the means or expertise to run collective farms efficiently. Over the next two years, 1.2 million of them were to die of starvation.

This dreadful catastrophe did not, however, become as rampant that year in the northern, north-western and agricultural mountainous areas of Eastern Kazakhstan as in the rest of the country. But as the popular Kazakh saying goes: 'Once one family's going hungry, soon the whole aul is, and once one aul's going hungry, soon there's a famine nation-wide'.

By summer, droves of starving refugees from the republic's other regions started heading for Eastern Kazakhstan. After hearing that the people there had plenty to eat, that there was work to be had in the towns and mining districts, and that food rations were being given out, they poured into the villages and into the towns of

Zyryanovsk and Ust-Kamenogorsk. However, instead of organising famine relief, certain top officials in these places looked for ways of getting rid of the refugees. There is archive material in the form of written reports from various meetings at which these officials requested authorisation to have the refugees forcibly removed from the town by the militia, on the grounds that they were putting an excessive strain on the system providing locals with food. This attitude persisted until June 1932, when a Resolution of the USSR Council of Ministers was passed on organising relief for the starving population of Kazakhstan.

Grain from the State reserves was distributed throughout the countryside; the most needy were transported from remote regions to towns and other places where there were sufficient stocks of food, and local authorities were committed to feeding a certain number of refugees. Tragically, this action came too late: the famine had already struck hard and taken a great many lives. Even after the passing of the resolution, many of the starving died because of the length of time it took for the relief to reach them, or because it was insufficient.

Let me explain how relief was administered to the first organised group of famine victims brought to Ridder.

One day, without warning, the local authorities ordered all of us in the barrack to move out and camp 'in to the fresh air'. Each family, depending on how many members it had, was issued with some planks of wood to knock together some sort of makeshift shelter. Two days later there was a whole stretch of wooden shacks covered with grass roofs. The only way of getting inside was to crawl in; but at least you could sit down with your family inside and eat meals together. People were willing to put up with these conditions because they were relieved to escape the stifling, musty and cramped barrack.

The adults kept talking about the starving refugees being brought here and housed in the barrack. As a child, I had no idea what the Kazakh word for 'starving', 'asharyk', meant and when I asked, Father and Mother started flapping their hands and exclaiming fearfully, 'Be quiet! Don't say that word!' And then they began whispering, 'O Allah, may this misfortune pass us by!'

Meanwhile the local authorities began cordoning off a small area next to the railway line. Inside, they set up three open hearths with cauldrons, and three sacks of flour next to them – a commodity that locals had not seen for some time. The cordoned-off area was then placed under guard.

We children, though we were going hungry, still did not understand what the word 'starving' really meant, and we could not wait to see what the 'starving' looked like. Hearing that they were about to arrive at the station, we rushed over to have a look.

God! What an appalling sight! Some of the young children got such a shock that they ran off straightaway.

Out of the train's freight wagons came not people but walking skeletons. The skin on their faces looked as though it had been stretched and then stuck tightly to their bare skulls. It was impossible to tell whether their faces were black from being in the sun or smeared with dirt. Their arms looked unnaturally long and their eyes, sunken and terrifyingly lifeless, like sheep's. They could hardly stand, let alone walk, and kept stumbling and falling over. Some, dreadfully weak, were being helped along, while several others were being carried – but the people doing the carrying had hardly any strength left themselves, and kept falling over with the other person in their arms. For the most part they did not say anything, only exchanging a few short phrases in very hushed voices.

There were no elderly people or small children among the living corpses emerging from the wagons: they had not made it this far. They had either starved long before the resolution on famine relief, or they had died during the journey. The corpses of those who had died during the last few kilometres were left behind in the empty wagons after the survivors had got out: their relatives were simply too weak to carry them out and bury them. The authorities organised their funerals with the help of local workers.

The famine victims who had managed to get out of the wagons were led into the cordoned-off area and each given a small portion of broth. Every few hours the portion size was gradually increased under doctors' supervision. The victims were kept outside like this for several days, and then moved into the barrack we had vacated for them. And then a week or so later, before they had recovered or were anything like back to normal, they were deemed well enough to take on the same jobs as all the other workers and receive the standard food rations.

Those who believe that the famine in Kazakhstan was deliberately orchestrated by the Soviet Government should bear in mind these efforts to help the starving population, which – though in insufficient quantities and greatly delayed – certainly saved lives. Despite the losses on the journey to Ridder, the refugees who survived felt tremendously grateful for the care they had received. However, the relief organised by the Government in 1932 did not end the famine in the republic, but merely reduced its scope and number of victims. Kazakhs continued to die of starvation until the harvest of 1934.

ii

We 'special migrants', as we were now known, spent nearly a month in our makeshift shelters. We were happy enough to have some fresh air – but most people seemed to have forgotten all about the coming winter. As far as they were concerned, they were in the hands of the State, and the State was thinking about them and knew what to do. Exactly how the State dealt with working people, we now know full well: nobody, for example, considered it necessary to inform deportees in good time about decisions over their future, which is why far-fetched rumours used to do the rounds.

This time the authorities informed us that we were to move into new accommodation within 24 hours. The accommodation in question was located seven or eight kilometres from Kirpichnaya in the large settlement of Pozdnopalovka, now the site of the Tishinsky Mine in the Ridder coal-mining complex. The management had decided to use the 'special migrants' on the construction of a hydro-electric station on the River Ulba, a tributary of the Irtysh flowing out of the Altai mountains, that had just got underway. Several large one-storey houses had been built for us, each consisting of one room measuring eighteen square metres, a quarter of which was taken up by a so-called 'Russian stove'. This room had to accommodate two families, no matter how many people that meant – and sometimes there were as many as ten per family. We were accommodated in a room like this with Uncle Mukatai's family of five.

Worse, these houses had been left unfinished, because the management had sent the builders off to make hay. Instead of being insulated, the walls inside were lined simply with planks, while a few stakes nailed at intervals to the outer walls at intervals created the effect of a fence. The builders and decorators had obviously intended finishing the houses off by insulating the gaps between the planks and stakes in the walls with wood shavings and earth, and puttying and plastering the stakes outside; the ceiling inside also needed to be insulated in the same way. But they had not got round to it, and the houses were clearly not ready for winter habitation.

What's more, the men were sent off to work some distance away, also making hay, which meant the women, children and old people were left to fend for themselves in their new accommodation. Since there was no work for them there, they remained on a ration of 200 grams of bread. Naturally, every newly arrived family in the settlement grew deeply concerned about how they were going to get sufficient food to survive. But nobody in the village of Pozdnopalovka seemed concerned about how we were going to get by on such meagre rations; nor could our menfolk be contacted – none of us were allowed to visit them, and they were forbidden to leave the fields. Like convicts, they were guarded round the clock by militiamen.

Faced with the threat of malnutrition and, increasingly, of starving to death, the women and children started walking out to the Tishinsky Hills, picking berries and filling their empty stomachs with them. When the cereal crops were harvested, they began picking up the grain left on the fields to supplement their rations. Then, much to their joy, the time came to harvest the potato crop, which meant that they now had work, if only temporarily.

On 1 September, the children of Pozdnopalovka (near Ridder) and the children of the Russian special migrants started school. Teaching was, of course, conducted in Russian. None of the Kazakh children went to school: just as before, it was something I could only dream about. Anyway, I had no time to attend lessons, as every day – from morning until nightfall – Mother and I were out looking for food. I used to watch other children of my age enviously as they made their way to school, and sometimes when I spotted them playing noisily during break, I could not stop tears welling into my eyes. I longed to study with them – but it was not to be.

The men did not come back until late autumn. In the meantime, the women and children who had been left behind went on living in the chilly houses. A few of the Russian tried to make them habitable for the winter, but the Kazakhs seemed simply to hope that either Allah would send them mild weather or the authorities would look after them. The fact was that most of them could not adapt to their new environment because they were so naïvely and hopelessly nostalgic about their former life.

In addition, because they did not speak Russian, they were unable to strike up close friendships with the Russians they worked with, let alone the local residents (who did not particularly trust the families of kulaks). In the entire village of Pozdnopalovka, there was not a single adult Kazakh who spoke even one word of Russian, or a Russian who could understand even a smattering of Kazakh. This made communication practically impossible. Conversations – which were often quite comical – involved a lot of mimicry and a hotchpotch of Russian and Kazakh words.

All ten Kazakh families living in Pozdnopalovka at the time needed the help of the only boy who knew a few words of Russian: me. They dragged me all over the village, getting me to interpret all sorts of important and urgent things as well as the totally trivial. Sometimes one of the Kazakh women would call me over and ask me to explain what a Russian was saying to her; another time, a woman, not daring to say her surname aloud as it was also the name of her husband's father – which, according to our customs, she was forbidden to use – would ask me to say it for her. Russians always used to roar with laughter at the way I interpreted what Kazakhs were saying to them. You can judge for yourselves how good my interpreting was from the following episode.

One day, several Kazakh women who had worked during the potato harvest went to the Ulbostroi cashier's office to collect their wages. The office was at the construction project's headquarters, some three or four kilometres from Pozdnopalovka. One of these women was my mother and she had taken me along as her 'full-time interpreter'.

When we arrived at the main block, the door to the cashier's office was open, so we all went inside. The doors of all the rooms were closed and there was nobody about so we sat down in the corridor to wait for the cashier. A sheet of paper was stuck to the small window in the wall of one of the rooms, and some words in capital letters were scrawled across it in red ink. No matter how hard I tried, I could not make out what they said. So we went on sitting there and waiting for the cashier. There was nobody around to ask. It was gone midday by this time. At long last, a woman from the house next-door came into the office and asked if we were waiting to collect our wages. I replied that we were. Then she explained to us that there was no money left and the cashier would not be there that day. She pointed to the sheet of paper over the window and then I realised what it said: 'No cash available'. If it had said: 'No money today', I would have understood at once. So much for my good spoken Russian – though as the Kazakh women could not, of course, understand what the Russian was explaining to me, I managed to get away with it.

Work on the hydroelectric power station had yet to begin, though a drainage canal from the River Ulba to the station was already underway. The canal started one kilometre from the village, and we children used to go and gawp at the amazing, brand-new excavator which was digging it. The excavator seemed

141

to us as big as a house. It was operated by steam, someone explained to us, produced by the water inside its large boiler; there was a stoker whose job was to shovel coal into its fire-chamber every now and then. The excavator emitted clouds of smoke through a pipe and occasionally hooted like a steam engine or boat – something we loved.

Ulbinskaya Hydro-Electric Station came into service in 1937, and has been providing cheap energy ever since. As someone who looked on admiringly as work got underway digging the canal, I still feel a sort of bond with its builders.

Chapter Sixteen

Fleeing Back Home

October arrived. The distant peaks of the Altai mountains looming above the town of Ridder were covered in snow, signalling the onset of winter. The heads of the families at last returned home from harvesting the hay – but Father was not among them. According to Uncle Mukatai, he and two other workers were being kept on in the fields to finish off some small jobs and drive back the draught horses. He assured us, however, that Father would be back by the end of the week.

The first party of men came back full of resolve not to stay any longer in their place of deportation, but to escape back home. They had secretly agreed this among themselves, and on the very first day of his return, Uncle Mukatai started making preparations for the journey with his family. He let Mother in on the secret.

'Shayakhmet will be back any day now,' he said. 'We'll set off as soon as he arrives. We must be packed and ready before he gets here.'

The preparations for our escape consisted of making food for the journey from the scanty supplies we had at home, and packing whatever essential household goods we could carry as far as the railway station. A week passed and, according to Uncle's calculations, Father should have returned; but though everything was ready, there was still no sign of him. Several families from the group who had made the pact started secretly leaving Pozdnopalovka, and Uncle Mukatai began getting agitated:

'If we stay another week waiting for Shayakhmet, we won't make it to the Irtysh before it freezes over and the steamers stop running,' he said. 'Then we won't be able to leave here this year and we'll have see the winter through. And if we're late leaving, we won't get further than Ust-Kamenogorsk and we'll get stuck mid-way with winter coming.'

Mother, however, refused to leave without Father, and suggested that her brother and his family should go on their own. But Mukatai would not give in, and eventually persuaded her.

'Shayakhmet gave me strict instructions that if he was delayed at the harvest, I was to take you with me when I left,' he said. 'He could see it'd be easier for him to hide if he left here on his own and followed us back to the aul. If you stay here with the children, you'll make things harder for him. And if you dilly-dally, you won't get any further than Ust-Kamenogorsk, because the steamers will have stopped running. Then you'll be like a lead weight round his neck. But if he's on his own, he'll be able to walk from Ust-Kamenogorsk all the way back to the aul.'

I should make it clear at this point that I was by now the only child left with our two families. Uncle Mukatai's two surviving children (a thirteen-year-old daughter and five-year-old son) and my little brother had been sent back to relatives in the aul. At the time, the adults had explained that this was because of the poor quality of the food we were getting in Kirpichnaya; but it now seems to me that they were already planning to escape as soon as the time was right.

While we were waiting for Father to return, our Kazakh neighbours secretly slipped away, too. Only the day before the house next door had been packed with two families; now it was completely empty, although the doors and windows had been carefully closed as if its inmates had only gone off to work or to visit someone. The fugitives left at night while the villagers were fast asleep: they loaded their belongings onto their backs and, as there were no tracks, set off in a straight line to get as far away as possible from the village and other people while it was dark. And that is exactly how we left as well.

When the village became silent at night and all its residents were fast asleep, we slung our bundles onto our backs and set off in the darkness, winding our way between the bushes across the trackless land. However, despite all our efforts, we made very slow progress. My bundle turned out to be much heavier than I could manage, and I had to keep pausing for breath and holding up the others. So we lost a lot of valuable time and covered very little ground.

Our main aim that night was to cross the bridge over the River Ulba by dawn. In those days, bridges – particularly those around Ridder – tended to have sentries guarding them. Exactly who they were being guarded against remains a mystery, but our adults were afraid that the sentries would presumably be checking people's documents before they crossed the bridge on horseback and on foot. They were worried that we were walking too slowly, and would not make it across the bridge while it was still dark; in the end they tossed part of my load into the bushes to help me walk faster. As it was, we reached the bridge just as dawn was breaking – only to find that it was not being guarded after all. After crossing over without any hitches, we managed to reach the pinewood alongside the station before it grew light, and lay down and hid there.

Gromotukha Station consisted of a small house that served as both a ticket office and lodgings for the stationmaster, who was also the ticket clerk and cleaner. A passenger train from Ust-Kamenogorsk stopped for one minute at the station just once a day; none of the freight trains stopped there at all. Very occasionally, two or three people from the surrounding villages would get off, but sometimes there was nobody for days at a time. I could not understand why the adults were afraid of walking up to the station and why we were not waiting for the train on the platform. Who would notice us there? I queried this with my uncle and he replied, 'Oh, don't be daft! There're always militiamen from the commandant's office on the lookout there. We mustn't be seen there during the day. We'll hang about in the wood until the evening, and then walk up there just before the train from Ridder's due, quickly buy the tickets and then get on the train straightaway.'

So we waited for the train in the dense pinewood.

Writing these words now, so many years later, I find myself thinking long and hard about the past. For years our ancestors lived under a tribal system where relationships were based on mutual help: they were convinced of the enduring worth of their centuries-old principles, and perhaps as a consequence used to regard any innovation with suspicion, fear and even disapproval. They were conservative by nature and clung to what was familiar: why else, in 1932, when the population of Kazakhstan was in the grip of a terrible famine, did our two families of fugitives head for a starving aul – where a year before they had been robbed, prosecuted and deported – instead of staying in Ridder, where they were getting limited but at least regular food rations?

It might be argued that they were they trying to escape from being discriminated against as 'special migrants' and not being allowed to choose work and move around freely. But by the time of their escape, nearly all of them had already served two thirds of their sentences: if they had waited a little longer, they would have been able to enjoy the full rights of citizens again. Some of them, in fact, had already been freed.

My 22-year-old cousin Aiken was a case in point. Sentenced a year before to two years' imprisonment as the son of a prominent kulak, Aiken was released a year early from a timber-felling camp near Ridder, and came to see us the day we arrived in Kirpichnaya. After spending the night with us, he declined to stay on a few more days, as my parents begged him to, and rushed back home instead to his mother and younger sister: after hearing much talk about people starving in the aul, he was desperate to rescue his family from starvation. Of course, this resolve did him credit: but there was a more rational way of rescuing relatives, and that was to stay on as a hired worker in Ridder and then arrange for them to be brought over to where he was living. His wages would have been enough to support two dependants – but instead Aiken travelled to his aul, where no one was going to give a convicted kulak work, to add to the number of starving people there.

The way we Kazakhs have always clung to the past has proved disastrous for our people – and yet this stubborn habit still sometimes obtains at the start of the twenty-first century. To say that the fear of innovation hampers our development and leaves us lagging behind is an understatement.

But let us return to our escape attempt. We lay there all day waiting for the train. There were six of us in three families, and a seventh man without a family. We did not dare cook any food because the smoke would certainly have attracted unwanted attention such as militiamen's – fugitives with no identification papers are afraid of everyone and everything, and we feared militiamen most of all. Just before the train was due to arrive we clambered up to station with our things; we put them down by the ticket office window and hid behind the stationmaster's house, out of sight. The men were reluctant to go up to the office for the tickets, again in case they attracted unwelcome attention, so they filled me in on what to do. Although I was ten years old, I had never heard the word 'tickets' before and had no idea what they were, but they explained to me how to purchase them, and then handed me the money and told me to hold onto it tightly in case of thieves.

There was one other customer in front of me at the ticket office. Copying him, I handed my money through the window; in return, I was given a whole wad of papers. A few moments later the train drew in. We hurriedly jumped on board, trying not to be noticed by anyone – though in fact the only other people on the station were the man who had just purchased a ticket in front of me and the multi-tasked stationmaster. Without identification papers we were even afraid of our own shadows. Still, we were over the first hurdle and on board the train.

Off we went, taking all our worries and cares with us, and collecting even more on our way.

'Checks are carried out on the train, I've heard, and everyone who's travelling is asked to show his ticket and documents. Recently a group of people like us were checked and then detained and turned over to the militia,' said a passenger, frightening everyone who was listening.

'The large station of Cheremshanka is ahead. There's a militiaman on duty there who always checks passengers' documents,' added another.

We all grew alarmed listening to these conversations: I felt as though I was going to be taken off on my own and handed over to the militia. The upshot of it all was that even though it was after midnight, none of us could get to sleep. Our fears about the militiaman in Cheremshanka were borne out when a 'blue-collar' (as they were known) came into our carriage in the middle of the night; my heart sank, but fortunately he turned out to be accompanying a passenger. Just before the train moved off, he went out of the carriage without taking any notice of the rest of us. The adults heaved a sigh of relief and I instantly dropped off to sleep.

'Get up, wake up, we've arrived!' Mother kept saying to me. When I opened my eyes and came to my senses, I realised that we had arrived at Ust-Kamenogorsk. As a boy brought up in a small aul, I marvelled at the great many different carts standing at night by the station. I heard the adults repeating the word 'quay' several times. Not understanding what they meant, I walked sleepily beside Mother and the other adults, following a cart full of our belongings.

From early morning until the following evening we sat on the Ust-Kamenogorsk quay on the River Irtysh at the very foot of the mountains. Mother, my aunt and I perched on top of the pile of our belongings, guarding them from thieves – we had been warned that there were masses of them about. We saw quite a few scary-looking, ragged, homeless people wandering about begging for food; there were also crowds of people waiting, like us, for the steamer. The men in our group were afraid of staying with us in case they caught the eye of the blue-collars and were asked for their documents. Once in a while, however, one of them would come up to enquire how we were and tell us news – for instance, that the last steamer of the season would be arriving from Semipalatinsk that evening, heading up the Irtysh. All navigation on the river would then cease until the following spring. This came as worrying news for everyone sitting on the quay for whom the steamer was their last hope of getting away – and by then there were a great many of us hopefuls. I was staggered by the numbers. Where were they all going?

In the late afternoon we caught sight of the steamer's black smoke in the distance. The hordes of people who only moments ago had been sitting quietly on their luggage started seething like the sea during a storm.

After finding out how many tickets were on sale for the trip up-river, and that there would not be enough for everyone there, people instantly lost all their dignity, humanity and reason. They started rushing towards the ticket office in a frenzied stampede, barging, pushing and stamping on anybody in their way. None of them took any notice of anyone else or kept anything in their sights except the precious window of the ticket office.

Vigilant as ever, the adults had made sure I joined the queue in front of the ticket office early that morning. While the queue was still intact, they taught me how to purchase the tickets and counted up enough money for seven tickets, and again put it in my fist, telling me only to open it in front of the cashier. Just when it was nearly my turn at the ticket counter, the seething crowd – who were oblivious to everything by that stage – decided to resort to survival-of-the-fittest tactics. There was a swell in front of the counter caused by sudden jostling to the left and right. Tossed from side to side, I completely lost my bearings. Just then a group of people surged forward, hemming me in and carrying me with them towards the ticket counter. Several hands shot through the window. Copying them, I raised my fist clutching the money and thrust it towards the window. My small fist must have caught the cashier's attention among all the others because he opened it, took the money and instead of just asking, shouted out loudly, 'How many?' 'Seven,' I managed to gasp in reply. The cashier then gave me some pieces of paper in return for the money, carefully closed my fist and then pushed it gently away from the counter as if to say, 'Off you go!'

Elbowing my way back from the window and getting out of the crowd proved no less difficult than getting there. A dense wall of people kept surging frantically towards the ticket office. By good fortune, I found myself between two burly young men who had just purchased tickets. Accidentally pressing against either side of me, they forced a way through the crowd, taking me out of the hellhole with them. Had it not been for them, the demented crowd would probably have crushed me to death.

As for boarding the steamer, everyone just started barging onto it, whether they had tickets or not. The pushing and shoving by the gangway was even more frenzied than by the ticket office. And when the steamer's horn first sounded to warn of its imminent departure, the people trying to force their way on board began struggling even harder. As Mother and I reached the gangway, a mass of people surged towards us, pushing me away from her; and while she just made it up the gangway and onto the deck, it now looked ominously as if she was going to leave on the steamer while I was stranded on my own on the quay.

At that very moment some of the sailors on board started removing half of the gangway, which meant it was almost departure time. The people at the front of the crowd rushed frantically forward again, sweeping me with them. Although the sailor standing at the end of the gangway on dry land tried to stop them, they kept scrambling onto the narrow plank to get on board. Just as the sailor was leaping onto the gangway himself to run up and lift it off the quay, I managed to call out to him, 'Please, I've got a ticket, but it's with Mum. She's on board. Let me on or I'll miss the boat and lose my mum!'

Just then, on board the steamer, Mother let out a piercing cry of despair and panic. The end of the gangway was already clear of the quay, so the sailor grabbed hold of my back and my bundle and tossed me over the railings so that I thudded onto the metallic floor of the lower deck. By the time I had come to my senses and struggled to my feet, the steamer was slowly gliding away from the quay, its paddle wheels gently splashing through the water. A great many people who did not make it on board were left wandering aimlessly about the quay: among them were women and babes in arms, elderly, weak and needy people. You could tell how desperate and inconsolable they were by the way they kept flapping their arms confusedly and sobbing hysterically.

The lack of rainfall which had caused the harvest to fail had also made the river levels sink dangerously low. Islets, sandbanks and shallows had gradually appeared in the Irtysh, and these now hampered the progress of the steamer we were so happy to be on. Designed to function at low speeds, it was sailing against the current at about five knots; but even so, it spent less time forging upriver than getting stuck on sandbanks or backing away and searching for alternative passages through the shallows. Every now and then it would plough into a sandbank and get totally stuck: then the crew would make all the passengers stand in the stern to make the prow lighter so the steamer could slide off the bank. Sometimes a convenient place would be found to set all the passengers ashore so that the boat was light enough to negotiate a stretch of shallows; it would then pick us up again further upriver. In the end the journey took four whole days instead of the usual one and a half.

As Mother and I were going back to the aul where Manap's family lived, we disembarked earlier than our companions, at the quay by the village of Baty from which Father had originally been sent off to Ridder. Uncle Mukatai and his family and travelling companions continued further upriver to their various aul, where they were to be welcomed and taken in by their close relatives. We did not have such close relatives in our aul and so, as Mother put it, we were 'going to the aul of someone else's clan where her daughter was married.'

By the time Mother and I ended up on the bank of the River Irtysh on our own, she had already gained quite a lot of experience living among strangers in 'far-off' Ridder: she had spent an entire summer working with people of different nationalities, and learned to socialise with them as well. However, she had not managed to lose her shyness and reticence, or the narrow views of an aul woman. Whether because of what she was used to, or because she did not know another language, she was rather scared of Russians, when she actually needed to become more outgoing and resourceful and learn ways of communicating with strangers if her children were to survive. As she possessed none of these skills, she grew very anxious and agitated when the two of us found ourselves on dry land and on the other side of the fence cordoning off the quay. It was already late afternoon and we did not know how we were going to get to the aul or which road to take.

Anxious and confused, Mother told me to get directions from some locals. I started asking people we met the way to Kargaly aul, where my sister was living. I phrased my question as well as I could, using all the Russian words I had at my fingertips – but nobody could tell me, since they had never even heard of the place. How were villagers leading isolated lives in their community to know one of the numerous auls consisting of only a few households scattered around the steppes, valleys and hills?

Night was falling. There was nobody in the village we knew. What were we to do? Who could we turn to? We had no idea.

Noticing our frightened faces as we sat huddled on the riverbank all alone, the watchman at the quay asked us who we were and where we were from. Then his face lit up and he began saying something in a mixture of Russian and Kazakh, as local people tended to when they did not speak both languages well. This is what he was trying to say: 'How am I to know your Kargaly? On the edge of the village upriver, however, there's a place where all the grain is delivered from the collective farms. I'd go there, young man, and ask them which way to go. They're bound to know. You may even meet a Kazakh from your Kargaly there.'

Luck was on our side. When I reached the storehouse the watchman had directed me to, I met a driver I had worked with ploughing the fields that spring. It was already dark by the time he had delivered the grain and we had driven over to the quay, and I do not need to describe how my mother, sitting alone on a riverbank at night, was feeling; but the watchman turned out to be a kind man. Appreciating the predicament the frightened Kazakh woman was in, he had allowed her to wait inside the secure quay area. Delighted by his act of kindness, Mother came to the following conclusion: 'It turns out that some Russians are Moslems, too.'

Chapter Seventeen

Hunger Comes to the Aul

Manap, his mother and grandmother were delighted to see us back again. Their initial elation, and especially my sister's, was only spoiled by the news that Father was not with us. Along with all the other members of the collective farm brigade, they were living in a temporary camp on arable land, and helping to gather in the disappointing harvest. Various things had happened in their aul over the summer during our absence. Dear Aunt Batish had died and Uncle Zhantursyn had got remarried to a woman from a neighbouring aul and gone to live with her. One of the first few days after our arrival Mother took me with her to visit Aunt Batish's grave. On her way there she recited prayers to the deceased woman's soul and then uttered the following words at her graveside:

'Unforgettable, dear Apai! Dear Tate!' she cried, using the traditional Kazakh forms of address for an older woman. 'You did not wait for your loved ones to come back. May the earth gently cradle you. May your kind, radiant soul take up its place in Heaven. Your kind deeds on this earth have earned you the gratitude of everyone who knew you and the approval of your ancestors' spirits. During the most difficult times you came straight over to help your brother's children and took them under your wing and fed your nephews all winter long. We, your close relatives, were not beside you when you took your last breath. We did not hear your last words and did not ask you for the last time to forgive us. Your brothers could not be there when you were committed to the earth – God willed it so. Farewell! Never stop caring for your relatives still on this earth.'

Mother's speech made a big impression on me and set me thinking. Experiencing town life and food shortages, cramped living conditions and what it really felt like to be in dire need had made me think long and hard – possibly, for the first time – about Aunt Batish and her husband's generosity. Mother's heartfelt words of gratitude were etched on my memory, and I promised myself there and then that when I grew up, I would do my duty as far as my family was concerned, and help all those who were in need.

Recent reforms, bringing change to our society, remind me of the importance of this. The transition to a market economy since 1991 has resulted in factories grinding to a halt, arable fields going uncultivated, livestock numbers being cut back and unemployment levels rising in both urban and rural areas. Villagers abandoned their homes and smallholdings and poured into the towns, swelling the ranks of the unemployed. I have tried to contribute by at least reminding my children (who have always lived in towns) of the duty families have towards needy relations. Every living creature has to take care not only of itself, but also of its descendants who will ensure the survival of the species. And as a popular Kazakh saying puts it, 'There is no life without movement': constant activity is required to sustain it.

Mother, it appears, had taken this saying very much to heart. Three or four days after our arrival she called me over when I was playing with some local boys and said, 'Darling, we can't go on living here any more as though we haven't a care in the world. It's impossible to say when your father will arrive: it won't be easy for him to get to us now that the steamers have stopped coming here. Winter is on the way. We've got to think about how we're going to live from now on and how we are going to get food. Manap can't look after us all – look how many other mouths he's got to feed. We've got to do something until Father gets back so we're not a burden round Manap's neck. There are still a lot of ears of corn left in the fields near the camp: let's pick them all up so we've at least got a small amount of grain put by for us all. We'll start work tomorrow morning.'

I did not dare object because I had been taught to obey my parents and elders, but I was not particularly enthusiastic about doing the work. I thought to myself, 'Last year Aunt Batish and her husband took us in and fed us until the spring. Why can't Manap and our Zhamba do the same?' And I was sure I was right. I did not realise just yet that the drought had ruined the crops for the second year running and in some places the collective farms had not even managed to cover the costs of the seeds that had been sown in spring; nor that people living in the region were already facing a grim future with insufficient food to last them until the next harvest time. How was I to know that Manap's family of seven were faced with this terrible dilemma?

Our work gathering up the ears of corn from the fields did not continue for long. Now that it was late autumn, the days started getting colder and in the mornings the fields were covered in hoar frost. It was on a day like this that my other brother-in-law, Kairankazhi, who had married my sister Altynzhan the winter before, turned up with his horse and cart and announced that he was taking us to live with them at Kokzhura aul. Then he helped us pile our belongings into the cart and drove us off. You see, a Kazakh man was traditionally duty-bound to look after his wife's parents or, as the Kazakh saying put it: 'Once you've cut the corn, you mustn't burn the straw left behind'. Even though he did not have adequate housing, Kairankazhi took the three of us into the home he already shared with the four other members of his family. To take in your mother-in-law and two children in such circumstances you needed not only a sense of duty and responsibility but also, most definitely, a kind heart and conscience.

So, where was he living exactly? As the watchman and stoker respectively of the collective farm office, he and Altynzhan had been allocated literally a corner of it to live in. The office consisted of a large, spacious room in a house consisting of two apartments. For some reason or other, all three identical houses built in the farm's new centre over the summer were heated by means of an ordinary Russian stove. The one in the office was screened by a wooden partition – and it was in the small area between this partition and the side of the stove, measuring four metres square, that the eight of us had to live in. During the day there was scarcely enough room for us all to have our meals there. At night the mothers of the two families slept there with one child each. The rest of us – the young couple, Kairankazhi's sixteen-year-old brother and I – slept in the office space.

Every morning we used to get up early to vacate the office, clear away our bedding and carry it all into our corner behind the partition. Then all day long there was a constant flow of people coming into the office: chairmen, vice-chairmen, secretaries, accounts clerks – as well as regional officials who kept appearing one after the other, chatting, arguing, sometimes shouting at each other, and even coming to blows. There was always a blue haze in the room from tobacco smoke, because although smoking was not yet popular among Kazakhs in those days, it was regarded as the height of sophistication by anyone in an official post or aspiring to one: it set them apart – you see – from ordinary people.

These were the conditions we lived in that winter – thanks be to merciful Allah, as the mothers of our families always used to say. To get by in such circumstances you have to be patient and count your blessings, which we did. We had enough clothes and footwear still in fairly good shape, and we did not have to worry about food; the room we were living in was warm, no matter how cramped. What more did homeless people need?

When times are hard, a small fillip is something to be really thankful for, and one came in December 1932 when we learnt that the USSR Council of Ministers had passed a resolution permitting every collective farm member to take a dairy cow from the communal herd. This was a very joyful event. The farmers who had cursed the Soviet authorities for collectivising their private property now started celebrating and praising 'their' Government for carrying through a policy that 'took account of the people's aspirations'.

On the appointed day, the cows selected from the herd were brought to the collective farm's office. The chairman explained to the assembled farmers how things would proceed: a family with five or more dependants would get a cow, a family with three or four dependants a heifer, and all the other families a heifer that was going to calve the following spring. Everyone grabbed the cow offered to them by the horns without any objections or criticism and led her home as fast as they could.

Why had this action been taken? One of the reasons was that – because of the drought – the collective farms did not have enough hay put by to feed the communal herds, and there was a serious threat of them dying of malnutrition. So the Government decided to give part of the herds away to the collective farmers, presuming that each family would look after their cow as it was now their private property. But in the event, many of the peasants lacked winter stocks of fodder, and the cows died anyway. Other peasants, fearing that the Government would make them hand their cow back when spring came, simply slaughtered them and ate their meat. So, during the third winter of the collective farm system, there was a significant decrease in the numbers of livestock throughout the country, and in Kazakhstan in particular. This in turn had a serious knock-on effect on food stocks throughout the country. By the end of winter, there were ominous signs that famine the famine was beginning to affect the population of the upper reaches of the River Irtysh and the adjacent foothills of the Altai mountain range.

This, however, lay in the future. On the day when Kairankazhi's cow was led into the yard beside his house, everyone was absolutely thrilled. His elderly mother walked towards her and hugged her round the neck as though she was a favourite daughter who had returned to her father's home after a year of marriage. Shortly afterwards, the cow produced a calf, and again we were over the moon.

Then, as if to prove what people used to say about God's bounteous nature, yet another joy was bestowed upon us with the arrival of Toimbai-ata.

We had not seen my uncle since he gave up his fugitive life and turned himself in to the authorities. After serving a two-year prison sentence, he had been sent to a small, isolated aul consisting of four or five households on the shore of Lake Zaisan. It was from there that he – a 63-year-old man who in better times had never gone anywhere on foot – had just walked over 150 kilometres along sleigh tracks to visit us, his brother's family.

I cannot speak for the others, but I was more pleased to see Toimbai-ata than I would have been to see my own father. I stuck by his side during his entire visit. Even though he could see we were living in very cramped conditions, he still praised Kairankazhi for looking after us: 'The fact that you've taken in your in-laws' family and are getting on well despite having so little space is worthy of God's praise,' he said. 'You've done a good deed, and you'll definitely be repaid in kind. You may be living in cramped conditions, but you're not miserable. If a person has a big heart, he can never feel hemmed in!'

In keeping with a Kazakh custom, as a relative through marriage he received invitations to the homes of Kairankazhi's relatives. I accompanied him to these meals in his honour. Each time he was about to leave, it was customary for the head of the household who had invited and entertained him to say, 'As an honoured guest, we ask you to forgive our rather meagre offerings and hospitality. You deserve more. But I hope you will not hold it against us. Perhaps you have some request to ask us? Please don't be afraid to ask.'

It is another Kazakh custom that when a revered person – and particularly a relative through marriage or a close friend – is invited into a home, presents are given along with the specially prepared food. What's more, the recipient is always asked if he or she is pleased with the present. Even if there were no presents, the hosts are always anxious to know whether his guest minds or not. If, in keeping with tradition, such a guest considers he is owed something by his host, he may lay claim to a present reflecting the closeness of their relationship and his own personal standing. The guest is given the right openly to express his wishes, or to ask for a present – although such requests are not always made.

In this instance, after the master of the house had asked him various questions of this kind, Toimbai-ata's reply was, 'What can I say? I do not need anything from you. I have travelled a long way to see my little nephews. Now I've seen you and become acquainted with the new relatives through marriage God has granted me. Thank you for your hospitality – I shall pray to God for your health and prosperity. May your children always bring you joy. You've mostly likely heard about me: I was released from prison not long ago, and sent to a place far away where you never see a soul. It's tough living there. But what can you do? Such is the will of the powers that be and of God.' He finished his speech with an apologetic request, 'We haven't got enough food or grain there. If there was a bit of grain…'

I swelled with indignation. How could he be asking for something so trifling when his host had entertained him in a suitable manner and showed him all the respect he deserved? I did not want to see our wonderful Toimbai-ata asking for what was, to all intents and purposes, charity. However, I did not dare speak up or interrupt the adults' conversations. One of the hosts gave him between five and ten kilograms of wheat grain, saying by way of an apology, 'Forgive us, most honoured brother-in-law, but this is all we can do for you. We can't help you any more. It's the same for us: we spend all our time wondering what we are going to eat tomorrow.'

Other people there asked for his forgiveness and then lowered their eyes, sombre and ashamed.

After staying with us for a week, Toimbai-ata loaded the gifts he had received – a sack just over half full of grain – on to his sleigh and set off on his long journey back home. I walked with him from the aul as far as the main sleigh track. I really did not want to say goodbye to him: in fact, I wanted to go with him. Before setting off, he hugged me tightly with what seemed to me particular warmth, kissed me several times on the cheeks, and shed a few tears. I could scarcely hold back my tears either. What I did not know then was that this parting was to be our last; but recalling our goodbyes, I now think that Toimbai must have somehow sensed this. I stood there for ages watching him gradually disappear in the distance, stooping and wearily pulling the sleigh behind him. This is the lasting memory I have of him. Six months later, we heard that he had died.

ii

It was now the middle of winter, and several months since we had left the area we were deported to and settled in Kokzhura aul. Father had still not turned up; nor had we had any news of him. However, I did not notice my mother seeming unduly alarmed – either because we had already lived without Father for over two years and got used to it, or because she was just good at keeping her worries to herself.

Meanwhile, we continued living behind the plank partition in a corner of the collective farm's office. We had all the bare essentials, even though our living conditions were so cramped: we were in the warmth, and always had enough of everything to eat except meat. Certainly, I never heard any complaints from the adults about the food situation.

Living in the office meant that we could not help but witness all the goings-on there. From the raucous discussions and arguments we knew exactly what instructions were being issued from above, what plans were being put in place to implement them and how these were carried out, what problems cropped up and who was responsible and why. We also used to overhear conversations of a non-business nature and on a whole range of different subjects, not intended for public consumption. The noisiest part of the day was usually the morning. Then the officials would go off in different directions, leaving behind the secretaries, clerks and various other office workers until the end of the working day.

I always used to hang about nearby, and far from chasing me away, they would give me various bits of paperwork to copy while they chatted among themselves, puffing away on their long roll-ups. As a young boy with nothing to do all day, I found this work interesting and good fun. I tried to do all their jobs neatly, and so they started giving me more and more complicated business documents to copy and various forms to fill out; I also learnt how to write different kinds of business letters. Sometimes, too, they sent me on errands here and there and to fetch different things. I felt flattered when the office boys started calling me their helper. It was all an education for me: that winter I gained plenty of practical experience of life.

However, for reasons unknown to me, one day in mid-winter Kairankazhi suddenly decided to look for other lodgings for Mother and us. Later on, from the adults' conversations, I gathered that the family of a class enemy was not allowed to live in the collective farm and aul council's office. Consequently, Kairankazhi had been told he had to move the politically unreliable family out or vacate the office entirely. As it was extremely hard for a family of eight to find any living accommodation in mid-winter, and in order to keep the jobs of office watchman and stoker, the adults decided that my mother, brother and I should move out. We were, after all, already used to going wherever Destiny and the authorities decided to send us.

In whose way were we getting and how were we preventing Soviet policy from being implemented? When I recall those days now, it occurs to me that we were moved out because the local officials needed to be seen to be acting vigilantly, and not because they were carrying out instructions from above. Certainly, there was nothing to suggest that internal tensions between our two families had anything to do with it. As far as I could tell, the adults all got on very well together.

Unable to find anywhere for us to stay nearby, Kairankazhi took us over to Manap's house about seven or eight kilometres away. Before we three arrived, there were already four people in the house: Manap's parents, grandmother and seven-year-old daughter, the only one of five children to have survived the previous year's terrible smallpox epidemic. Manap and my darling sister Zhamba had been sent by the collective farm to do compulsory work for the State all winter at the Kuludzhun mine.

At Manap's house we ate separately from his relations, since it was now vital for each family to manage and conserve its meagre food supplies. It has to be said that Kairankazhi had given us enough food to last us until the end of the winter, which is why I never heard Mother complain about being short of it; what's more, his family continued to supply us with milk, which would be left outside to freeze until I could collect it, as I did once a week. Still, it was possibly the first time in the history of the Kazakh people that two families living under the same roof – and, what's more, related through marriage – did not eat together.

iii

It was the spring of 1933, and Kazakhstan had been in the grip of famine for over a year. It had already taken a great many lives. Until the very end of winter, it was not as widespread among the population living in the foothills of the Altai mountain range, the Kalbin range and along the banks of the Irtysh in Eastern Kazakhstan as in other areas of the republic. But then it finally hit the aul of the Samara region where we were living.

Apart from the increasingly frequent incidents of families running out of food, there were growing numbers of people roaming around begging. To start with, these beggars were greeted in the aul with alarm and quickly given something to eat and anxiously asked how they had been reduced to such a state; but it did not take long for the residents to tire of their increasing numbers and offer them less charity. When the snow had thawed and the fields dried off, the famine victims started gathering the ears of corn from the fields and cooking them. Once there were none left and the fields had been ploughed and summer arrived, people started shaking the straw chaff on the old stacks and searching for edible grain.

Famine now gripped an area that had only ever heard rumours of it before. Everyone was now preoccupied by the problem of getting something to eat for the following day – or the same day, or that very moment, to relieve their hunger pangs. Even the kindest-hearted people and closest friends and relatives could no longer help one other. Our Manap had not returned to his collective farm from the mine as he was supposed to: he had managed to stay on in his job there, and arranged for his parents to join him. As for Kairankazhi, he had been sent off somewhere far away by the collective farm, and so we were unable to contact or seek help from either family any more.

By the spring, we were not only all on our own but our food supplies had nearly run out. So we too started collecting the ears of corn left behind on the fields. We used to dry the damp ears we had collected during the day and husk the grains; then Mother would wash and leave them to dry again. We only ate the grains after she had fried them.

What we did not know then was that grains became toxic from lying under the snow all winter, and could affect people badly if they ate them without cooking them properly first. We found out about this later when the first cases of poisoning happened. What had evidently saved us was the fact that Mother had washed the grains carefully before cooking them. Whole families were poisoned in this way because they had nothing else to eat and had thrown caution to the wind.

Mother put some food by in case the situation got really bad. Once a day, mostly in the evenings, on our return from collecting the ears of corn in the fields, she used to feed us from her old stocks; and twice a day we would eat the grains we had picked up. When we first started scavenging like this, Mother tried to conserve our meagre supplies by not allowing us to ask for food between the three meals we had a day. She explained it like this:

'If we don't do it this way, we'll eat up our last supplies and die of hunger. If we're clever and strong, we'll learn to get by and stop ourselves eating between meals, and then we'll last out till the next harvest and stay alive. We've got nobody to rely on now. We've had no news from your father. We don't know where he is or even if he's alive. Let's hope for your sake that he turns up soon. He's already served his time away from home. If he was with us, we wouldn't go hungry.'

At the time I did not wonder why we had heard nothing from Father, even though seven months had already gone by since we last parted.

iv

Oriental peoples who live by the seven-day calendar believe in seven supreme values. A person's love for their home and country is one of them. The story is told of Nebuchadnezzar's wife, who fell ill because she missed her distant homeland so much; no cure could be found until a huge garden built on hills was built as an exact copy of the one she had been used to as a child in her own country. Even though more than two years had gone by since we had left our aul, I still missed it terribly. I often used to imagine my friends and the places we used to play together in, and our relatives, and I constantly longed to see them again.

One day a man named Abdul, who had lived next to us the year before, arrived on foot to see his relatives. Shortly before he was due to leave for home, I suddenly had the idea of going with him as far as his aul and then walking on by myself to my family's aul. I asked Mother to let me go. She was shocked at first and tried to frighten me by saying, 'You'll get lost on the way! You'll get eaten by starving beggars! I heard of a boy just like you getting eaten not so long ago on the banks of the Irtysh.' However, when I started explaining how much I was missing home, she eventually agreed to let me go on the long journey with the unexpected visitor.

And so off I set on foot with Abdul. Instead of following the main road, Abdul took a short cut along an old nomadic path leading to the Irtysh. There was not a soul to be seen. Every now and then we came across abandoned houses that local people had once used as winter stopping-places; now they were all living in a collective farm centre and nobody had been here for over a year. There were holes in the roofs and ceilings and parts of the walls were caving in. The dreadful scene of dereliction sent shivers down my spine and made me feel fearful and sad.

After we had walked across trackless countryside and around marshy stretches of land, we came out onto the bank of the Irtysh at a place where there was a small house on the opposite bank. I found all the unfamiliar sights here fascinating. Without warning, Abdul shouted out twice at the top of his voice: 'Boat! Boat!' A moment later someone started rowing towards us in a boat from the other bank, his oars splashing through the water. It was the beacon-keeper. In those times, there were beacons at regular intervals all the way along any navigable river, showing the safe route along the channel. Most of the beacon-keepers were Russians and lived with their families on plots of land allocated to them beside the river. Before nightfall they would row out to the beacons and light the kerosene lamps mounted on them, before returning to extinguish them at dawn. They were always pleased to meet anyone because they led such isolated lives. This was certainly true of the beacon-keeper who rowed us across the Irtysh.

After crossing the river and walking another three or four kilometres, we came to Abdul's house. By then it was midday. When Mother had agreed to let me go with Abdul, she had arranged that he would let me spend the first night at his house and feed me, and then the following morning show me the way to our relatives' aul. After walking for half a day, we were naturally very tired and hungry. Unfortunately, Abdul's house was empty and there was nobody about to offer us a meal – or perhaps there was nothing to serve up. Abdul was so weary that he lay down to have a rest, and I did the same.

I do not know how long I slept for. When I woke up, Abdul was still snoring with his back to me. I went outside. Judging by the position of the sun, it was already mid-afternoon. I wondered when, or indeed if Abdul's wife was going to show up. The house certainly looked untidy and rundown. And I did not like the way Abdul was sleeping with his back to me as though I was not there.

What's more, I was famished. As it seemed highly unlikely that I was going to be fed by Abdul, I decided I had better continue on my journey before it got too late.

I reckoned I could walk as far as the next aul, Ust-Kurchum, before dark, spend the night there and then quickly run the rest of the way to the home of Uncle Kozhakhmet. I did not expect to get supper in Ust-Kurchum where I was planning to spend the night because I did not know anyone there. Even though I had not eaten since the morning, I decided I could go without food until the following morning. Having made up my mind, I woke Abdul and told him of my decision to go on with my journey. Abdul seemed delighted. As though afraid I might change my mind, he hurriedly explained to me how to get there. Although I was very much hoping he would say something about feeding me before I set off, he avoided the subject completely.

It turned out that I already knew the way from my travels in the autumn of 1931. I walked along the same wide dusty road I had ridden along several times two years before. I kept glancing back in the hope of spotting a cart coming up behind which I might be able to hitch a ride on. The sun seemed to be moving faster than usual towards the western horizon. As I did not want to be out after dark, I took off my boots in order to walk more quickly and continued barefoot with them in my hands. At a place Abdul had told me about, I turned off the main road onto a narrow path that was short cut to the aul I heading for and started walking up a long, steep gorge. By the time I had got up to the top, the sun had set. I had another five or six kilometres to go before I reached Ust-Kurchum. I speeded up again, breaking into a run, afraid of the descending darkness.

Then, in the gloaming, I noticed the silhouettes of two people walking in the distance ahead. With a sense of relief, I started running even faster to catch them up as soon as I could. They turned out to be a man and woman, most likely a married couple. They were thin like all the local people affected by the famine, but dressed in clean clothes. The man asked my name and where I was from and on my way to. When I told him, he shook his head and exclaimed, 'How could your parents let you go at a time like this? It's dangerous, you know.'

We were now getting close to Ust-Kurchum. The man asked if I knew anyone in the aul. When I shook my head, he added, 'Then stick with us, lad. We know a family here. You can spend the night there with us.'

This was a real spot of luck. I knew that traditionally Kazakhs never turned away any traveller asking to stay the night, and sure enough, the acquaintances of my new companions let us in. However, contrary to another Kazakh custom, our hosts did not offer us any food. Judging by the late hour, they must have already had supper and none of them mentioned it. We were not offered beds either. So, still hungry, we all lay down to sleep on the floor without getting undressed. I ended up sleeping near the porch.

When I woke up, it was already light inside but not yet sunrise. All the family of our hosts and the other guests were still asleep. I slipped outside. It was early spring and the bitterly cold wind cut through me and made me shiver all over, as I had not eaten for 24 hours. Realising I would not get a crumb to eat there, I hurried off without going back inside or thanking my host for letting me stay, and ran towards where my uncle should still be living, about five or six kilometres further on from Ust-Kurchum.

When you have not eaten for over a day, your stomach keeps reminding you that you are hungry. I could think of nothing else. Longing for food, I raced towards uncle's place. However, when I eventually reached the aul he had previously been living in, I found that there was not a single family left among my mother's relatives. In an attempt to escape the famine, some had gone off in various directions – even as far as China – while the others were now living on different parts of the collective farm.

I was so disappointed and shocked that I simply collapsed with exhaustion. I must have used up the last ounce of my strength on the final stage of my journey that morning. I felt dizzy and too tired to even stir and my wretched stomach went on demanding food. It dawned on me that I should perhaps go up to one of the locals and ask for some, even though I did not know anyone there.

But that was begging! Ravenous I might be, but I could not beg.

I did not know this then, but during those times of famine quite a few people disappeared without trace, especially children and youngsters like me. They travelled great distances to find their relatives, only to learn when they arrived that their family had moved on and they had nowhere to seek refuge. They were by then too weak to go back home, and often ended up dying of hunger. Recalling all this now horrifies me.

As I was sitting there exhausted and confused, one of the elders came up to me and, after enquiring who I was, where I was from and what the purpose of my visit was, replied: 'You're in luck, lad. You see that house over there with the haycock in the yard? It belongs to you Uncle Mukatai's daughter. Her husband is the vice-chairman of the aul council. They're well off. You go to them, son. But do you know your aunt? Will she welcome you as one of the family? Some won't have anything to do with their relatives any more, you know.'

As I walked towards the house he had pointed out, my doubts grew and I started feeling very nervous. How was I to know what sort of welcome I would get? I had not seen that side of the family for three years. Perhaps my cousin would turn out to be one of those who had disowned their relatives, as the elder had warned me.

I need not have worried. As soon as she set eyes on me, my cousin Boldekesh looked pleasantly surprised and immediately started firing questions at me:

'Lord, where have you come from? How did you get here? Where are you all living? Do feel well? Are your parents alive and well? Where's your father?'

This welcome made me feel much more relaxed. I stayed overnight with her, getting my strength back and filling my hungry stomach. I ate plenty of delicious food at Boldekesh's house, some of which I had not tasted for ages and other dishes I had never tried before. They ate like royalty – or at least, that is how it seemed to me as I savoured the long-forgotten taste of good food. I could not help wondering where it had come from: there seemed to be so much, at a time when so many people were suffering from malnutrition and dying of starvation. I told myself it had surely been sent by God.

I should also mention Boldekesh's husband, Adilkhan Sikimbayev, and his reaction to me turning up at his door. When my family was living in our aul and my parents were running a profitable smallholding, Sikimbayev – who had only recently married into the family – used to pay us visits and bring presents to us children. He used to joke and have fun with my sisters, and we were always pleased to see him. But when he saw me in his house after such a long time, he did not bother to ask after my family, what our circumstances were or where my father was; he did not seem to even notice me. I sensed this at once because I recalled how affectionate he used to be with me. People change the way they behave amazingly fast, depending on where they happen to be on the social ladder at the time, and Sikimbayev seemed to prove this theory; but he may simply have been scared of being accused by the authorities he served of associating with a kulak's son.

According to Boldekesh, Uncle Kozhakhmet was living somewhere in a small settlement at the collective farm's winter stopping place. Following the faint outline of the steppe track that was hardly ever used, I reached his home in the afternoon.

I found him working as a watchman at the farm's winter cowshed, which although empty needed, apparently, to be guarded against 'enemies of socialism'. He and his wife were living there by themselves, so in an emergency they were unable to alert anyone or seek help anywhere.

Observing them, you could get a very good idea of the way simple, honest, rank-and-file collective farmers lived in those difficult times. They kept no food supplies at home, and lived off the meagre rations that were doled out by the collective farm every now and then; unlike other collective farmers, Uncle did not even own a cow. The collective farm management not only provided him with meagre provisions, they also took advantage of his diligence by putting him in charge of clearing the irrigation ditches so that they could be used to water the crops in the summer. As he and his wife could not survive on their official rations, he used to work on two jobs during the day, and then in the evenings he would go and shake the straw and chaff on the old stacks to get a few grains to eat. This was also a laborious task, but if you worked really hard, you could get enough grain in a day to make a single meal. People were driven to these extremes when there was no other way of getting food.

Apart from consistently not having enough to eat, what drove my uncle to despair was the way Communism had undermined the foundations of family life. He did not have any children of his own, but he had adopted his brother's young daughter and his elder sister's son. It was a common practice among Kazakhs to adopt a relative's child, even though the biological parents might still be alive, in order to reduce the strain on a family which already had a lot of mouths to feed: the parents for their part took an oath that they were giving their children up voluntarily, and would never demand them back or consider them as their own. This was strictly observed even after the adopted parents' deaths – although the biological parents might take their children back, the children retained their adopted parents' surname and continued to be regarded as their offspring. It was not just that people were afraid of breaking an oath they had made before God: their principles also forbade them from doing so.

But at the time of my visit, Uncle had recently been forced to give up his adopted son. It was a terrible blow for a man who had gone through agonies finding enough food to save his children from starving to death. What had happened was that his elder nephew Arshabai, who was on good terms with the new authorities in his region, had turned up and persuaded his brother to leave his adopted father and go away with him. This was quite scandalous as far as Kazakh traditions were concerned. The young man caused his uncle considerable grief by violating his parents' oath; what's more, he also demanded that Kozhakhmet give him a share of the household goods and the money supposedly owing to him for grazing the flock of sheep, a task all the aul children helped their parents with. He ended up taking away Uncle's last two goats as compensation.

A second blow to Uncle was that his adopted daughter also chose to ignore the old traditions by secretly getting married without his permission and blessing. Uncle Kozhakhmet had to put up with all these affronts to his dignity because there was nothing else he could do; as he said himself, he had been 'stamped on all over' as a human being. Yet when he told me all this – since there was nobody else to pour his heart to – he still showed extraordinary generosity of spirit. 'The children of your sisters and daughters, as people used to say, come from another clan, while your own daughters are destined for another clan,' he said. 'My daughter Kauariya certainly was. I do not curse her or feel upset with her. I hope she is happy. If you really think about it, what could I have given her at home? Certainly not enough food to live on. What joy can I offer her now? Her husband is the chairman of an aul council, I've heard, so perhaps she'll have enough to eat at least. It's just a shame that my new son-in-law and his close relatives have not been in contact over the past three months since the marriage. They haven't bothered to come and sort things out with me. After all, they're my relatives now and evidently plan to remain so forever. But they obviously do not consider me their equal. That's what I find so upsetting and confusing! That's what's getting me down!'

Recalling Uncle's complaints over sixty years later, I have come to the conclusion that he would have had every right not to let me anywhere near his home, since his other nephews had treated him so badly. But on the contrary, he seemed very pleased to see me. Despite being very hard up, he insisted on me staying with him for a week.

When I told him that I wanted to visit my father's aul, he approved of my plan and wished me well, saying: 'I've heard that your father's cousins Rakhimzhan and Alzhan Mukazhanov are quite well off. The younger of the two, Alzhan, is in charge of the keys to the collective farm's granaries. They, of course, have plenty to eat and a lot of food put by. Go and see them. At least you'll have enough to eat for a while.'

Then, after a moment's thought, he added, 'It's not on the way to your aul, but go and see my Kauariya and spend a bit of time with her. Find out how she is. Then come and see us on the way back and tell us all about what you've discovered.'

I did as he had asked me to.

I had not seen my cousin for two years, but she greeted me in the usual way in such circumstances and then spent a long time asking me all sorts of questions about the family. When she found out that I had come straight from Uncle Kozhakhmet's house, she started weeping silently. Then she wiped away her tears and started anxiously asking, 'How's Father? Is he furious with me? What kind of food have they got to eat? I'm sure they don't have enough, do they?'

I told her how I had gone to the old threshing-floor with him to shake some grains out of the straw, but did not mention how upset he was with his son-in-law and the young man's relatives. After hearing this, she must have realised how famished I was, for she stopped asking questions and ran off and fetched me a whole cup of yoghurt and a plate of cold fried fish. After putting it all on the table, she told me to help myself while she went and made the tea. In those hard times it was a tremendous honour to be served a meal like this, not just for a boy like me, but even for the most distinguished guest. And what a meal it was, too! I wolfed down the whole lot and felt full for the first time in ages. After I had drunk all the tea I could manage – fresh tea with tea leaves, whose taste I had long forgotten, not the usual boiling water with tea dregs – I sat back and rested and marvelled at how well some people lived compared to my family and our neighbours. However, I did not dwell on where the food on the table had come from at a time when people were dying of starvation. I came to the conclusion that God must have answered Uncle Kozhakhmet's prayers to give his daughter Kauariya enough food for her not to go hungry.

The people whose names are mentioned in this memoir have all long passed away, and it is considered unseemly to criticise the dead. However, this is not the only reason why I want to mention the great concern shown to me by Kauariya's husband Nugman

Mukushev, even though he had neglected my uncle. On the morning I was due to leave, he found time before going to work to get me across the river by boat and then drive me to the road leading to my father's aul, explaining to me how to get there. I felt truly privileged to be shown such attention by my cousin's husband, especially as he was the chairman of the local aul council, and I decided he was a good man. I have always remembered his act of kindness, although later on I was never to hear any of his acquaintances describe him in such glowing terms.

v

In the days of that appalling famine, you would see hordes of homeless beggars wandering along the main roads between the towns and villages. But the roads between the small aul in isolated areas were uncannily deserted. There was very little movement between the main estates of the collective farms, and the traditional socialising that went on between people in neighbouring aul had almost ceased due to the lack of transport.

It was along one of these deserted roads that I walked fifteen kilometres without meeting a soul, until I reached the aul that had once been the centre of the Topterek collective farm. I had never been to it before, because it had only been set up over the past two years, during collectivisation – so I did not know how to find the houses of my closest relatives. I stopped by the first hut I came to, unsure whether to go inside and ask directions. Fortunately, a boy came out of the next hut, pointed to the one I was standing beside and told me it belonged to Rakhimzhan and Alzhan Mukazhanov – the cousins who had looked after our hidden rugs, and sent me off on my terrifying ride across the frozen Irtysh.

I did not know what kind of reception to expect. Though renowned for their hospitality, Kazakhs react differently to guests they have never set eyes on before, particularly when they turn out to be relatives from some distant aul asking for charity 'in God's name' and calling themselves 'God's guests'. The welcome extended to these guests depends first on the host's financial circumstances and then on his generosity and sense of obligation. It was two years since my relatives in this village had seen me: how was I to know if they would guess that the emaciated lad was the same boy they had known? Then you had to take into account that the famine had forced many of the most welcoming people to renounce their national traditions of hospitality and duty to close relatives. I went into the two brothers' house with great trepidation, like a hunter creeping up to the den of a sleeping bear.

I carefully opened the door into the front room and quietly stepped inside. There were three women sitting in the room who, I could tell at once, were the grandmother and her two daughters-in-law – Aimysh, the elder of the two, and Nukhan. Catching sight of me in the doorway, all three stared at me with eyes full of wonder and fear. A second later, as though at the wave of a magic wand, all three gasped in unison, 'Oibai-ai [My God], it's Mukhamet! Is it really you?'

Sitting up on a bed, wrapped up to her waist in blankets, the other grandmother Maria called me to her in a quavering voice, embraced me and hugged me tightly to her for a long time, kissing me. Her daughters-in-law then came up and did the same, if less effusively. Then they started bombarding me with questions: 'Where have you come from? How long have you been in these parts? Where are you living? Have you had news of your father? How's your mother doing? How are things? Do you have enough food? You're not going hungry, are you?' All three were desperate to know all about our daily lives.

The two Mukazhanov brothers' families lived all together. The elder brother, Rakhimzhan, was 49 and the younger, Alzhan, 37. Their father had had died when they were young, and in keeping with tradition his brother Aitlembet – my grandfather – had taken their mother as his wife and treated his nephews in the same way he did his own sons. We, their cousins, used to call their mother our 'younger grandmother', because she was our grandfather's third wife.

The men in the Mukazhanov household were less enthusiastic about my arrival than the women had been. Was it because men are naturally more reticent, or because they were afraid of having ties with a kulak's family? I can't say. To make up for it, though, their children were genuinely thrilled to see me. Rakhimzhan's son Mubarak was five years my senior, and Alzhan's daughter Altynsar a year younger than me. Mubarak in particular did everything he could for me all the time I was staying with them.

In terms of the food supplies, the Mukazhanovs were relatively well off by the standards of 1933: they had a dairy cow and – because Uncle Alzhan had access to the collective farm's granary – grain stocks that were quite substantial for those days. What's more, unlike most people, the brothers' family was not subject to any rationing. Compared to what I had seen at our neighbours' when we were living with Uncle Kozhakhmet, and how we ate at home, life at the Mukazhanovs' was, to my mind, simply heaven. I had not realised then that they lived so well compared to the rest of the aul residents

Other relatives in the aul gave me a warm welcome. All were anxious to know about our daily lives and, first and foremost, about Father. When they heard that we had not heard from him for eight months, they stopped asking me questions and began sighing instead.

After staying just over a week at my relatives', I got ready to go home. However, the Mukazhanovs – especially my grandmother and the other women – started trying to make me change my mind:

'Why are you in such a hurry to get home? Stay a while longer with us. You know what it's like back at home. Why take your meagre rations away from your brother and mother when you can live here with us? Whatever we have to eat, you'll eat with us.'

They did not have to twist my arm much, as I knew I would never go hungry at their place. What's more, there were a lot of boys of my age in the aul who I knew from my school days. In the end I stayed for three weeks.

All the members of the Mukazhanov brothers' families got on well. They had lived under the same roof most of their lives and worked on the same smallholding. In a patriarchal family such as theirs, it was customary for the younger brother's wife to be responsible for all the housework. In this case, it was Aunt Nukhan. As she was at work on the collective farm all day, she had to do the household chores early in the morning and all evening after work. While I was staying with them, I tried to relieve her of some of her work. During the day I would fetch water from the river half a kilometre away from the aul; I would also collect firewood along the riverbank and carry it home.

Of course, in those days I did not know all the intricate rules that had to be followed in the relationships between people of the same clan. The day before I left the Topterek aul for home, a man called Nurgalii Kystaubayev – who was related to the Mukazhanovs through marriage, and so to my family as well – said something to me about the Mukazhanovs' duty to us. He considered that as soon as I showed up, they could at least have put by a sack of millet grain, and – once it had been ground into flour – taken it to the local market in the next village and sold it. Then my family could have used the money to buy the same amount of millet at our local market, which would have really helped us.

'You're too young to know about this sort of thing,' he told me, 'but your relatives here haven't shown any concern over what might happen to your family and do not appreciate what a difficult position you're in. They must all be skinflints, or must have forgotten all about their duty as relatives. In the past your father Shayakhmet did plenty of good deeds for each and every one of them.'

As if to confirm this, neither of my father's cousins enquired about the route I would be taking home, or whether I needed anything for my journey. Nurgalii was the only one to give me some useful tips:

'From what you've told me of your journey here, I can see that you had to walk long distances all on your own,' he said. 'Never sit down, let alone lie down, to rest on your own on a deserted road. If you're tired, you may fall asleep and sleep through the daylight hours, and even end up spending the night in the steppe all by yourself. God forbid that that should happen, as it's dangerous. Always try to make it to a village before dark.'

When I did reach home, Mother echoed Nurgalii's criticisms of the Mukazhanovs. Three or four days after my return, she said indignantly, 'The neighbours want to know if our relatives have helped us in any way and whether they've sent any food back with you. They reckon they haven't done enough for us. I feel ashamed that they've shown themselves up like this to outsiders! What a pity your father has cousins like them!'

Chapter Eighteen

Days of Mourning

It was now the middle of 1933. All the ears of corn left on the fields after last year's harvest, which had provided the hungry with a temporary source of nourishment, had been picked up and the fields ploughed. The last grains left in the straw and chaff in the old stacks had also all been taken. People's meagre sources of food had run out. Famine now swept through the entire region as far as the outcrops of Southern Altai and the upper reaches of the Irtysh, parts of the republic that were renowned as grain-producing areas. There were more and more famine victims roaming about in search of food. Mother had reduced the portion sizes of our three meals as much as possible; but how was my six-year-old brother to understand that this harsh regime had to be stuck to? Apart from the few minutes a day when he was gobbling down his miserable ration of food, he spent the whole time pleading for food and crying. Appalled by the sight of his tears, Mother was forced to give him something extra to eat.

Just at this point during the famine we received an unexpected visit from Toimbai-ata's son, Aiken, who had made the same 150-

Part of a Kazakh family's horse and camel train, fully loaded, in the course of a seasonal migration in pre-Soviet days, in a rare photograph (**above**) which endorses the somewhat idealized record made by the Russian painter Nikolai Khludov in the late 19th century (**below**).

Left and below:

1927. The last migrations. Kazakh families arrive at their summer pastures for what was to prove one of the last seasonal migrations before the imposition of collectivisation.

Below left:

An early camera (1920s) catches a Kazakh couple with their three young children during the construction of their summer yurt, showing a panel of felt cladding in the foreground.

Above:

*1929. A rally of nomadic Kazakhs, whose horses graze the steppe, is harangued by a Party official (**centre, left**) on the requirement to join* kolkhozes *– collective farms.*

Left:

1928. A certificate in Arabic script (until then the customary medium of writing among the Kazakhs) records the owner's membership of the 'Kosshy' farm labourers' union, upon which employment came to depend.

Right:

Enforced settlement and collectivisation was accompanied by attempts at mechanisation and the allocation of new roles to women.

Below:

The milk yield of the single cow permitted for any one family had to be delivered in a standard pail daily for collective distribution.

Right:

The most feared man among the Kazakhs from the mid-1920s and throughout collectivisation was Feodor Goloshchekin, Stalin's Party chief for the territory.

Below:

The coming of the railways to Kazakhstan gave a new dimension to Soviet power, including deportation of unwanted families.

Left:

Mukhamet Shayakhmetov in Red Army winter kit, December 1941.

Below:

*The author in 1938, aged about 16, with a school friend (**below left**), and in 1939 with a cousin (**below right**), both of whom were killed at the front towards the end of the War. Shayakhmetov is on the left in both pictures.*

Left:
Mukhamet Shayakhmetov's wife with daughter Aliya and son Bagdat. Seated, right, is the author's mother.

Below left: *The author at school in 1940.*

Below right: *Denied, as a boy, the education he craved, as 'an enemy of the people', Mukhamet Shayakhmetov was to become a schoolteacher, serving the cause of education among his own people in Ust-Kamenogorsk (today's Oskemen) with distinction. He is pictured here displaying medals awarded for his service to education along with his military medals.*

kilometre walk from Lake Zaisan that his father had. I was so dismayed by his appearance that at first I very much hoped it was not Aiken at all. Standing before us was not the pale-faced young man we knew so well, but an emaciated man with a sallow complexion. Not so long ago he had been a handsome young man dressed in the European manner; now, wearing a dirty, tattered old coat draped over him like a bedcover, he looked to me like a complete stranger. Instead of the calf boots he used to wear, he now had thick cloths wrapped round his feet and rawhide shoes.

Still, we were very pleased that he had come to see us, and eager to learn news of his family, whom we had not heard from for a long time. As it turned out, though, the news that Aiken brought us was anything but good.

It is an age-old Kazakh tradition that the news of a person's death is conveyed to his or her close relatives in a particular way and according to set rules and rituals. The most respected close friends and acquaintances of the deceased get together and then go in a group or one by one to the house of the person they have to convey the sad news to. When they arrive, they engage in conversation on general topics, gradually broaching the difficult subject and reason for their visit. They only break the sad news to the family after they have prepared them for it. The most revered person in the group is entrusted with the task of conveying all the necessary details; once they have broken the news to them, they express their condolences and stay to comfort and mourn with them for the first few hours of their grief. Neighbours or close relatives living nearby then bring hot dishes of food from their houses, and offer them to everyone else present. After comforting the bereaved, the visitors all go home a few hours later.

Aiken did not dare break with tradition and tell us the sad news as soon as he had arrived. Without us realising it, he first went and told our neighbours.

The day after his arrival, our neighbours started calling into our hut one by one and talking with Aiken because he was our guest.

I was under the impression that the neighbours had come to greet him in keeping with the Kazakh custom of calling upon any guest who has come from afar; but I could see that Mother was not her usual self. I thought she was not happy about the neighbours coming to greet Aiken, because she kept stonily silent; but it turned out that she had sensed something was wrong. And indeed, the visiting neighbours proceeded to tell first Mother and then us that Father had died.

According to Aiken, it had happened the previous December. Someone who had worked and lived with Father in the same lodgings had written to his relatives in Kumashinko with the news, and from them it had filtered through to some of our relatives in the Topterek aul. However, for some reason or other they had kept this information to themselves. Aiken had only found out about Father's death when he called in to Topterek on his way to us, and that is why it was he who informed us about it.

It seems that, while trying to make his escape from Ridder, Father had been stopped by a passing militiaman, who decided quite by chance to carry out a spot check on him. As a result, he had been separated from his companions and unable to leave the town, where he then fell ill and died. More than that, we simply do not know.

I wept so bitterly that I found it hard to breathe. I could not bear the idea that Father had died far from home and those who loved him, without anyone to give him the care he desperately needed. I imagined him missing us – and me in particular – in the last moments of his life; and I wondered what was to become of us without him in this time of starvation and death.

Our next-door neighbours arranged a small memorial gathering for us with food from their meagre supplies. The gathered company said prayers at the table for the soul of the deceased, and for the future well-being of his loved ones.

Mother was wracked with grief and, left without a husband at such a difficult time, retreated even further into her own world. What tormented her greatly was not only that Father had died in unfamiliar surroundings, but also that the death of a man who had been a highly respected member of the community had been commemorated in such a low-key manner by a few mourners in a small aul. 'In the old days,' she would say regretfully, 'hundreds of people would have mourned his death, and close relatives and friends would have honoured his memory by coming over with camels and horses and organising a lavish funeral for him.'

She was also sad that she had not been able to commemorate her husband on the seventh and 40th day after his death, as tradition demanded. Nor could she afford to pay for prayers to be said for his soul: how could she, when she was struggling to keep her children from dying of starvation? A true believer, she was deeply upset that since his death the previous winter not a single word of prayer had been said to comfort his tortured soul.

ii

During the summer of 1933, the numbers of adults, old people and children roaming around the aul asking for charity and food increased by the day. They were grateful even for a handful of grain (to say 'crust of bread' would be misleading, since bread was a rarity in those days, and if someone got hold of any, they kept quiet about it). Whereas in the early spring it had been unsettling to hear that some family or other had had to go without supper or breakfast, we were now facing the appalling sight of starving people with bloated bodies.

As for us, we had nearly used up our small supply of food and had no means of getting any more. Mother was not expecting any help from her sons-in-law, for Manap had a large family of his own and was not earning much, while Kairankhazi and Altynzhan had been sent off by the collective farm to a timber works somewhere far away in the *taiga*, and we had lost contact with them.

After Aiken had set off home from our aul, I started thinking more and more about our relatives in Topterek. In the end I suggested to Mother that we move there. She replied by saying that we had nobody there to go to. 'These relatives of your Father,' she continued, 'didn't help you one bit when you were with them in the spring, so I doubt if they'll help us now. Anyway, how are we going to get there?'

A while later, however, when she was sitting at home worrying herself sick about what was going to happen to us, I repeated the suggestion. This time she kept quiet instead of objecting as before. Two or three days later she called my younger brother and me to her and asked us in a serious tone, as though we were adults, 'Do you want to go to your clan's aul?' And my younger brother and I at once shrieked in unison: 'Y-e-e-s!' 'All right,' she said, 'I'll take you to your relatives. I am not expecting to get any help or charity from them. They're not capable of such things, I know. But if you are destined to die of starvation, let it happen among your close family in your home region.'

My little brother and I were completely delighted. We were moving back home! It turned out, however, to be easier said than done.

Mother heard a rumour from a neighbouring aul about someone about to travel to Ust-Kurchum – an individual peasant farmer by the name of Shaken who owned his own horse. She went to see him and got him to agree to take us all the way there in his cart, free of charge. He was in such a hurry, however, that we did not even have time to say goodbye to our relatives.

My mother, brother and I sat in the cart while Shaken and his partner rode the two horses harnessed to it. We travelled very slowly, taking the whole day to cover between 40 and 50 kilometres. The long, bumpy journey in the heat made us all so drowsy that we boys kept nodding off to sleep – but we only managed to doze a little before the driver would wake us up again by shouting out: 'Wake up, lad! You're making it harder for the horses!'

In the late afternoon the men turned off the road and rode towards a meadow in the middle of the rushes along the bank of the Irtysh where the horses could rest and graze. Just then, two other men rode up with a cart of their own and started unharnessing their horses with the same intention as our drivers. Then they lit a fire, heaved the plump carcass of a sheep off the cart, slashed it in half and started cooking a large chunk in a cauldron. Our drivers, who turned out to be acquaintances of theirs, began chatting with them and waiting for the meat to be cooked. They sat by the fire, talking ever more animatedly and laughing raucously, until long after they had finished eating the steaming, fatty meat.

As for us, we sat a little way away in the rushes waiting for them for what seemed like ages. All we could hear was a lot of loud noise. As we were half-starved, we could not get over the fact that these travellers were carrying fresh mutton with them on their journey and treating their friends to a feast washed down with strong alcohol, while all around us people were dying of hunger, unable to find even a scrap of food to eat. How lucky these people were! Where had they got hold of the meat, when most people had not tasted it for over a year? This is what I kept wondering.

A month later we discovered the answer. It turned out that they were agents who drove around purchasing gold and gold articles from the general public on the State's behalf. Starving people were giving away everything they had, including gold, in exchange for something to eat – and these rogues were fleecing them.

Delayed by this long halt, it was the middle of the night by the time we arrived in Ust-Kurchum. Nobody was expecting us, of course. We were just a few of the masses of people struggling to find ways and means of staying alive. We had no idea where we were going to live there, so Mother asked Shaken to take us to the lodgings we had stayed in two years previously, which was the home of the only people we knew in the aul. Not daring to wake up the house's owner, Akhat Sabitov, we sat outside in his yard until morning. The man, God bless him, gave in to our pleas and let us stay for a while in his winter cowshed. Mother regarded this as the act of a true Muslim.

iii

Now that we had reached Ust-Kurchum, Mother was in no hurry to move to Father's family aul, and did not even inform our relatives of our arrival – though she was sure that the news would reach them instantly by word of mouth. She explained her decision like this:

'We are in mourning for the head of our family, and so it's not right for us to go calling on acquaintances or sending them news of ourselves. Anyone who had even a grain of respect for us or Father's memory would come and see us first to express their condolences in the traditional way, and say a prayer with the family of the deceased. Until this happens, it would be wrong for us to try and make contact with our relatives. If they fail to behave towards us in a dutiful manner as set down by tradition, it means they no longer consider us close relatives or value us as such. It might just be, though, that they are no better off than us. Either way, we can't expect help from them. They, of course, already know that we are here. Perhaps they're scared of having contact with us as a kulak's family and that's keeping them away. As far as that goes, we really could cause your father's relatives at Topterek some harm.'

Meanwhile, the ring of famine was growing ever tighter around us. Everywhere you looked, you could see starving people with swollen faces wandering about or, worst still, living skeletons, all skin and bones, in tattered clothing. There were corpses lying in the streets, the steppe and the roads, and the sight of them even touched the hearts of people on the verge of starvation themselves who could feel virtually nothing any more except pangs of hunger.

During the first stage of starvation and especially in the second (when the person is no more than a living skeleton), most people lose all sense of conscience and human dignity. The victim's thoughts are concentrated entirely on getting something to eat. Moreover, they no longer care what they are eating – they are totally in thrall to the blind demands of hunger. In those days it did not take long for a respectable mother of several children to turn into a wretched old beggar; for proud young women and pretty girls to turn into skeletons and be reduced to marrying men unworthy of them; for widows to become second wives to anyone at all just to save their children, or to marry their fourteen- or fifteen-year old daughters off to someone more prosperous. Famine made people forget the traditions that made their nation so special.

But no matter how much havoc the famine was wreaking, you could still come across people who had retained their sanity and self-respect. Such people refused to give in to their instincts, and whenever they found something new to eat, they would try to eat it sparingly and with the next day in mind. In this way they kept going longer.

Fortunately, Mother was one of them. She sat us down in the cowshed and then said, as though giving a lecture: 'This is how much food we've got left, and that's all.' She pointed at a sack with about eight kilograms of millet in it, and another with about three kilograms of half-rotten grains of wheat which we had gathered in the summer from the straw and chaff in an old stack. 'No matter how hungry you are, you're not to touch the millet without my permission. For the time being we are going to eat the wheat grain. When needs be, I'll give you the millet to eat as well. If you don't do as you are told, and if you start poking your hands in the bag of millet, you've got to realise, it'll all be gone soon. And when the millet's gone, there'll be nothing to eat and you'll die of starvation. Don't forget that: you're my clever ones.' From that day on we had to make do with even smaller portions of half-rotten fried wheat grain. Occasionally Mother gave us a meal of watery millet porridge.

The other source of support Mother hoped to find in the area was Uncle Kozhakhmet; but as I had seen in the spring, he was hardly managing to make ends meet, and had nothing left to share with us.

So Mother started looking for job openings – another reason why she had agreed to move to Ust-Kurchum. She looked for work as a boiler stoker, cleaner and home help. She managed to find the odd vacancy, but as soon as her prospective employers found out that she was from a kulak's family, they refused to take her on. Wherever she went, she took me with her as her 'interpreter and secretary'. I remember going with her to Berdikhozh Kalybayev, the chairman of the Topterek collective farm where people from our aul were now living, and him saying to us: 'We aren't allowed to take a kulak's family into our collective farm. We could only do so if we were to get a letter of authorisation from the regional authorities.'

So off we went to the regional executive committee with a written request to be taken into the collective farm, since we had been left without the head of our family, a kulak now deceased. The chairman returned it at once with the following comment written on it in red ink: 'To be decided by the collective farm's management and collective farmers' general council.'

We took this reply to the collective farm chairman; but he was illiterate, so he handed it over to his secretary to read. When he had heard what it contained, he exclaimed, 'It says you're not to be allowed in! Of course, you should join some collective farm: the regular grain rations would help you get by until the new harvest. But we can't take you into ours. If I was to admit you, I'd be given the sack and even prosecuted. I want to stay alive too, and I've got children of my own. I'm sorry. No offence meant.'

By this time we had only one kilogram of food left, and were in serious danger of dying of starvation. But, constantly searching for ways out of our dilemma, Mother at last managed to find a small and not very reliable means of income to tide us over. One of her acquaintances had tipped her off that some of the regional office workers liked to buy bunches of hops to use as yeast when they baked bread, and bundles of birch twigs to beat themselves with at the steam baths. As soon as she found out about this, she took us both off to pick hops. After picking a sack of them the first day, we carried it back to Ust-Kurchum and then walked from door to door offering it for sale. A woman took the whole sack in exchange for half a round loaf, which was a lot of food during a famine. The bread made a meal for the three of us. It also gave us hope that we might be able to survive and cheered us up immensely.

Encouraged by this, we carried on. We would go out in the morning and get back to town towards the evening, walking from house to house in search of customers; and whenever we found one, instead of asking for money, we took whatever food they offered us in exchange.

Every day we had to walk across the turbulent River Kurchum to and from the place where we picked the hops. It was a dangerous crossing, and Mother and I used to hold onto my younger brother's hands and wade across the fast-flowing mountain river, nearly up to our waists in water. On our way across on the third day, Mukhametrakhim somehow slipped out of our grasp, and we only just managed to catch hold of him to save him being swept down-river. From then on Mother stopped taking him with us, leaving him in the aul all on his own as there was nobody to look after him. That was also quite a risky thing to do, and Mother spent the whole day fretting about him. However, she had no choice: we could still very easily starve to death.

When it came to the bartering, it was the men who tended to be difficult. They would say to their wives, 'What do you need them for? You haven't got any flour to make bread with, have you?' In the end, though, the women would often talk them round and take our wares.

What we got in return depended on people's generosity. One day Mother hurried home instead of taking the hops round the houses as usual and got me to do it. I managed to find a customer in the very first house I tried on the edge of town. As soon as I called out in Russian, as I had been taught, the owner of the house appeared, took one look at the hops and invited me inside. His wife started haranguing him, but he ignored her objections and went over to a trunk, raised its lid slightly, took out a brick of tea and handed it to me. I left in a hurry in case the woman made him change his mind.

On my way home, I kept thinking about the deal I had just struck and worrying over it. All I had got was a brick of tea – and not even a full brick, since it had a corner missing. Would Mother be angry with me for accepting it instead of food?

When I handed it to Mother, however, she cried out in delight, 'Oibai-ai, what a gem! It's a gift from God! Do you know how much this brick is worth? The same as a man's wages for two weeks' work!' Tea it turned out, was a much sought-after commodity: it was not usually for sale on the open market, and even if it did appear, ordinary people could not afford to buy it.

One of the few places it was available was a 'closed' shop – known locally as 'Dvadstatka', from the Russian word for twenty – which was set up and run purely for the region's twenty most senior officials. The men were supplied on a regular basis with all the different goods and food products they needed, so they never knew what it was like to feel hungry. It should be said, however, that it was not their fault that they did not have either the financial resources or the authority to help the victims of the famine: everything was in the hands of the Soviet Government. Even the Government of the Kazakh Autonomous Republic did not have the authority to resolve all the problems involved.

Unfortunately, our hop business came to an end after only ten days: we could find no more customers, and we had pulled all the hops off the bushes within walking distance of Ust-Kurchum. So we started making bundles of birch twigs and bartering them instead. They were harder to carry than the hops, but they kept us going for another week, getting one meal at a time. Our goal was to survive until the new harvest, which was now not very far off: the collective farmers would then have something to eat, and something or other was bound to come our way as well.

The scene that greeted us as we sold our goods from door to door was a harrowing one. Wherever we went, we came across starving people begging for crumbs as they wandered along. Some of them would even ask us for food.

Besides feeling permanently hungry, a starving person gets extremely thirsty and drinks a lot of fluid. This soon causes swellings on his face and then over the rest of his body. After a week or two, depending on his food intake, the swellings go down and he is just skin and bones. He will not last long without a minimum amount of nutrition. If he gets it, he may survive for a matter of months.

Small children and older people always die of starvation first, because when they are weak their resistance to all sorts of illnesses is lower. Starving children develop potbellies and wrinkled faces and looking increasingly like old dwarves on spindly little legs; eventually they grow so weak that they can no longer walk, and have to remain lying down all the time. It is terrible watching a baby who is too exhausted to cry any more, and makes strange little sounds instead; it is terrible watching his suffering before he dies, and the despair of his mother, helpless to do anything to save him.

Dying is never easy, but starving to death is extremely painful. A person suffers both physically and mentally, for it takes a long time to die, and he is constantly anticipating his own end. And yet it causes starving people even more pain and suffering to watch their loved ones die than to experience death themselves: they suffer not only because they are unable to help, but because they are too weak to bury the body of their loved one. May God prevent anything like this ever happening in our country again!

Mother advised the beggars we met to follow our example and find something to do in exchange for food; but though they used to nod their heads, they would then go on begging just as before. Hunger had caused them to lose their reason.

Not until much later did it come home to me that in 1931-34, when millions of people were dying of starvation in Kazakhstan and other parts of the USSR, the Soviet Government was still pursuing its policy to industrialise the country with reckless and ruthless intransigence. All public capital, State gold reserves and other revenue went on buying foreign equipment for major construction projects. If only the authorities had put a temporary halt to this and helped the victims of the famine instead! But no, our 'people's' Government had to live up to the slogans it had invented to speed up the industrialisation process.

When you look at archival documents relating to those tragic years, you can see how much public money was spent not only on industry, but also on endless conferences attended by thousands upon thousands of people all over the Soviet Union. The funds squandered on these alone would have been sufficient to save many lives. Tragically, however, our leaders were more concerned about receiving accolades from Party delegates than they were about the deaths of working people.

Chapter Nineteen

The New Harvest

As the end of summer approached, everyone waited impatiently for the crops to be harvested: the half-starved aul residents; the collective farmers living off meagre food rations from the farm's general stocks; the tramps and beggars who had somehow miraculously clung on to life and now had only this harvest to save their lives. The same was true for us, and my mother kept talking about its advent to help my brother and me bear our dreadful hunger pains.

When nobody in the regional centre wanted our goods any more, Mother decided to move to the Topterek collective farm aul, as their residents would be the first to taste the new harvest. Our move was brought forward by another unexpected event.

Aiken, his mother Onal-apa and his ten-year-old sister Zhametai suddenly arrived in the Topterek aul. Following the death of Toimbai-ata earlier that year, his family had regained their right to live wherever they wished to, and so they moved back to the area they had originally come from. This meant that our two families could be together again.

The new arrivals gave us a strange account of Toimbai-ata's passing. It seems that when Aiken had returned home after being with us and told Toimbai-ata of my father's death, Toimbai-ata had literally lost the will to live. Watching the sunset every evening, he would pray to Allah to let him die and take his soul. And, sure enough, on the seventh day he passed away.

The first crops of wheat now ripened and the collective farms set about harvesting them. But this did not mean an immediate end to hunger. Government policy dictated that as soon as the grain was threshed, it was sent to the State procurement stations: only after a certain amount had been delivered were the collective farms allowed to issue their own members with a share of it, which was barely enough to see them through to the next harvest.

In those days the crops were harvested with scythes and horse-drawn mowing-machines, and the cut corn was tied in sheaves and then transported to the threshing floors. There were always quite a few ears of corn left on the harvested fields that could save people in dire need. When the harvest first got underway, people were forbidden to collect the grain left behind; but once the corn had been taken away to the threshing floors, hungry people would force their way onto the fields and collect just enough grain to keep going for a while before the watchmen could catch them.

My mother, however, had a more far-sighted approach. Gathering ears of corn, as far as she was concerned, was not just a stop-gap measure, but a reliable means of building up our food stocks for the future. So she hunted for fields a good distance from any human habitation, where we would have little competition and all the corn would be ours.

The first isolated area of land she chose was called Kainar, some 30 kilometres away from the collective farm's centre, where, according to reliable sources, the fields were empty and there were plenty of ears of corn left behind after the harvest. Off the two of us went on foot (having left my younger brother with Onal-apa), carrying bundles of clothing, utensils and other things we would need during our long trip.

We walked past the places where our aul used stay in spring and autumn in happier days, on the way to and from the meadows up in the Altai mountains. Three years earlier, my mother had ridden a white horse along this same route, sitting astride her silver-edged saddle studded with precious gems, with a child in a travel cradle fastened to the front of her saddle, leading a camel by a long rein attached to her left wrist. It was impossible to know what she was thinking now as she traipsed along in a state of semi-starvation: she must have longed for the past, but I believe that she, my younger brother and I survived that famine-stricken winter and summer only thanks to her perseverance and will power, and her sense of responsibility for our future.

As for me, someone once said that unless you had a hard childhood, you could not understand what adult life was all about. It is certainly true that a tough upbringing helps you grasp early on the difference between good and evil. It was the simple, character-building catch phrases that children usually ignore, such as 'do as you would be done by' – repeated to me over and over again in my early teens – that stayed with me when life was difficult, and encouraged me to help my mother as much as I possibly could.

The fields we eventually reached were totally deserted. We came across a light shelter made of branches that must have been built by a watchman or a hunter. It was here we kept our things and slept at night. The very next morning we set to work. As soon as we got up we would heat up some water to drink, have a small breakfast, and then start picking up the ears of corn. At midday we would have a short break and eat a frugal lunch of fried wheat grain and boiling water before working right through to the evening. Mother would prepare supper from the grains we had picked that afternoon, while I threshed the ears of corn and husked the grain. By 'threshing' I mean stamping on the ears of corn on a flat stone and then separating the grains from the chaff through a sieve. This was less laborious and time-consuming than the alternative method, which involved tossing the chaff in your hands over a flat dish until eventually the husks got blown off the grain by the currents of air.

Even so, it was not easy for me to husk the grain after picking up ears of corn all day long. I tried to keep in mind Mother's goal of creating food stocks, but I sometimes felt too tired to do the threshing in the evening, and then she would do it for me.

So there we were, just the two of us, with the vast and empty rolling hills all around, as far as the eye could see.

Not far away there was a collective farm threshing floor that still had some threshed grain waiting to be taken away. It was guarded by a watchman, who was the only other person in the area besides us. At first we did not even realise he was there; but when we tried to spend the night on the threshing floor (feeling too scared to sleep outside all by ourselves), this man started yelling at us: 'Heaven forbid! Don't come anywhere near here again! If anyone finds out that you have,' he added in a frightened voice, 'I'll be accused of giving the collective farm's wheat away to a kulak's family and be put on trial.'

We received slightly better treatment from a collective farmer we knew, by the name of Musagozhii Mukii, who showed up a week after we got there in a two-horse *britzka* to collect a load of grain. When he came across us, he said to Mother, 'The corn's just been cut in the irrigated fields down-river and the sheaves have been taken off to the threshing floors, so the ears of corn can already be picked there. And what's more they're thicker, juicier and longer there in the fields than up here in the hills. If I was you, I'd move down there.'

After thanking him for his kind advice, Mother asked Mukii for a lift as far as our aul.

'Oh, come off it, my dear!' he said. 'How can I take you in my *britzka*? The activists in the aul will be onto me in a flash for moving a kulak's family instead of delivering the collective farm's corn to the State.' Then after a moment's thought he said more gently, 'If you haven't got too much grain, I don't mind taking your things and putting your son in my cart. But I can't take you, my dear.'

'Thanks for your offer. I can walk behind the cart.'

'Don't be daft, my dear!' exclaimed Mukii in alarm. 'If our wicked activists see you next to the *britzka*, they'll write a report on how I was taking the corn to your place and how they saved a load of collective farm corn from being stolen. For God's sake, don't let any of them see you – you'd better stay here today. Walk to the aul on your own tomorrow.'

So the carter took my things and me with him, leaving Mother to follow. Weighed down by the collective farm grain, the *britzka* moved along very slowly and only reached the aul towards evening. Half a kilometre outside it Mukii stopped the cart and said, 'Stay here with your sack of grain, lad. You can carry it through these bushes. If I take you in my *britzka* into the aul, you'll have your sack taken off you and I'll get done for giving you collective farm grain.'

Then he dropped my sack of grain on top of a bush and said anxiously, 'Wait here until I've got to the aul. Then don't you dare walk along the road with your sack. Go through the bushes and try not to be spotted by anyone on the way back home.'

There I was, then, standing in the road with the sack. I had to get it home safe and sound, which meant keeping out of sight. Leaning towards the bush the carter had dropped the sack on, I heaved it onto my back and began staggering towards the aul, trying to keep to the undergrowth and out of sight. But after 40 or 50 metres I could no longer bear the weight, and had to drop it on the ground. I was simply not strong enough to carry fifteen or so kilograms.

After a short break I tried lifting the sack onto my back again, but without success. Then I tried lifting it into my arms – but I could not get it off the ground. What was I going to do? Bewildered and terrified of losing the precious sack, our only source of food, I mustered all my strength and started rolling the sack like a barrel; but I was too weak to do it for long, and did not get very far with it.

I began feeling more and more desperate. I was scared that any moment now a passer-by would appear on the road, spot the sack of grain and take it off me, as the carter had predicted. After suffering the torments of hunger for so long and knowing how much effort every single grain had cost, and always dreaming of having a little food put by for, say, half a day, I feverishly tried to think of a safe way of getting it back home where Onal-apa and the little children were depending on it.

It occurred to me to go back to how I'd started. The easiest way to get the sack on to my back was to take it off the top of a bush;

so if I rested it on another bush whenever I stopped, I would be spared the effort of heaving it up off the ground each time. In this way, staggering 50 to 100 metres from one bush to the next, I managed to carry it all the way home. As she helped me haul it into the makeshift wattle hut we were living in, Onal-apa exclaimed in amazement, 'How on earth did you carry something so heavy? You surely must have hurt your back? You've had a tough time, my little one, and really suffered. Oh, Creator,' she wailed, 'what sins are you punishing us for?' Then, changing tack instantly, she continued, 'I'll fry some grains of wheat right now and fill you all up. God has sent this in answer to the little orphans' prayers.'

No sooner had Mother reached home the following day than she started getting ready to set off again for the place where the ears of corn were 'bigger and juicier'. This time she got ready for a long trip and decided to take my younger brother as well. It turned out that when he had stayed behind with Onal-apa, he had kept giving her the slip and skulking off with the local boys to swim in the dangerous river.

But when the three of us arrived at our destination, we found a whole crowd of other people intent on picking the ears of corn as well. They all slept overnight on an old threshing floor, in the light shelters previously used by the collective farmers during the threshing. We also took up residence in one of them. We spent all the hours of daylight picking ears of corn, and the evenings threshing and husking them. My brother would start the day by helping us diligently, but, being only six years old, he soon got fed up and started playing games instead; and because there is only so much fun a little boy can have in a field of stubble, he would wander off into the undergrowth around the perimeter and hide in the grass and bushes. Then Mother would have to stop working and go off after him, or send me to look for him. This was so disruptive that in the end Mother was forced to take him back to the aul, despite the river's dangers.

There were a dozen men and women working in the fields, and they were all Kazakhs. The most fruitful area was one where half of the new harvest had been cut manually with scythes and raked into piles on the ground like hay, instead of being tied together in sheaves and taken off to the threshing floor. Unfortunately, we had to contend with a watchman who kept chasing us off his territory.

'Why doesn't he let us pick them up? If they're left, they're only going to rot under the snow. What's it to him?' one of the other scavengers would ask.

'He's acting like this because he's Russian,' someone else would declare.

'If only God would do something bad to him,' another would add, before praying earnestly to Allah to let the hateful watchman die.

Later on, though, we discovered that he was not to blame for being so obstructive. He had simply been told that if the regional authorities heard that trespassers were gathering ears of corn in their fields, the collective farmers would be accused of mismanaging the harvest, and made to pick up the ears of corn themselves: that was why he chased people away, even though he realised how ridiculous and mean it seemed.

We remained in this place until there were no more ears of corn left in the fields nearest the threshing floor, and we had to walk to fields further away, which took even more time and energy. Our pickings dwindled and the nights grew colder. There were now fewer people about, as some had given up on this wild and primitive way of life – if you could call it life – and started drifting away. Eventually, only the two of us remained.

'Everyone else like us has left. Why don't we?' I pleaded with Mother. 'How can we stay by ourselves in these empty fields? Let's go back to the aul!'

But she replied, 'We have to stay. Those who've left must have some help or support or other source of food to see them through. What or who have we to rely on? Your cousin Aiken can't be counted on – he's got to feed his elderly mother and little sister. We can only rely on ourselves. That's why we've somehow got to keep at it right up until it starts snowing.'

So on we went; but with every passing day our task became harder. We had to walk further to find new fields, and there were no longer enough hours of daylight to scour them. Nor was it possible to start work earlier, as the ground was covered with hoarfrost and our hands froze. We could not warm up until we had got the fire blazing.

At night, ice began to form on the irrigation canals around the fields' edges and on the bowls we left out. We also began to feel the cold in our light shelters. Trying to warm up, I went over to the stacks of straw on the threshing floor, dug myself a hole and – with Mother's permission – spent the night snuggled up in the warmth there. From then on I slept there every night. It was so warm that I slept better without my coat on. The only things that kept me awake were the wisps of straw tickling my face, and the rustling and squeaking sounds of mice. No matter how much I enthused about sleeping in the straw, Mother refused to sleep there; but at least she could use my outdoor clothes to keep herself warm in the chilly shelter.

It never ceases to amaze me how a small, naturally delicate woman and a boy, both undernourished and lightly clothed, coped with such a harsh way of life in the cold steppe over a long period of time without falling ill. A piercing wind was now blowing from the distant snow-capped mountains all around: I remember well how I used to rush to the edge of the field and shelter from it under a bush for a few moments. After I had warmed up a little, I would hurry straight back to work; yet my mother kept picking up the ears of corn without a break.

A further anxiety was where we were to spend the winter. We had no home of our own, and we could not stay in the makeshift wattle shed where we had left Onal-apa and the little children. As the weather grew colder, Mother fretted more and more about this problem.

Then – one cold autumn day at the beginning of November, I think – Aiken turned up at our camp with a wheelbarrow he had knocked together out of some heavy cartwheels. After finding out from someone where we were and what we were doing, he had come to take us home. 'You can't stay here any longer,' he said. 'It's going to snow any day now. I've brought this wheelbarrow along to take you back.'

'Where do you want to take us?' Mother asked. 'Do you have a roof over your head yourself?'

'I've found some lodgings in the village of Kamyshenka. True, we've got to share them with someone else. But where could we find separate lodgings, seeing who we are? It'll be cramped, but at least we'll be together, and with each other's help we'll get through it all.' Then he started loading our things onto the wheelbarrow.

Later, he told us how he had searched for ages before he found temporary work on the collective farm he was now taking us to. Unable to cope with the harvest because of insufficient manpower, the farm was hiring temporary workers and paying good wages. Acquaintances had advised Aiken that he would be better off moving to a Russian village: it would apparently be easier to get through the winter there than in a Kazakh aul, with occasional opportunities for him to earn a little money.

In retrospect, Aiken's choice of lodgings was exceptionally successful. It is, I believe, thanks to being in a Russian village such as Kamyshenka that we stayed alive during that harsh, famine-stricken winter, for reasons that I shall explain.

Chapter Twenty

The Milk of Human Kindness

I am writing this memoir for the rising generation in order to give them some idea of what their grandparents' lives were like, and what they endured during a certain period of our country's history. It is important for them to realise, too, that people can get through any ordeal as long as they persevere, and have some notion of what they want to achieve in life.

The autumn of 1933 had brought some temporary relief from the famine, and there were better crops of wheat in the higher regions of the Altai mountains and along the right bank of the Irtysh, where it was relatively damp and rained at least once in a while. Elsewhere, however, the harvest had failed to live up to people's hopes, thanks to the third successive summer of drought. Worse, because of the quota of grain that had to go straight to the State, many collective farms were left without any seeds to sow the next crop with, condemning their farmers to a half-starved existence until the following autumn. So people from the upper reaches of the Irtysh and the Kalbinsk Ridge started pouring into the grain-producing Zyryanovsk region in the hope of finding salvation there.

They walked all the way, taking their children with them. In many cases, the elderly chose to remain at home and face starvation rather than be a burden to the rest of the family on the journey. This was a tragedy on a national scale – relatives saying goodbye in the knowledge that they were unlikely to meet again in this lifetime.

So many migrants poured into the Zyryanovsk region that its inhabitants faced a further threat. One can still read several resolutions passed by the District Executive Committee on tackling the smallpox epidemic that had broken out: regional authorities were instructed to send representatives to all the places were homeless people had congregated and either help them to get settled or return them to the regions they came from. However, these resolutions were never implemented, and during the winter that followed a good number of migrants died of starvation and disease.

The situation in Russian villages and collective farms was slightly better than in Kazakh ones. The famine had not been so widespread among the former, and even during the drought the farms had managed to grow some meagre crops and put by some emergency stocks for their farmers. What's more, unlike the Kazakhs, the Russian villagers had their own allotments providing them with additional food.

Ever since the times of the first settlers, and especially since the turn of the twentieth century (when reforms were introduced to regulate transmigration within the Russian Empire), the Russian population had farmed the most fertile arable lands in Kazakhstan. When the collective farms were first organised, those with Russian populations were therefore at an advantage; they also had superior agricultural equipment and tools (ploughs, winnowing-machines, harvesters, threshing machines, *britzkas*, and so on). Moreover, as Russian peasants had devoted themselves to growing cereal crops for generations, their farm were run more efficiently, with a higher standard of management and a more disciplined labour force.

The result was that they earned better wages – even though collectivisation was supposed to have made all farmers equal – which, in turn, increased their incentive to work.

On the Kazakh collective farms, however, the complete opposite was true. Stockbreeders were expected to grow cereal crops on the very same land their animals used to graze, which was quite unsuitable for the purpose; and they had to make do with hardly any equipment, as very few of them had previously owned harrows and ploughs, let alone winnowing or threshing machines. The result was low productivity and a badly paid, demoralised workforce. Unfortunately, the same shameful difference in living standards between aul-dwellers and villagers continued until the collective farms became State farms at the end of the 1950s.

But for all their advantages, the Russian villages were suffering too, and could not possibly take in all the famine victims; besides which, having previously lived apart from the indigenous nomadic people, the villagers felt ill at ease with them, and were particularly alarmed by the starving vagrants who kept turning up at their doors, because of the health threat they posed. In such a situation it was very hard for the Kazakh migrants to get a roof over their heads, so it was extremely fortunate for us that Aiken had managed to find lodgings in the village of Kamyshenka.

The few Kazakhs living in Russian villages before collectivisation had mainly worked as herdsmen and as hired labourers. When the Soviet authorities dispossessed the wealthy villagers who had employed them, the labourers in Kamyshenka started working at the local grain procurement station, and organised a separate aul on the edge of the village. It was here that our acquaintance Kabyl Kilybayev had rented a vacant log hut until the following summer.

Kilybayev had been declared a kulak and deported to Ridder at the same time as Father. For health reasons, he had been released ahead of time, and he had then gone back home to rejoin his family. But the local authorities had started persecuting him again, and so he had moved to Kamyshenka in the hopes of being left in peace. His offer to put up Aiken made sense for both of them, because by pooling their resources it would be easier to pay the rent and get enough fuel to see out the winter.

But while we had solved the problem of where to live, there

remained the challenge of replenishing our small supply of grain to last us until the next harvest. Our answer was to prepare and sell winter fuel to the Russian villagers. You see, these villagers, like all the others along the banks of the Irtysh, did not use firewood: instead, they burnt rushes, which they could only get hold of when the river had frozen over. What's more, they were not generally very skilled at cutting the rushes themselves, and preferred to buy them.

Unfortunately, there were plenty of others doing the same as us, and so the price of the rushes fell to almost nothing. In exchange for a full cart that had taken several adults a day to cut to the right size, the seller would get enough food to feed an average family once. This fell far short of what was required for a family of five. We needed to add something, no matter how small, to what Aiken was earning.

Not far from the village and the Irtysh there were two lakes with narrow marshy strips along three of their shorelines. These marshes had dwarf rushes, willows, birches and various bushes growing in them. In winter the lake water used to flood the tussocks sticking out of the marsh; it would then freeze and form a perfectly flat crust of ice over the surface.

Aiken got an axe that was small and light enough for me to chop the small bushes and rushes out of the ice. Most of the rush-sellers left these alone (preferring the denser thickets of tall rushes growing along the banks of the river and lake, as they were in great demand); the only people who collected them were me and an old man by the name of Akhmadii.

To begin with, it took me three to four days to cut down enough to fill a cart. With practice, however, I got this down to two days. Aiken used to find a buyer in the village and accompany him in a cart to collect the load I had just cut down. I have no idea how much Aiken used to charge, but he would come home with extra food such as potatoes, bread, flour and sometimes simply wheat grain – whatever he could get in exchange for the rushes.

It was not the easiest of work for a twelve-year-old boy, chopping away all day and every day, without a break. What's more, some of the fuel was needed to keep us warm at home, which meant that it took longer to collect a cartful for sale. But I put up with it because we had to stay alive somehow. We owed a lot to the Russian Kamyshenka villagers who had managed to put enough by to buy our wares.

And what was the State doing at the time of this national disaster? It was removing all the grain from the collective farm threshing floors under the system of obligatory deliveries, and deliberately leaving the country folk to go hungry. True, it then gave the collective farms interest-bearing loans of seeds – but this was the same grain that had been taken from them the previous autumn, which they now had to bring back from the State procurement stations in carts drawn by emaciated horses.

In March the problem of where to live recurred yet again. The owner of the house we were in decided to move back to the village from an aul, and demanded that we vacate it – though he allowed Kabyl Kilybayev to stay. Because Kilbayev had sub-let it to us, there was nothing Aiken could do except search for somewhere else. But who would take in a family of five in midwinter?

Aiken searched for ages, while the owner kept repeating that he wanted us out without further delay. As if that was not enough, he started accusing Kilybayev of letting a kulak's family into his house without permission, and threatened to make him leave with us if we did not vacate the hut within 48 hours. So as not to make life even harder for the kind man who had given us shelter at a time of dire need, the adults in my family took extreme action.

Next door to where we were staying was an empty hut that was considered unsuitable for habitation in winter. It had thin walls and ceilings, only one window, and a plank door with no lock that was propped up on the outside with a stake. Its owner apparently lived there in summer and somewhere else in winter. Astonishingly, by the standards of today, it had not been broken into or damaged in any way, so out of desperation we decided to move into it – despite the fact that it had been standing empty for several months and was draughty, damp and icy cold. We had no other choice if we were not to freeze to death in the open air.

The first thing we had to do was warm the place up. This was a miserable business which took ages. Recalling those days now, I can only marvel at how we managed to stay alive: it is one thing to be hungry and malnourished when you are in the warm, and quite another in the cold. Although there was a stove, the chimney refused to draw, so when it was first lit all the smoke came billowing into the hut and we had to let it out through the open door. And when the chimney finally did begin to draw and the stove had warmed up slightly, its walls began to crack. The black smoke started seeping through the cracks and filling the room, stinging the eyes of the person who was trying to keep the rushes ablaze.

The cracks got so wide that we knew we had to seal them if the stove was to function. Finding and mixing a clay solution to do this took a long time and a lot of hard work. (We also had the task of repairing the window frame and erecting a cauldron in the hearth to cook our food.) First, the clay had to be dug up from under the snow; then the clods of earth had to be heated and dissolved in boiling water to make the solution. Once the cracks had been sealed, the chimney began to draw again, but the stove got so hot that the hut was filled with clouds of steam, as thick as fog; and a day later, when the 'fog' had disappeared, the ceilings and walls remained covered in condensation, with droplets of water dripping like rain from the ceilings and streaking down the walls onto the floor.

On the fourth or fifth day the droplets dried up and the walls and ceilings became a damp shade of grey that showed, according to the adults, that they had partly thawed out. The floor was still entirely frozen. However, the owner of our previous lodgings wanted us out so badly that we were forced to move into the damp room with its frozen floor covered with a layer of rushes. Even though the stove was alight nearly all the time, the room was still unbearably chilly. You had to keep your outdoor clothes on inside, and sleep in them as well.

These new lodgings were bound to affect our health. For Onalapa, who had fallen ill while we were still in our warm house, the cold, damp air proved fatal. Once the wife of the most respected elder in the aul, with a reputation as a generous hostess, she had always enjoyed a comfortable way of life; now, at 65 years of age, she could no longer stand the appalling conditions we were living in. She died lamenting the cruelty of fate.

Like other peoples, the nomads kept a calendar with their observations of annual, monthly and daily changes in the weather, on the basis of which they attempted to make forecasts. Every type of extreme weather was given a name – for example, the 'six-day *akpan*' (the first few days of January) and the 'seven-day *otamal*' (a changeable spell of weather in mid-March). Livestock breeders were particularly wary of the *otamal*, which used to come just when all the people and animals were worn out and undernourished at the end of winter. They used to say of it, 'If your luck's in, it'll pass in a flash; if your luck's out, it'll rant and roar.' Within a matter of days, it could wreak havoc and kill off large numbers of stock, making paupers of rich breeders.

Such extreme weather came out of nowhere that winter. There were heavy falls of snow and blizzards continuously for a whole week. All communication between the populated areas was cut off. The blizzard started so unexpectedly that it caught quite a few travellers on the road and herds out at pasture. A good proportion of the livestock perished by being stranded outside in their pens without fodder, while people who had kept alive by begging were forced to stay indoors and starved to death. The *otamal* also deprived us of our income, for the wind raged so much that it flattened everything in its way, letting the heavy snow cover all the bushes and rushes so that they were impossible to cut them down. For a while we had to eat our emergency stocks of food, reducing our rations to the very minimum.

Onal-apa's funeral took place just as the blizzard started raging. Kazakhs always used to attach great importance to helping families in mourning, and thanks to the efforts of our neighbours, her body was finally committed to the earth on the third day, when the snow abated slightly. A mullah and an elder officiated. Devastated by her death, Aiken spoke movingly at the funeral:

'Not so long ago, dear Mother, when you were respected and revered by all your relatives and everyone who knew you, could you ever have imagined that you would die at such a terrible time and that I, your only son, who you doted on all your life, would accompany you on your final journey without performing all the traditional rituals in your memory? At this time of national disaster when people are dying of starvation, those of your acquaintances who have not been informed of your passing away and funeral will think that you died of hunger, too...'

At this point one of the guests interrupted him, searching for the right words to console him:

'When so many people are dying of hunger in the streets and roads and in the steppe, lying there unburied, your mother at least died in bed at home. At her bedside she had someone to give her water and listen to her last words. Not just anyone is granted such a death by God: only those who are pleasing to Him deserve such an end. Surely every mother prays to God to die in the presence of her son? And so God answered your mother's prayer. He has taken her to His kingdom. For this we should offer our thanks to Him. It is His will, and it is a sin to mourn such a death too much. It may anger our Creator.'

Afterwards, contrary to custom, the mourners did not visit the house of the deceased to pray for her soul, share a meal to honour her memory, and express their condolences more fully to the family; instead, they went straight from the cemetery back to their homes. They knew that if they came to us, we would be giving up our last crumbs to entertain them and be left without food for the next few days – so they graciously went on their way. The mullah and elder did visit our hut to perform the traditional rites there, but they had to make do with a meal consisting of two handfuls of wheat grain and a cup of boiling water.

March was drawing to a close. Once the first milder days of the thaw set in, our hovel became noticeably warmer and drier. We could now take our overcoats off indoors. Our sense of relief was not to last long, however. Just as before, the owner of the hut we were living in suddenly decided to move back to the village, and demanded we vacate his property. Unable this time to find even a corner in the village to shelter in, our family was forced to move to the nearest aul. I have to say that for once we were lucky: just when Aiken was searching for a new place, a man in the aul was appointed chairman of a collective farm elsewhere, and decided to let us move into his warm and comfortable little house. If he had not been given the post, who knows how long we would have been left homeless.

ii

So we found ourselves living in a former winter stopping place called Kyzyl Kaiyn, where the aul residents were all members of my mother's clan, the Zhauotei-bur. Despite this, the chairman – who also happened to be married to one of my first cousins – did what no one else had done in our three years of being homeless, and insisted that we produce a residence permit from our last domicile.

'Unless they are officially registered as residents, migrants are strictly forbidden to live within the territory of this aul council,' he said bumptiously. 'And they cannot be registered without a document from their previous place of residence. If it becomes known that a kulak's family is living right under the noses of the aul council without the right papers, I will be accused of harbouring you and be removed from my post. Either you produce the documents within a week, or you must leave.'

Since the bad spring weather made travel difficult, we asked for an extension – but he refused us even this. 'You have just one week!' he insisted.

How were we to get hold of this document we so desperately needed? We had no idea whether we had been registered in the places we had stayed in over the past three years. We came to the conclusion that we would have to apply to the aul we had originally been deported from.

Aiken – who fortunately for his family already had the necessary documents from another place they had lived in – had misgivings about going back there, knowing how unjustly the council treated returning former kulaks. But in any case, he was not be entitled to receive the papers on our behalf. As it was dangerous and difficult for Mother to walk 30 or 40 kilometres along the slushy spring roads, the adults decided that I should go instead. So off I set.

Along the way, I saw how people you think you know well can change beyond recognition. Close relatives and friends can sometimes behave just as callously and unkindly as strangers, and complete strangers can sometimes help you out.

I had already had some experience of this a month before, when at Mother's request I had paid a visit to Uncle Kozhakhmet in Zyryanovsk. It turned out that Uncle Mukatai had gone to live with him, and after waiting until the two of us were alone in the house, Uncle Mukatai suddenly started yelling at me for no reason at all, 'Get out of my sight! All of you will be the death of us! Haven't you all been cursed enough already? Get out of this house!'

Because I did not understand what he meant, I went on sitting there in silence until another member of the family came inside, whereupon Uncle went quiet. I never told anyone about this unpleasant incident, not even Mother: somehow I felt ashamed of Mukatai and what he had done. But twenty years later, in 1954, a year before his death, he once spoke about it when the two of us were alone. 'I was wrong,' he said. 'Forgive me. I was in a state of shock at the time because of the dreadful things your cousins Bazar and Arshabai had done, going against tradition and depriving Kozhakhmet of his last means of earning a living. I was furious with them, and when you turned up I poured out all my anger undeservedly on you.' I hurriedly reassured him that I had long since forgotten, even though this was not so. There was no point in upsetting an old man over something he had done in the past.

I started out for our old aul just as the spring thaw was at its worst. Although the snow had still not completely disappeared, it was melting so rapidly that there was a layer of water underneath it in the steppe. My feet kept sinking through the slushy surface of the country track: as vehicles seldom went this way, the surface had not been compacted by passing wheels. The whole of the natural world seemed debilitated after the long and severe winter: the livestock were now emaciated on account of the fodder shortages, all the vegetation was rotting under the snow, and people were exhausted from not getting enough to eat for so long and expecting at any moment to starve to death. Every living creature was waiting for the warm sun and new spring.

Because of the tough going, I hardly managed to cover the fifteen kilometres to the next aul, Topterek, on the first day. I knew that if could I spent the night there, I would reach the office of Aul Council Number Six by the following evening. So I went to see Uncle Yeskendyr, a man of around 50, who was father's cousin and had always been kind to me.

I found him, however, in a bad mood. Instead of returning my greeting of 'Assalaam aleikum!', he started yelling at me to get out of his house at once. Then he began ranting and raving about everyone dumping themselves on him and always being worse off than anyone else and one day ending up ruined.

But I was too young to work out why he was angry with me, and since I had nowhere else to go and it was nearly evening, I stayed put. Fortunately, it was soon time for evening prayer. Uncle calmed down, and when he had finished praying, he suddenly called out: 'Nurdykha, have you any *talkan* [small fried grains of wheat] left? Feed Mukhamet – he must be hungry after walking all day.'

Aunt Nurdykha, who had been watching her husband disapprovingly, but had not dared object openly, eagerly handed me a small bowl of *talkan* in milk. I do not know what had got into Uncle, but I reckon that as he was praying to Allah he must have realised that he had broken the sacred oath of every Muslim not to offend anyone of the same faith, and to help relatives and friends and the poor.

For the rest of the evening, though, he said not a word to me or to any of his family. Only when I was going to bed did he ask me what I had come to the aul for. When I told him where I was going and why, he simply said, 'Then get up really early and set off while the ground's still frozen. If you wait sun's up and it starts thawing, you'll find it hard going, and you won't manage to get back here in the day. It's hard spending the night in other clans' aul these days: nobody may let you in.'

I followed his advice and made an early start. There was nobody else around, for in those days few people ever rode along the roads between auls. However, it had been a warm night, and the ground was not frozen at all. There were puddles and rivulets trickling all along the track. I started trudging along more slowly and squelching through the puddles. My old boots looked as though they were going to fall apart at any minute. Water kept seeping in through some of the holes in them and then oozing out of others. It was fresh cold water from melted snow and my feet became chilled to the bone. Fortunately, they warmed up in the gaps between puddles, and I continued walking briskly along towards my destination.

By midday I had reached the aul. After asking someone the way, I quickly found the council office.

I had never been in an aul office on business before, although I had lived half a winter in another similar one. The terrifying name of the Aul Number Six office had stuck in my memory ever since Father's arrest and the confiscation of his livestock and property three years previously, and the doubts I was now having about getting the document made me even more frightened. I stepped warily through the doorway to find a man sitting at a desk in silence.

As people in offices apparently disliked the traditional greeting of 'Assalaam aleikum', I said, 'Salamatsyzba?' (meaning 'Are you in good health?') and then anxiously blurted out, 'I am the son of Shayakhmet Aitlembetov. Three years ago my family were dispossessed as kulaks and my father got a two-year sentence and was deported. He died there and never came back. We've just settled in the Ust-Kurchum aul council's area and we've been asked for documents from our previous place of residence. We don't have any. I've come to get the document we need. Will you give us a paper to say we used to live here?'

The man sitting at the desk asked my mother's name and our surname and silently began to write. When he had finished, he handed me a small sheet of paper and said, 'Here, I've written the document you need. Take it to the house of the chairman of our aul council. He's already left and won't be back here again today. He'll sign it and stamp it at home.'

'But will he let me inside his house?' I asked doubtfully. 'Will he really sign and put a stamp on my paper?

'Off you go and don't worry. He'll do everything that needs to be done,' replied the man reassuringly.

As I walked towards the house, I doubted very much that the chairman of the aul council whose officials had ruthlessly confiscated everything from us would now allow me through his door and sign my document. I reckoned that he would say that we had not been registered with them for ages and tear up the sheet of paper. I entered his yard with a sense of dread.

The sight that awaited me caused me to stop and rub my eyes. There was a cow standing without a head collar on, munching at a large haystack, and slightly further away, a round-bellied dark bay horse standing drowsily by a manger. The owner of this yard was certainly well off, that was for sure. The haystack at the end of winter, the cow wandering freely, the well-nourished horse – all these set their owner apart from his neighbours.

There was nobody about in the yard, so I walked very cautiously into the front room. My nose caught the pungent odour coming off a calf tethered near the door and then the stronger, mouth-watering aroma of fried *baursak* [bits of pastry]. I was knocked for six by the smell because I had not eaten since the morning, and could not even remember the last time I had tasted this scrumptious Kazakh snack.

I crept through the doorway of the next room and there, reclining on a soft mattress on the floor by the window (the most honoured place, usually reserved for guests) lay the council chairman, Madine Yesengeldin. I recognised his face: he had been one of the aul council's activists, and I remembered him visiting our house before Father was branded a kulak. Afraid of what his reaction might be, I shyly mumbled a greeting and then loudly and clearly rattled off the speech I had already made in the office. I also hastily added that I had come to his house on the advice of his secretary.

Madine looked up and, without getting to his feet, took the sheet of paper from my outstretched hand. He turned it over a few times – without reading it, as far as I could see – and then silently did what he had been asked and returned it to me. Meanwhile, the appetising aroma of fried *baursak* was not just tickling my nose, but about to burst my nostrils. My empty stomach had given me such a huge appetite that I could no longer think straight. I had to leave and get away from this tantalising smell as fast as possible. But as soon as I turned towards the door, Madine called after me, 'Wait, lad. I had the honour of enjoying your parents' hospitality on more than one occasion. Stay and have tea with us.'

Quite a few people had once enjoyed the lavish meals, aromatic tea and refreshing mare's milk prepared by my mother, and seen all the valuable work my father did in the community. Now, after three terrible years, Madine Yesengeldin was one of the first to recall my parents' generosity. We sat down at the table. A boy of my age in tattered clothes, who was obviously from another family, came in carrying a steaming samovar, placed it next to a low, round table, and sat down nearby.

I could tell that Madine's wife was really annoyed with him for inviting me to tea. She poured her husband and herself strong cups, and then gave the boy and me cups of boiling water with milk but no tea in them. Then she scattered a whole bowl of *baursak* across the table. As though remembering something, she hurriedly singled a few bits out of the main pile for the boy sitting by the samovar and me. This was her way of giving us to understand that these few were for us and that we should not dare grab any others.

We quickly got through them, and the delicious bits of pastry only whetted my huge appetite. Trying to warm up, I kept sipping the hot water. Our hosts' portions of the *baursak* were still lying tantalisingly close by, within easy reach on the table. I had to use all my will-power to stop myself from reaching out and snatching one.

When tea was finished, I felt warm and drowsy, and went on sitting at the table for a few minutes. In the end, my host enquired,

'Are you reckoning on spending the night with us, lad?'

'It's already late,' I replied. 'I won't get to Topterek before nightfall. Aga, if you don't mind, I'll stay with you tonight and then set off in the early morning while it's still cold.'

'No, my dear, you can't stay here tonight. We've got guests coming,' Madine replied. 'On the hill,' he said, pointing vaguely, 'you'll find the Bozhikovs' aul. Go over there. They all got on well with your father and any of them will let you in to stay the night.'

After being turned down so politely and given such good advice, I could not possibly stay there any longer or feel offended. So I set off for the aul.

I started thinking hard as I walked along. At a time when emaciated people with puffy faces were wandering about in droves begging for food, it seemed total bliss for the chairman to have *baursak* on his table. Everything I had seen at his house seemed like signs of immense wealth, and I could not help wondering where it all came from. How was it that God gave so much to so few of His humble servants?

Nevertheless, I regarded the aul council chairman's act as the height of generosity, and I still do. Back then, when not even close relatives could help one another out and everyone's top priority was getting enough to eat, it was extraordinarily kind to invite to tea a boy who had called by on an errand.

As I drew near Bozhikovs', I began wondering if anyone was going to let me into their house, and if not what I would do, as it was nearly evening.

The aul consisted of five or six houses arranged in the traditional manner and set apart from the collective farm's centre. Before collectivisation, the Bozhikovs had been on close terms with people from our aul; and since we shared a common ancestor, I knew all their names. The first house I went up to belonged to Sadyk, who happened to be in his yard. After greeting him respectfully, I said, 'I am Shayakhmet's son. I have been to get a document from the aul council. I spent a long time there and now it's already evening. I've come to stay with you, if you'll allow me to.'

'No, you can't stay here! Go over there to Nursadyk,' he replied, pointing to the next house. 'He was a friend of your father.' He put particular stress on the word 'he'.

So off I went to Nursadyk, whom I knew well. He had visited Father often, and every spring for several years in a row he had borrowed one of our dairy cows and several dairy goats for the whole summer. (Such loans were one of the Kazakhs' traditional ways of helping needy fellow clansmen.) I remember well helping him drive the borrowed animals back to his aul: he would ride his horse and lead a cow on his right side with a calf on a leading rein attached to her tail, and goats tied round the neck so they could only walk along in a file and not get tangled up. The animals would quickly understand what people wanted of them and walk quietly along, doing what the person leading them told them to.

It was because of knowing him like this that I strode more confidently up to his house, sure of being given shelter for the night there. I even regretted not asking Sadyk about Nursadyk straightaway, instead of requesting to stay at his house first.

Nursadyk, however, had evidently overheard our conversation, and he had a sullen look on his face as I walked up to him. As soon as I had repeated what I had just said to his brother, he replied in the same way, 'No, you can't stay here!'

I felt as though I had been struck by lightning, his words had such a terrifying effect on me. I immediately glanced towards the west at the huge red disc of the sun hovering just above the horizon. I suddenly imagined walking through the night alone. There were wolves in the steppe. In my mind's eye I could clearly see the fiery specks of light from their eyes as they pounded towards me; I felt a sharp twinge of pain in my muscles as I imagined them sinking their teeth into me. No, I could not leave this aul, not with the wolves out there! I would stay at Nursadyk's house. I still hoped he would take pity on me.

I started muttering something about it nearly being dark, but he coldly interrupted me and told me to get out. In despair, and still believing he might have a change of heart, I walked silently into his hut, leaving him and wife to get on with the evening milking in the yard. They soon came in, and Nursadyk yelled at me from the doorway, 'What are you sitting here for? Look, I told you, you're not staying here. Get out! Go to your father Zhagypar! There's his hut over there.'

I slunk slowly towards to the door like a dog. As soon as I stepped outside, I glanced towards the west again: the sun had now set, leaving behind a crimson glow all along the western horizon. I felt even more terrified of the descending darkness.

I set off towards Zhagypar's house. He was the eldest of the six brothers, and the same age as my father. Kazakh men who share the same year of birth are considered best friends and supposed to put up with anything from each other except deceit and betrayal; it was customary for children to call any of their father's contemporaries 'Father', and for the latter to treat them as they would their own children and call them 'sons' and 'daughters'.

When I arrived, Zhagypar was standing with his back to me, tidying up his yard with a broom. Walking up to him without him seeing me, I said, 'Assalaam aleikum!' He looked round sharply in surprise, automatically reeling off a greeting in response, and then asked at once, 'Who are you?' I replied that I was Shayakhmet's son. At that he tossed his broom to one side and folded me in his arms, mumbling, 'God is just, where on earth have you come from, apple of my eye, my dearest son?' Then he burst into tears. Tears started rolling down my face as well. They were tears of joy – not so much at meeting him again as at being rescued from the wolves.

'Magripa! Mukhamet's here!' my 'father' called out, loudly announcing my arrival to his wife as though I was a long-awaited guest. He took me inside and then noticed that I was soaking from almost the waist down. 'Why, my son, you're completely drenched! You haven't caught cold, have you? Take all your wet clothes off!' He helped me strip down to my underclothes, wrapped me in a large dressing gown, and sat me down by the blazing stove. After telling me to warm my feet over the fire, he started hanging out all my clothes to dry. Only then did he start asking me all about my family's present circumstances.

He already knew that my father had died a year and a half ago, but he started crying again at the mention of Father's name. When

I told him about our life during the famine and why I was visiting these parts, and how his brothers had kicked me out, he indignantly retorted, 'God will punish them. Our ancestors' spirit will harm them. They will not be happy on this earth. Each of the wicked scoundrels has several sacks of grain and flour put by. And they've the milk from their cow, goats and ewes – not a lot, but at least something. What harm would you have done them by staying overnight? None, of course! Both of them, especially Nursadyk, were always kindly treated by Shakhen [the respectful version of my father's name].'

Only among the poor does one experience true generosity. In his larder he only had a few glassfuls of fried wheat grains put by. Magripa and he divided this in half and decided to give half to their young son and me then and there, and leave the rest for our breakfast. They poured the glassful of fried grain into a litre or so of boiling milk, and let it simmer gently over the fire for a few minutes before handing it to us boys to eat. It seemed like the most delicious food I had ever tasted. All they had for their own supper was the milk we didn't finish. I should also mention that we ate by the light of the stove, as they did not have any kerosene for a lamp.

When it was time to sleep, Zhagypar told his wife to make up one large bed for us boys. He said to his son, 'This is your brother. You're to sleep next to him tonight.' Then he turned to me and said, 'Let my only son sleep next to you, and take care of him as your younger brother. Be friends like your father and I were. Look after him when you grow up and take him under your wing. Keep him safe and help him. I entrust him to God and then to you.'

However, as is often the case, man proposes and God disposes: I was never to meet my sworn brother again, for he died fighting in the Great Patriotic War at the age of nineteen.

I remained on friendly terms with his father, however. Even though we lived a long way apart, we always kept in touch and met up every so often. And I have never, ever forgotten that reunion in the spring of 1934, and all his heartfelt warmth, and the taste of the *talkan* I shared with his son. Later, as an old man of 82, he would walk twenty kilometres across trackless countryside in winter to the cemetery where my mother, the wife of his childhood friend, was being laid to rest. That, to my mind, was true friendship.

He spent many years grieving for the death of his son. Then Destiny smiled on him in his old age. When he was in his 80th year, his second wife gave birth to another son. The last four or five years of his long and difficult life were happy ones, because he was at least leaving behind an heir, even though he had nothing to bequeath to him.

During my journey I came across another example – an incredibly surprising one – of how someone's personality could change according to circumstances.

After spending the following night in Topterek aul, I set off on the last leg home. On the way I again had to face various setbacks, this time caused by the weather. The narrow River Umesh, which was usually dried up during the summer months, was now flooded with melted snow, and a swollen mass of murky water was rushing over the road. I was well aware that at the point where I had to cross, the water might come up as far as my chest – but I was taken aback by how cold the melted snow in the river was. I took off my boots and trousers and waded into the water, intending to walk across; but the water was so icy cold that I shot straight back out again. After standing still for a few minutes, I decided I just had to grit my teeth and wade through the freezing cold water, so I stepped in again. This time I managed to get perhaps a metre further, but then hardly managed to wade back out again. Not daring to go into the water a third time, I pulled all my things back on and sat down on the bank.

I did not know then that you could wade through water in boots, and that the water would not feel so cold if you did. In those days I was young and naïve enough to take the Kazakh folk saying literally: 'Only in an emergency should a young dzhigit [warrior] enter water in his boots, or should a horse be allowed to drink in its bridle.' I was also worried that because my boots were so old, they might simply fall apart mid-way.

Even if I had wanted to, I could not go back to Topterek, for the simple reason that our relatives there were also having to cut back on their food. I very much doubted any of them would have been thrilled to have me for a third day. So I went on sitting on the bank and wondering what to do next. I hoped a traveller with a horse and cart would come along. Instead, a pinched-looking man came up and stood there, obviously not intending to cross on foot either.

A little while later a couple turned up: the man leading a cow by a rein, and the woman driving it on from behind. I recognised them as Izameddin and Katipa Akhmetov, with whom I had boarded during my brief time at school. As an imam, Izameddin had always led a pious life: during all the time I lived with him and his family, I never heard him say anything remotely unpleasant or even patronising. No matter where he was or whom he was speaking to, he always adopted an edifying tone and advocated a code of behaviour befitting a Muslim, and always practised what he preached whether he was with his family or outside the home.

When they reached the bank, husband and wife both mounted the cow and rode through the torrent. Then Izameddin came back on the cow and told me to get on behind him so that he could take me across.

The man waiting beside me asked to be taken across as well, but Izameddin started asking what he could give him in exchange. The poor man had nothing to offer except an attractive pocket knife; Izameddin decided it was not enough, and asked for something more. The other man implored him to accept his knife, but Izameddin snapped, 'If you haven't got anything else besides the knife, you can stay here on the bank' – and then he urged the cow forward into the ford.

The other man started begging him for help, invoking God's name and the prophet Mohammed's, saying it was very important and his fate might depend on it. I began feeling sorry for him, but Izameddin would not give in.

Whoever would have thought that a former cleric would refuse to do a small favour for an impoverished, starving man? How did he dare ignore the name of Allah? I was deeply shocked to see someone I had once regarded as a paragon of virtue behaving in this despicable, callous manner.

Nevertheless, I was still grateful to him for carrying me across the torrent and not leaving me stranded. Once on the other side I walked with them for a while, since we were heading the same way. Now it was my turn to help by driving the cow on from behind and giving Aunt Katipa a break.

As we trudged along the slushy spring road for what seemed like ages, we kept slithering about in the snow and getting our feet stuck in the mud. We were caught up and overtaken on the way by a flushed, healthy-looking, well-dressed man on an equally healthy-looking, well-bred horse. Instead of cantering past, he slowed down and rode alongside us for a few minutes. However, not once did he even glance at us, but kept staring into the distance in an openly contemptuous manner. We, on the other hand, could not take our eyes off his rosy cheeks and his stomach bulging over the pommel of his saddle. What a contrast between him and us, who were so weak with hunger we could hardly shuffle through the snow!

Once the stranger had ridden on ahead a fair distance, I asked Izameddin about him, and learnt that he was an investigator from the public prosecutor's office. As I did not understand the word 'investigator', I asked if the man was the prosecutor himself; and when I learnt that he was not, I began thinking how fine the prosecutor must look if this was one of his assistants. Watching him disappear into the distance, the same kind of naïve thoughts crossed my mind as in Madine Yesengeldin's house: 'What a lucky man!' I said to myself. 'He's riding along a wet road and keeping dry on his horse. He doesn't have to worry about going through water. And when he gets home, there'll be some hot tea waiting for him. What have the likes of him done to deserve God's gift of happiness? How come some people are starving while others are eating wonderful food, and some are wandering around on foot while others are riding well-fed horses? After all, all people are equal before Allah – that's what I've heard the adults say.'

I got so immersed in these reflections that I forgot where I was and who I was with and that I was supposed to be driving the cow. It was only when Izameddin ticked me off that I snapped out of my day-dream. They were childish thoughts, merely outlining the way things were – thoughts which trailed off with me wondering if my family would ever be happy.

Most poor people in those days could not find answers to these fundamental questions either. They believed that God determined everything. This same mass of people swallowed the propaganda that their ordeals would soon end, and paradise would come to earth in the form of Socialism. They thought that this would lead to equality – meaning, first and foremost, equal prosperity: 'He who was a nobody, will become everybody,' in the words of Marx and Engels. But there had never been equality in any society before, and nor – as it turned out – was there any in the legal, political or economic institutions of Socialism.

Chapter Twenty-One

The Last Days of Famine

The famine in 1934 was no less serious than in previous years. By spring, even the most prudent and thrifty families had run out of food supplies. Official aid to the so-called organised working population (in collective farms, State enterprises and institutions) was reduced to a minimum; the situation became even more acute for those of us who were not provided for by the State. As soon as the roads became passable again that spring, increasing numbers of starving people began roaming about in search of food. There were more and more famine victims' corpses lying in the streets and on the steppe.

In early spring, shortly after my gruelling trip to fetch the residency document, I went down with malaria again. Such a serious illness could have had grave consequences for my already weakened body, though of course I did not understand the danger I was in at the time. I had bouts of fever every other day between nine and ten in the morning, as regularly as clockwork. Here once more were the sudden sensations of freezing cold, the impossibility of warming up: the mounting shivering which took over my whole body, my teeth chattering continuously. I would go on feeling dreadful like this for a couple of hours; then came the second part of the attack. I would gradually stop feeling cold, but then my temperature would shoot up and I would start running a fever. Burning with heat, I would try all sorts of ways of cooling down, but nothing would work: I just had to wait for the fever to go down, and then I would begin sweating heavily and sink into sleep. By the time I woke up towards the evening, I would feel so weak that I could not get up without help. Worse still, I would feel totally disorientated. I would remain lying like this until the afternoon of the following day.

One spring morning, when there was no longer any snow about but the earth was still frozen hard, I started going through a fit of the shivers, and tried to warm up by throwing on everything I could find in the house and curling up on the floor, cocooned from head to foot. Nobody else was at home. I was so muffled up that I could barely hear anything, but I somehow became aware of the sound of footsteps. I could sense someone getting closer and opening the small trunk just behind me, and then banging its lid shut again. I thought it must be Mother, just arrived back home and moving around. But then I heard the footsteps growing fainter as the person moved towards the doorway.

Despite feeling dreadfully ill, I suddenly became suspicious – for if it had been Mother, she would definitely have asked how I was feeling and covered me up with something warmer, as she always did. I decided to have a look and see who was there, so I pulled back the covers and lifted my head.

What I saw was a stranger walking off with the small bag that had been stowed away in the trunk containing the last three kilograms or so of wheat grains we had managed to put by. I shrieked in alarm as loudly as I could, 'Where are you taking that bag? Put it down right now!'

But instead of breaking into a run like a thief, or even flinching, the stranger went on plodding slowly and unhurriedly towards the door.

Even though I was so feverish, I somehow managed to stagger to my feet and limp unsteadily after him. By the time I got outside, he was plodding just as slowly across our yard. 'Put the bag down!' I shouted again.

He slowly turned his head towards me, and I could see he was an emaciated lad of about eighteen or nineteen, but he calmly went on walking. I caught up with him a few steps later, still yelling, 'Put the bag down!' and pushed him with one hand from behind. He dropped the bag and then immediately fell face-down onto the ground. I snatched up the bag, limped back into the house and, just to be on the safe side, put the grain under my head as I lay down again, greatly relieved that I had managed to save my family's precious supplies.

A while later, when I was burning up with fever all over, Mother came rushing in with a terrified look on her face and said in alarm, 'God help us! There's a dead man lying in our yard! Where on earth did the poor wretch come from? What are we going to do?' When I told her what had happened, she grew even more alarmed – this time, I think, at the idea of having left me all on my own when I was so ill, and not having padlocked the trunk.

After Mother had notified the authorities of the unknown person's death, a special team of local people responsible for picking up and burying the bodies of homeless famine victims came and collected the dead man. As usual, none of the team or the authorities enquired who he was, where he was from or why he had died. It was obvious: he had starved to death like all the others.

When a person has starved for so long that he has no strength left, he falls forward as he is walking along, as though tripping, and never gets up again. That is why the bodies of the famine victims in the streets and roads were mostly lying face down. The young man in the yard would not have lasted more than an hour, even if I had not pushed him; nevertheless, however unwittingly, I was responsible for hastening his death.

ii

My family was now in grave danger of 'going to bed without supper and starting the next day without breakfast', to use an expression popular at the time. Aiken searched tirelessly for additional ways of earning a living, and eventually stumbled across a novel method of getting hold of food.

Even when the country was in the grip of a famine, there were some people – mainly Russians – who used to buy vodka for special celebrations and get-togethers. Others did so merely out of habit, as a way of relaxing, while a third group (including Kazakhs, who until the 1930s, thought vodka to be the drink of the devil and would not touch it) wanted to experience something new. These were minor officials who considered themselves part of the educated élite, identifiable by the 'refined' habit of drinking vodka and smoking.

Finally, there were those such as Aiken who bought vodka to exchange for other things, primarily food. As it could not be purchased anywhere in the area except at one shop in the regional centre, there were not always sufficient supplies of it on sale to satisfy demand, and as a rare commodity it sold well – though to trade in it as we did was illegal and therefore dangerous.

Aiken used to buy two three-litre bottles of vodka at a time, put them in the two pockets of his saddlebag, and carry them off somewhere to sell. Two or three days later he would return with the bag's pockets stuffed full of wheat. Half of it – eight kilograms or so – was used to feed us, while the rest was sold for cash to buy the next batch of vodka with.

On the days I was not ill with malaria, I used to go with Aiken to the vodka shop, as the management had imposed a limit of one three-litre bottle per customer and he needed to buy two of them. We used to go to the shop in the evening and wait overnight in the long queue.

Most of the people queuing were poor Kazakhs like us. To make the night pass more quickly, they would compete with each other to see who could tell the funniest joke or invent the most amusing catch-phrases or limericks, or recite whole stories and poems by heart: no matter how wretched their lot, Kazakhs have always had wonderful storytellers, poets and improvisers, musicians and comedians to cheer them up. We would all doze off to sleep some time after midnight.

Thankfully, the nights were warm. When the shop opened the next morning, we would buy the bottles and hurry home. Aiken would set off the same day with the bottles in his saddlebag; our task was to sell half the wheat we already had before he returned.

If I was feeling well enough, I would take the wheat to the market at the regional centre. It used to sell fast because there were always plenty of buyers and hardly any for sale. I remember always earning enough to buy our next batch of vodka.

So who were these customers buying vodka in exchange for food despite the widespread famine? They must have been people with access to the collective-farm barns, where reserve seed stocks and a meagre amount of grain were stored to supplement the farmers' supplies: in other words, the collective-farm management and their sycophantic activists. What's more, this was happening at the time of the spring sowing, which meant that the grain was being bartered away just when it was needed most.

Compared to some people, the amount Aiken was exchanging was just a drop in the ocean. There were others who would to bring carts along to the place where deals were struck and drive off with whole loads of grain. But however we came by it, the wheat we acquired saved us from starving, and enabled us to put a little by to see us through until the next harvest.

iii

After a while there was no longer any grain available to buy with the vodka, and Aiken had to give up his trading. But once again we were rescued, this time by an individual farmer with a smallholding of his own, who hired us to help bring in the crops and gave us some food by way of an advance payment. Recalling that most difficult of times and the famine victims who failed to get through it, my family were always grateful to Destiny for providing us with the opportunity of working for a good man at such a critical moment.

It rained a lot during the summer of 1934. After three years of drought we at last had a bumper harvest. The cornfields – full of ripe ears of corn, nearly waist-high – were a comforting and joyful sight to everybody. However, as always, after it was threshed, the first batch of corn was not distributed to the collective farmers or the other people most in need: it was sent straight to the State procurement stations. Despite this heartless policy, the situation generally improved once the harvest was brought in, and there were no more deaths among those displaced by the famine.

Our employer, Ivan Antonovich Ataikin, was from the village of Kamyshenka, where we had spent the previous winter. His crops were only about three or four kilometres from the village. The agreement was that our family was to cut his wheat with scythes, tie it in sheaves, and then arrange the sheaves in stooks, ten to each one. We were to live on the land for the duration of the work and take responsibility for the security of the harvested crop. Our employer was to provide our family with three meals a day throughout the harvest, and once the wheat was threshed, he was to give us three sacks of wheat grain.

We stayed out in a shelter that Ataikin had made for himself. He and his wife used to bring us hot food for breakfast and bread, milk and something else for lunch and supper. There was always enough for us all to eat our fill, and when he was about to leave for home in the evening, he always used to ask what we would like for breakfast and lunch the next day. You only have to remember the situation of most of the population at the time to appreciate what a humane employer and generous person he was.

Ataikin never disturbed us while we were working: he and his wife would spend all day working on another field, cutting oats. Sometimes he would come later and check the stubble to see how well we had cleared the field, and make sure there was not a single ear of corn left standing or lying on the ground; but he was always pleased with our work. He treated us as equals, possibly because he himself had once worked as a hired labourer for rich people.

As for me, I did not mind how hard the work was: all I cared about was having regular meals. My one and only dream over the past one and a half years had been to eat my fill, and now it seemed as if this dream had at last come true.

According to all the adults who saw Ataikin's crops, he had a record-breaking yield that summer. His wheat was tall, dense and healthy. We worked every day from sunrise to late evening, as long as we could see to work. We had only two breaks: one in the morning for breakfast when Ataikin used to come to the field from his home, and the other in the middle of the day for lunch. We tried to complete our work as quickly as possible so that the wheat did not stand too long and shed its grain. We also did a thorough job to ensure that the sheaves were securely tied and would not fall apart during transportation.

I had only used a scythe once before, four years earlier, on the occasion when Father had taken me with him to the wheat fields our relatives were harvesting. In fact, the only one of us with any real experience was Mother, which meant that she had to do most of the work. She had helped bring in the harvest every year when we had our own smallholding, and she used the scythe so effortlessly and expertly that you longed to be just like her. Some days, when the work on a designated area was taking longer than usual to complete, she would tell me to put down my scythe and tie up the piles of wheat she had just cut into sheaves, and I would only just manage to keep up with her.

After a month, our work was done. Ataikin paid us in full, and then drove us in his cart to the rented lodgings we had previously been living in, which had stood empty while we were away. We now looked and felt very different from when he had first taken us on. In body and mind, we felt like normal people again: eating properly had restored our health.

Aiken left us to rest and sort ourselves out, and got some seasonal fieldwork at Kamyshenka village's collective farm. When he returned home a month later, we hardly recognised him. Once emaciated and ashen-faced, he was now a well-nourished, clear-complexioned, handsome young man who looked even better than he had three years previously.

Now that the famine was over, and people were gradually starting to recover from their harrowing experiences, they could think for the first time in ages about things other than food. Mother began sorting out our clothes: she turned coats and altered things, making one item of clothing out of two and cutting large garments down in size. And while she was sewing, she would sometimes quietly sing snatches of the old folk songs she had once loved, able at last to stop dwelling on the bad times we had been through.

iv

Our troubles, however, were by no means over, and we did not have to wait long to be reminded of our lack of rights. First I went to the regional centre's school to see if I could enrol for the autumn term; but as soon as I told him about my family, the head teacher interrupted me by saying, 'You're the son of a kulak. You'd better go and attend a school in some remote aul, because all the ones here are closed to the likes of you.'

I was terribly upset by this rejection, and felt so depressed that I was ill for a whole week. Then the old familiar problems with lodgings surfaced once again. The owner of the house we had been renting, Tostambek Sabitov, was removed from his post as collective farm chairman in another aul, and told to return home, so despite having arranged to spend the winter there and carried out repairs to make it ready for cold weather, we had to move out. Instead, Sabitov allowed us to move into a tiny outhouse in his yard which he used for storing food and all sorts of rubbish; it needed a lot doing to it to make it habitable, but at least he promised to set all the work against our winter rent.

It was late autumn by the time we had insulated the ceilings, made a window, and found the bricks to build a stove and range for the cauldron to stand on. Not long afterwards, it started to snow.

Then, less than two weeks into winter, Sabitov asked us to leave. His explanation was brief and to the point. A relative was coming to live with him, and he needed the miserable little outhouse for him.

We had no recourse to the law whatsoever: in those days, the courts seemed interested in nothing except enforcing punitive measures against people like us. To complicate things further, my sister Altynzhan and her husband Kairankhazi had moved in with us for the winter. Where on earth could we find a shelter for so many? Everyone in the household was very despondent: we regarded what had happened to us as a most severe punishment that a wrathful God had inflicted on our long-suffering family. What could be worse than finding yourself in a position where anyone can do what they like to you, knowing you cannot defend yourself?

Aiken and my brother-in-law started looking for somewhere else for us all to live. They decided to try in villages rather than auls, because they knew from previous experience they would get odd jobs there. Eventually we found lodgings with a widow by the name of Maria Boronina, a collective farm worker in the village of Kamyshenka known locally as 'The Shrew'.

There were two rooms, twenty and fifteen square metres in area, in which the owner and her two children were already living with another family. When we all moved in, the number of occupants rose to fourteen, if you include a mongrel called Palma and a piglet that lived under the owner's bed. What it basically meant was that each family shared a living area that consisted of a single bed: here we had to keep our clothes and other essentials, take our rest, and eat our meals. The small gap between the beds was a communal space for all the occupants, and at night it served as a sleeping area for Aiken, a boy from the second family and me. Anyone needing to go outside during the night had to step over us, which meant they often trod on one of us in the dark.

Later on, when I read about the conditions in the barracks the Nazis kept Soviet prisoners-of-war in, I could not help comparing them to the one we lived in near Ridder, and this room in Maria Boronina's house in the winter of 1934-35.

Chapter Twenty-Two

A Home of our Own

According to the 1926 census, Kazakhstan then had an ethnic population of 4.2 million people. By the end of the catastrophic famine of 1932-34, this had fallen to just 3 million. There is a lot being written these days about its causes, and in my view the blame is justifiably attributed to the errors and excesses of the Soviet Government in forcibly collectivising the peasantry and making nomadic stockbreeders become settled arable farmers. If the Kazakh farmers had kept their livestock, they would have survived the failed harvests unscathed, as they had done in 1921-22, when a terrible famine ravaged the entire territory of Russia but did not affect the people of Kazakhstan, who were able to take in a great many starving children from the Volga region.

The bumper harvest of 1934 heralded the end of the famine and the start of the population's recovery from it. Although people's diets were still poor, they were at least now getting enough to eat, and for the first time in a long while they could start taking an interest in the country's current affairs.

One thing that captured their imagination in 1935, apart from the end of grain rationing, was the formation of new administrative regions in the USSR. The Samara region, for instance, was separated from the Kumashinko region, and this seemingly insignificant event gave rise to an animated debate about the reasons behind the changes, the actual location of the new boundaries, and the villages and aul affected. It was as though immensely important state borders were being fixed.

Life continued to be a struggle, however. Rural workers were still receiving low wages, there was unemployment, and there was nothing for sale in the shops; the trading that went on in the villages was paid for in kind, as neither the collective farmers nor the unemployed had any money. Since Aiken was not allowed employment in State enterprises, he carried on doing odd jobs on villagers' private smallholdings and cutting and selling rushes. But at least the demand for rushes now made it a seller's market, and since we had managed to put by substantial food supplies, Aiken no longer had to work as hard as the year before. He even let me off helping him.

'You're not strong enough to cut rushes,' he said, as though I had been stronger the year before.

Instead, he put me in charge of taking our wheat to the local mill, which was about eight kilometres from the village. Twice a month, throughout the winter, I would load between 30 and 40 kilograms of wheat onto our sledge and pull it all the way there. It was quite a busy track, and senior and low-ranking officials, travelling light, would canter by, impatiently overtaking anyone in their way. Ordinary people would catch me up with heavily laden carts, and they would always hitch my sledge onto theirs and pull it as far as the turning I needed, or to the mill itself if they were going in that direction. Every time an arrogant official went by, these men used to say, 'Just look at him: his horse belongs to the State, but he'd never give anyone a lift, not even women and children.'

One mill usually served several villages and aul, and in winter it always had plenty of customers, since the collective farm workers were finally able to get grain for the 'work-day tokens' they had been paid in. People had to queue for several days at a time to have their grain ground into flour, and they would pass the time in the wayside house next to the mill, resting on the plank benches set along the walls. You would hear them telling each other anecdotes and tales about the past, and exchanging pieces of folk wisdom in various different languages, though mainly in Russian. The talking went on round the clock with the subjects and participants changing as people came and went. Meanwhile, their sledges laden with sacks of wheat and their draught animals (horses, oxen, camels and sometimes cows) would be left standing in the open, unguarded yard outside; nobody, however, would touch anything that was not theirs.

The arrival of the long, lingering spring of 1935 brought an end to Aiken's rush-selling, and forced us to think of new ways of earning a living. While we were sitting at home with no work, Uncle Yeremenko – the head of the third family which shared our lodgings – taught me how to make the baskets he sold local housewives in exchange for food. First he showed me how to select the various different kinds of osiers from rose willows and bushes in the steppe, and then how to weave them together. It turned out to be quite easy and I quickly mastered it, though my baskets were not nearly as attractive as his. In the end I only managed to make and sell about a dozen, and then I called it a day; but I have never forgotten Uncle Yeremenko's generosity in teaching me the tricks of his trade to help my family out.

All the unemployed were going through a bad spell that spring. Once again, my family got an unpleasant surprise as far as our lodgings were concerned. Recalling our verbal agreement to rent until 'the beginning of spring', our landlady used the early thaw in March that year as a pretext to ask us to leave. For want of anywhere better to stay, we ended up moving into a cold, empty shed with a frozen earth floor. It is terrible to think now of the conditions we had to endure.

Shortly after our move, the planting season came round again and the villagers started hiring the unemployed to dig their allotments. For at least two weeks Mukhametrakhim and I were outside digging non-stop from early morning until nightfall. Then all May and June we were kept busy doing minor repairs to people's houses, fences and allotments.

By working flat out for two months we were able to stock up with plenty of food. (Many people still evaluated everything in life – including financial wealth – in terms of quantities of food supplies.) Comparing our situation in the summer of 1935 with what it had been, Mother often expressed her thanks to Allah for what He had send us, even though we were by no stretch of the imagination eating healthily. People's diets were lacking in variety and nutrition, and made them susceptible to all sorts of illnesses. As there was no proper medical service, sick people simply had to make do and pray to God to spare them.

I fell ill again, this time with night-blindness. I would go blind at dusk, and only regain my sight at dawn the following morning. I could not move around at all at night without someone's assistance, and yet I could see perfectly well during daylight hours. This continued from the middle until nearly the end of winter. None of the folk remedies I was given helped. 'Experts' insisted that the only possible natural remedy for this form of blindness was liver. Apparently, you only needed to eat it for a single day for your sight to be fully restored.

The problem was that, in order to conserve and increase livestock numbers after the disastrous fall caused by collectivisation, anyone lucky enough to own animals was officially banned from killing them for private consumption, or selling the meat to anyone other than collective farms and the State. The only way round this was to obtain a vet's certificate confirming that there was a good reason for the animal's slaughter; if he failed to do so, the owner could be sent to prison. But as luck would have it, one of our neighbours came up with a valid excuse to slaughter his one and only goat. Mother got the neighbour's wife to give her a piece of the liver, and immediately fried it for me on the fire. It was steaming hot and succulent.

Amazingly, a couple or so hours later, when night had fallen and I was sitting inside our hovel gazing at what seemed to be very dim and blurred lamplight, like moon on a misty night, I noticed it very gradually getting brighter and clearer. Another half an hour went by, and I had regained normal vision in the dark. That was the end of my night-blindness.

ii

No sooner had we somehow managed to settle in the freezing cold shed, thaw out the icy floor and warm ourselves up, than our troubles started all over again: the shed's owner decided to carry out repairs on it, and asked us to vacate it. But this time Aiken came up with a new solution to our housing problem: to build a makeshift shack in the aul that some hired labourers had organised on the opposite bank of the Irtysh, where we had spent the summer before. It only took a day to erect the timber-framed shack and cover it with a roof of rushes and dried grass, on a spot we had chosen directly on the grassy riverbank. You had to crawl through the entrance, but you could sit upright inside. The collective farm field brigades stayed in similar shelters during the spring sowing, summer haymaking and autumn harvest.

Slightly later, in early July, we were without work again for a short while. When we were all sitting in the shack one morning, Aiken came up with the following suggestion: 'We've got enough food supplies to last us a month. While we've got such a lot put by, and before we start helping with the haymaking at the local collective farm, why don't we build a simple hut for ourselves? Then we won't have to go on endlessly searching for places to live in. We should manage to get the walls up during the month we've got before haymaking.'

'But how are you going to build it? What with? You've got no materials or transport or even building tools,' replied Mother doubtfully.

'We'll make the walls from turf and we'll use a spade and the steel blade of my scythe,' Aiken replied. 'We should manage to cut the turf with them all right, and we'll carry it to our building site in the wheelbarrow I'm going to borrow off a neighbour. So that's our transport and building tools sorted.'

That was that as far as he was concerned. The building work got started without further delay. Aiken was the hut's architect, chief engineer and project manager rolled into one, even though he had no experience or training. It seemed like a mad idea. Nevertheless, having endured much suffering and humiliation on account of not having a home of his own, he would not budge from his decision.

Early every morning, before breakfast, Aiken would cut pieces of turf of the same size and thickness out of the dense grass along the banks of the Irtysh. This work was considered too responsible for me to have a go at, but after breakfast he and I would load the turf onto the wheelbarrow – which had been knocked together out of some old cartwheels – and push it over to our building site. This work was very hard too. Aiken would pull from the front while I pushed from behind, keeping hold of the handles and trying to help as much as I could.

I was not very strong in those days. Years of malnutrition had stunted my growth, and although thirteen I was still the size of a ten-year-old. Whenever we went over a bumpy patch and the wheelbarrow shook suddenly, I would stumble sideways and let go of the handles. Then I would exchange places with Aiken and try pulling the wheelbarrow from the front, and only push when I felt strong enough. Every time the wheels rolled into a rut or a patch of soft ground, our load would get stuck and Aiken would somehow have to pull it out. But no matter how laborious and slow our progress was, we still kept going.

Working really hard, we managed to erect four walls. We needed twenty to 22 layers of turf for them to be reasonably high. Once we had four layers in place, we had to go round cutting bits off here and there on both sides so that the base of the walls were smooth and the same height all the way round. This involved quite a lot of skill, and you had to make sure you stood on top with your feet the right distance apart, or else you might accidentally push the wall over. It soon became obvious that Aiken did not have enough expertise to do the work properly: we needed an experienced turf layer for the job.

Among our new neighbours was a middle-aged man by the name of Zeinold Bekdairov. He must have been watching us toiling away and not getting very far, because he came up to our building site one day and stood there shaking his head. Then he silently picked up the scythe blade and started expertly smoothing down the layers and cutting off bits of turf. When he had finished, he said to Aiken:

'God has made us neighbours, and He wants us to do our duty to Him by helping one another, as our ancestors bid us. Allah would not be pleased to see that one of your neighbours has transport, even if it is only a dairy cow, when you are struggling with a wheelbarrow. The way you're going about it, it will take you forever. From tomorrow onwards you can borrow my cow and cart to carry the turf in. Only you'll have to work with her after she's been milked and while her herd is resting and then let her out to graze after lunch: she's a dairy cow, after all, and we need her milk. Don't overwork her – she's tough, but she may refuse to pull the cart. This way you should have enough time to move two rows of turf every day, which is all you should be putting on the walls. The top row has to sink in and dry off before you put the next one on.

'The higher the walls get, the longer they'll take to dry, and so you'll need at least twenty days to finish the job off. Then you'll have to leave the walls open, without a cover, for another month and a half for them to dry off and set properly. I'll drop by in the evenings and smooth off the turf you've laid during the day. I hope you don't mind me telling you all this.'

Zeinold helped us every day until the hut was ready. He proved particularly valuable when we had nearly finished the turf laying. The higher the walls got, the less stable they became, and it was now increasingly difficult to climb up on top and level them off: one false move and they might come thudding down. But with Zeinold's kind assistance we had them successfully completed within the twenty days.

After finishing the first stage of the building, Aiken gratefully enquired what Zeinold would like in return for all his kind help and the loan of his cow. But he replied, 'Oh, Aiken! You're still young, that's why you're talking like this. Don't dream of paying me for such a small thing! I've simply been doing my duty as a neighbour, just as we Kazakhs have always tried to do.' He would not let Aiken mention the subject again.

Our other neighbours also rallied round by giving us various building materials such as poles, planks and logs. Mother was delighted with the way in which people had started helping one another again, just like in the old days, and she took it as a sign that life was at last getting back to normal.

We ended up with a squat hut measuring twenty square metres with a single window and a door opening directly outside. Sometimes in winter, clouds of frosty air would come billowing in from outside every time the door was opened or closed; but whatever its shortcomings, at least the hut was ours. No longer did we have to face the terrifying prospect of being left homeless.

iii

After the long period of drought, we had a good harvest in our area for the second year in a row. There was a substantial increase in the collective farms' wheat deliveries to the State. As a result, more manpower was needed at the local State procurement station in our village, and this time Aiken managed to get a job there. Overnight, the cousin who had taken such good care of us in times of trouble went from being a kulak's son to a fully-fledged citizen, on an equal footing with everyone else in the country. Apart from the interruption of the War, in which he was wounded, he continued working in the same place for a quarter of a century, earning enough money to raise a family, until his death at the age of 50 in 1961.

It was now September 1935 and the children of Kamyshenka village went back to their primary school. As I watched them, I once again dreamed of going to school myself. I had never stopped thinking about it. but now it began to really get to me. Even though I had missed four years (and was, strictly speaking, now too old for primary school), and my uniform was terribly shabby, I decided to ask Aiken about it.

I expected him to tell me I needed to do some work for a while to help support the family. Instead, he consented without a moment's hesitation. 'My father wouldn't let me go to school when

I had a chance to,' he said, 'maybe because he never went himself, or was too mean to do without me at home. If I'd been to school, we wouldn't be struggling the way we are now. It's too late for me now – but God willing, you can still get an education, and maybe become a teacher yourself one day.' Then he became lost in thought.

And so it was that at the age of thirteen I presented myself at the village school and, in my very limited Russian, asked to be allowed to start in the third year. With the harsh words of the headmaster in Ust-Kurchum still ringing in my ears, I very much doubted I would get a place. But the head teacher at the Kamyshenka school was quite different: by way of a reply, he took me by the hand like a small child, led me into the third-year classroom, and said to the teacher, 'This boy is going to be in your class.'

My dream had come true.

In the mid-1930s, relations between the different nationalities within the Soviet Union still had a long way to go. The Kazakh and Russian rural populations went on leading separate lives, with very little communication. The first Kazakhs to move into Russian villages tended to keep to the edge of them: their children hardly mixed with Russian children, and seldom managed to pick up their language. Since there was no provision for Kazakh children to be taught in separate classes in their mother tongue, only five of the fifteen of us in Kamyshenka attended school – one in the first year, two in the second year, and me and a boy by the name of Zhambylov in the third year.

Because I did not understand Russian very well, I found the lessons difficult. Those devoted to writing and arithmetic went way over my head: the teacher used to return my writing and dictation tests with his corrections scrawled all over them in red ink.

'Never mind, Shayakhmetov,' he used to say, 'it'll all come right in the end.' I could understand the words 'Never mind' because they were so common, but to begin with I had no idea what else he was saying. As the term went by, however, my Russian vocabulary steadily increased.

I remember our teacher with gratitude: he was a young bachelor aged 23 called Trofim Trofimovich Adamenko, who amazed us by being able to draw a perfect circle on the blackboard freehand. He was strict but fair, and though he used to smile gently at my incredibly mangled spoken Russian, he never let the other pupils in the class make fun of me. Instead, he would patiently make me practise the correct pronunciation straightaway. He taught me not to feel embarrassed, but insisted I never made the same mistake twice.

Chapter Twenty-Three

Adolescence

The summer of 1936, a tragedy befell my family. My clever and beautiful sister Zhamba, who was now 23 and living at a well-known gold mine in the neighbouring Samara region, fell seriously ill. As soon as we heard the news, Mother set about packing to go and visit her.

It did not take long for people like us to prepare for a journey: our feet and walking staffs were always ready. We did not even have to waste time on getting the gifts that guests traditionally gave their hosts, as this custom had not yet been revived after the terrible years of famine. With me as her travelling companion, she set off on foot.

I will never forget the long journey to Kuludzhun. The first day we crossed the Irtysh and walked half way, as far as Kokzhyr aul, where Zhamba's sister-in-law was living. That evening, when we arrived at the house where we were going to spend the night, we heard the dreadful news that Zhamba had died exactly one week before.

Devastated, my mother sobbed inconsolably all night long. In the morning she somehow managed to summon her strength and pick up her staff, and we set off again. We walked all day without exchanging a single word; Mother just kept sighing heavily and wiping away her tears. She was now in a hurry to get to her beloved daughter's grave and recite sura from the Koran, although inwardly she did not want to believe that Zhamba was really dead. When we arrived at the fresh mound of earth that was to be my sister's eternal resting place, she wept and grieved with Manap and his parents and relatives. The one small consolation was that Zhamba had left behind an eighteen-month-old son; but although everyone in the family prayed to God to grant the little boy a long and healthy life, he died six months later.

Kazakhs are superstitious, and always inclined to find links between omens and events that take place at a later date. I tend not to believe in such things myself, but there is one thing that has always baffled me.

According to Kazakh lore, it is bad luck to gaze after a relative or a friend for a long time as they are leaving. Partings before long journeys should always be kept brief. The person leaving is also not meant to look back. There may be serious consequences if these rules are not kept to, particularly for the person travelling.

I still remember how I said goodbye to my sister Zhamba after staying with her during the winter of 1935, some eighteen months before her death. I remember her coming out onto the porch and staring after me in a strange manner as I walked away and finally disappeared from view. I cannot forget her sad expression in the cold early morning light; and as it turned out, we never saw each other again.

A quarter of a century later, I said goodbye on two separate occasions, first to my cousin Aiken and then to Mother, before they set off on long journeys. In both cases, without realising it, I found myself gazing after them for a long while, and for some inexplicable reason feeling particularly uneasy. In both cases, it was to be the last time I saw these loved ones alive. It was only much later that I learnt of the superstition attached to such partings, and when I did, I recalled that frosty morning in 1935, and my sister Zhamba staring after me. I now believe it was not by chance that she did so.

I should mention that after Zhamba's death, we did not lose our close ties with Manap and his family, and indeed went on seeing him even after he had remarried. He was a remarkable man who was naturally well disposed to others and highly perceptive, with a real gift for detecting people's true worth and respecting them for it; he could also tell true friends from false ones, and the difference between good and bad, truth and falsehood. He was energetic, active, and had wonderfully skilful hands. Tragically, he was killed at the front in 1943.

ii

Life is never a straightforward journey. It takes you on through quicksands and marshes, ditches and gullies, over high mountain passes and up and down steep slopes. It is such tough going that you sometimes feel like a climber with a heavy backpack pressing down on your shoulders, gasping for air. Then all of a sudden you come to an easy road and you are able to relax and enjoy the scenery for a while.

One piece of good fortune in my boyhood concerned the village school at Kamyshenka. Not only did it have some good teachers, but while I was there it expanded from a primary school into a secondary school. It is impossible to say how things might have turned out for me if this had not happened, but my family would definitely not have been able to send me to complete my education further away.

It was here in this school that I met my future mentor, a good man by the name of Semion Akimovich Yakovenko, who was the head of the primary school. He was the one who gave me a place despite being a kulak's son; a year later, he taught me in the fourth form himself, before becoming head teacher. He helped me a tremendous amount with my schoolwork, and greatly influenced my ideas and view of life.

One day, at the end of my first year there, Semion Akimovich summoned me and told me about a Young Pioneers camp being held near the town of Semipalatinsk (now Semey). The All-Union Mass Children Organization of Young Pioneers organised out-of-school activities for children of my age; camps like this one provided good food for them, and gave them a chance to get fit and well again. With my family's consent, my teacher put my name forward to receive a free holiday there. I was the only one of his 200 pupils to receive such a recommendation – he must have guessed how poor my family were – and I found myself spending a whole month in a beautiful pinewood on the banks of the Irtysh. Not only was I able to eat as much as I liked, but I was even fed meat, the taste of which I had almost forgotten. In addition, all the children were given new clothes, with a lovely, crisp feel I had not known for years.

iii

After returning from camp that summer, I had the most dreadful piece of bad luck. My second cousin Mubarak Rakhimzhanov, who was five years my senior and had grown up in the same aul, was working as a teacher quite nearby and never missed an opportunity to call in on us. He had always looked after me, and used to write me letters to give me advice and find out how my lessons were going. One day he wrote to tell me he was on holiday and planning a shopping trip to the Kuludzhun mine, and invited me to go over to his house and then make the trip with him.

In those days you saw never material for clothes on sale in village shops. They did, however, appear once in a while in shops at the mines. Aiken agreed to let me go and borrowed 80 roubles – the equivalent of his monthly wages – from his work-mates. Handing them to me, he explained which fabrics to buy for whom, and what sort of clothes we would make out of them. So off Mubarak and I set on our mission.

We had been invited to stay there at the house of a distant relative called Nurzhamal whose husband was the chairman of the mine's village council. Then as now, it was common practice for someone in a position of power to pull strings, and this chairman set up a visit for Mubarak to a warehouse where he could pick out all the materials he needed. Meanwhile, I was advised to go to the shop, where I would be able to buy materials if I was prepared to queue for them.

The queue was a very long one. When, at about twelve o'clock, my turn finally came at the counter, I reeled off a list of different materials and measurements to the sales assistant, and stuck my hand in my pocket to get my money out. It had gone. While I had been standing in the queue, some wretched pickpocket had cleaned me out.

I cannot begin to describe how I felt. When I eventually got back to my relative's house, depressed and miserable, she exclaimed in fright, 'What's wrong with you? Are you sick? You look awful! And where's the material you were going to get?'

When I told her what had happened and she started wailing, 'Astapyr-allah! [Save us, God!] Oh, how terrible! What are we going to do? How could you let such a thing happen?'

But after a few moments she started trying to calm me down. 'Don't be upset! What use is it now? What's done is done. Crying won't change anything. Allah will make up for it.'

I was beside myself. I had gone there in the hope of getting new clothes for the whole family for the first time in years; I could not imagine returning home empty-handed, and I was terrified to think how angry my cousin was going to be after borrowing and entrusting me with a substantial sum of money.

I was dreadfully anxious all the way home, and the nearer we got Kamyshenka, the more upset I became. Seeing the state I was in, Mubarak – who had kept quiet until then – said to me as we approached the village, 'Don't worry, I've had an idea. Turn off into the wood here and let your horse eat the grass; we'll have a rest and I'll tell you what it is.'

He pulled the two sacks full of materials he had just bought at the mine off the cart and said, 'One sack's got the stuff I bought for myself, and the other is full of the stuff I bought on various neighbours' instructions and got paid for. I'm going to cut you off a large piece from each length of material. Back home you'll say you bought them for the 80 roubles: you won't say a word about your slip-up. We'll have to pretend everything cost more than expected. I'll back you up.'

The relief I felt was enormous.

iv

The most important political event in the Soviet Union in 1936 was the adoption of a new constitution. The whole country spent the entire summer and autumn studying the draft of the country's basic laws and discussing it.

Once a week, a watchman from the State procurement station named Orazbek Matayev, who had been appointed by the local Communist Party to head a study group, would get all the aul residents together and ask me (since he himself was semi-literate) to read the draft of the new constitution from a newspaper. The people attending the group would just sit there in silence. I have no idea what they made of it all or how much they actually took in: no questions were ever asked. Sometimes Orazbek would stop me reading to get to grips with the text himself, saying, 'Stop there, lad, read that bit again', or 'And now explain to the everyone what you think that last sentence means.'

After the draft constitution had been adopted by the Eighth Extraordinary Soviet Congress in December, we spent the whole winter going through it one article at a time. People would also discuss various rumours they had heard. One was that everyone was going to be tested on the constitution and the rights and duties of citizens contained in it: anyone who failed would be taken to the regional centre and made to learn it all over again. People in the group were terrified of this happening to them, since this was just when secret servicemen were knocking on doors in the middle of the night and throwing innocent people into prison. What everyone feared most was that their ignorance of the contents of the constitution might mean that they could be accused of not wanting to know them. Fortunately, the rumours came to nothing.

Orazbek was also the chairman of his procurement station's trade union, and he got me to take on its bookkeeping and paperwork. I discovered that the union subscribed to the Kazakh journal *On the Literary Front* – though none of the members actually set eyes on it, since it was kept, along with all the union's documents, in a trunk at Orazbek's house. I was able to read it, however, and it had an important impact on my intellectual development, giving me a strong interest in Kazakh literature – so I owe more to the badly educated watchman than he could ever have imagined.

Later, when elections were announced to the country's Supreme Soviet, Orazbek got all the aul residents together just as before, and again asked me to read the regulations. As I kept reading them over and over again, I soon learnt them off by heart. I cannot say how much I actually understood, but it did give me an interest in studying politics, and towards the end of my time at school I and three others in the top form joined the Young Communist League.

According to a resolution of the Party's Central Committee, all members were expected to study the newly published *History of the All-Union Communist Party*. So we found ourselves discussing Marxist theory along with the collective farmers, village council chairmen, brigade leaders and so on. It was ridiculous: what on earth could we schoolboys, or the semi-literate adults who used to read the words in newspapers one syllable at a time, understand about subjects such as empiriocriticism and dialectics? I remember us spending ages discussing and hopelessly trying to fathom the meaning of the words 'spontaneous movements'. But we had been ordered to study Party history, so study it we did.

v

My family's standard of living was now beginning to improve slightly, but it was still not good. We were all living off Aiken's wages, as we younger ones were at school and Mother looked after the house. What he earned was only enough to buy a small amount of food, and he was on a constant look-out for extra income.

Every now and then, steamers and barges delivered supplies of coal, salt and flour as emergency aid to the region, and the organisations responsible would employ local workers to unload them, paying by the ton. As the salt and coal were transported loose, they first had to be poured into sacks, and each worker was given a certain load depending on how much he could carry. The adults were given about twice as much to carry as us youngsters, so although I did this work several times during the summer, I earned next to nothing.

That autumn I started in the sixth year at school. I must have been quite a good pupil because to mark the twentieth anniversary of the founding of the Young Communist League in 1918, I was awarded a pair of canvas boots as a prize for my academic achievements. They were the first new boots I had ever owned in my life.

Even though nearly four years had passed since the famine, people had still not totally recovered from it. On the plus side, there was a gradual increase in the number of tractors on the collective farms, so virgin land could be ploughed up to provide more fields for crops; and in the villages work began on new public buildings. But there continued to be food shortages, with most of the grain from the harvest still having to be delivered to the State, and the ban on slaughtering their animals and selling meat still in force. Horses were in very short supply, because most of them had died of disease or neglect on the collective farms, so that the State was forced to start buying them in from countries such as Mongolia and China. In rural shops there were virtually no manufactured goods on sale, and in any case, people had no money to buy them with.

Of all the things we needed, what we most longed for was a cow. In the summer of 1938 we managed to save up enough money from Aiken's modest wages to buy a tiny heifer, which with luck would produce a calf the following year and provide us with milk. We had really missed all our livestock ever since it had been confiscated eight years before, and so we were all thrilled. In those days a cow was considered such a valuable commodity that relatives and neighbours would call by to congratulate us and tell us how happy they were for us. The very fact that villagers were now buying and selling livestock also indicated an improvement in their living standards. The same could be said of the fact that people started building new houses for themselves.

In the spring of 1939 it must have been fairly simple and cheap to build wooden huts, because all the residents in our aul decided to cross the Irtysh to the village on the opposite bank and settle all together on the edge of it. Building work on the new houses got underway as soon as the snow had melted and it was slightly warmer. Over the summer, all of the aul's fifteen households managed to build small houses and outbuildings to their own design and with their own hands, from whatever materials were then available. In our case, we built a house with two rooms. This time we borrowed a horse and cart from relatives to help carry the building materials.

During the construction work neighbours did what they could to help one another with materials and labour. We were even more grateful for the Kazakh tradition of mutual support when, during the course of the summer, our much-loved little dairy cow suddenly fell sick and had to be slaughtered. Hearing of our bad luck, all the other residents of our aul got together and gave us an advance payment for all the meat at market price. It was a tremendous help, for in the July heat we simply could not have managed to get the meat to market in time or keep it fresh at home. The money our friends collected was enough for us to buy another cow. But it was not only our Kazakh neighbours who helped: my head teacher Trofim Akimovich, for instance, got me a temporary job at the village council, enabling me to earn some much-needed money for the family.

vi

That year, Aiken finally got married at the age of 28. I realise now that the reason he took so long to find a wife was largely to do with the family's financial problems. But as things improved, Mother started saying with annoying persistence that it was high time for Aiken to find himself a bride, and coming up with the names of suitable candidates. Aiken would then explain why, as far as he was concerned, none of them would do. This wrangling went on for nearly a year before he succumbed.

It was not a lively or noisy wedding. The bride did not arrive with a traditional retinue of matchmakers and maids of honour, nor did she have any dowry except the clothes she was dressed in. She was greeted by sashu, a kind of confetti; the five or six neighbouring families who made up the guest list congratulated the couple, wished them and the rest of the household happiness and prosperity, drank a samovar of tea with us, and then said their goodbyes. That is what nearly all weddings were like in those days.

Our self-built wooden house had twenty square metres of living space, which seemed plenty to us. As the newly-weds did not have their own bed yet, they slept on the floor behind a traditional Kazakh printed cotton screen called a shymyldyk. Aiken's bride Nurlygain coped well with her new responsibilities as a young housewife, and won everyone's approval – including, most importantly, Mother's. We younger ones really liked her, as she used to go out of her way to fuss and spoil us.

The new school year began. Although I was in a new form in the seventh year, everything else seemed to have remained exactly the same. I was now a young man, a *dzhigit*, and I longed to have some money to spend: I wanted to throw out my old rags and replace them with smart new clothes, and go out in the evening to dances and films, or even to the two concerts given during the summer by touring artists. But I did not have a single kopeck from the money the council had paid for me over the summer, as it had all gone on building materials for the new house. The way I saw it, my family's financial situation had got worse rather than better, since we now had an extra person to feed.

After thinking it over, I decided to give up school and go out and earn a living. It was wrong for an eighteen-year-old lad to be living at his cousin's expense and always wearing cast-offs. Aiken, of course, cared a great deal for us, but it was not as though he was my elder brother: it was really up to me to support and feed my mother.

When I told him of my decision, he replied without a moment's hesitation, 'Stop talking nonsense. You'll stay on at school and keep going with your studies even if you have to go barefoot. You're not going hungry, and that's all that matters. We'll pull through somehow. Don't bother me with daft things like this again.'

I didn't argue with him, but I was still determined to stick to my plan. Then one day I mentioned it to some of my classmates; the headmaster came to hear of my intentions, and he called me in and asked about the rumours. I told him they were true, and explained my reasons for wanting to leave school.

In reply, Semion Akimovich told me of how he had studied a long way from home during the terrible years of famine, of the clothes he had worn, and of how much he had suffered from hunger.

'There's no comparison even between the way things were for me then and the way they are for you now,' he said. 'You've got to put up with everything and just get on and study. Don't give up school, whatever you do. We'll do what we can to help.'

He kept his word. Not long afterwards he called me back into his office and said, 'The regional education authorities have decided to allocate sufficient funds for us to have a Young Pioneer leader at the school. We're offering the job to you so that you can work and get paid for it. I've brought the contract over with your name already on it. You're to start work on the first of October. You'll do fine.'

'But what about my studies?' I asked uncertainly.

'You'll just have to work very hard at them. You can attend lessons in the mornings and then work with the Young Pioneers in the afternoons and evenings. We'll show you what to do, and give you lots of help.'

I was simply overjoyed at the prospect of staying on at school and having a job at the same time. So, on 1 October 1939, I began my new duties, organising educational and artistic activities for ten-to-thirteen-year-olds out of school. It was my first day in State employment. Like so many others, I saw no contradiction in working within the system which had persecuted my family, choosing to believe that our sufferings were attributable to unscrupulous individuals, beginning with Stalin's Soviet Party chief in Kazakhstan, Feodor Goloshchekin, and then the underlings down the scale, rather than to Stalin himself and the ruthlessness of the ideology he worked to or the true nature of his personal tyranny. The 'will of the Centre' assumed in us a sense of ineluctable destiny involving the whole USSR with which the only course was simply to comply and whose promises for a better future we all had to trust, to keep hope alive. However evil the practice of the system, which led to mass destruction for the Kazakhs, I neither fostered nor harboured hostility for the system itself. Indeed, I clung to its merits. Education in a Marxist-Leninist frame was in significant measure education, and for that I was thankful.

I think I carried out my duties quite well, while working my way through the seventh and eighth years at school. The job was a gift from heaven: apart from the financial benefits, it gave me an opportunity to work on public events in the region and get to know a great many activists in the Young Communist League and other organisations. I know that but for my perceptive and kind-hearted mentor, I would never have got it or been able to complete my secondary education; and I have recalled Semion Akimovich's kindness and generosity of spirit every day of my life since.

PART THREE

WAR

Chapter Twenty-Four

The Coming of the Great Patriotic War

In the autumn of 1939 the Red Army invaded Poland. As a result, it was able to occupy the territories of Western Belorussia and Ukraine that had hitherto been under Polish control, before Germans advancing from the west could reach them. But whereas in Western Europe these military actions were heralded as the first campaigns of World War II, the population of the Soviet Union did not initially attach much importance to them, regarding them as yet another border conflict.

Soviet historians used to contend that all the campaigns the Russian armed forces ever engaged in were conducted out of necessity, to defend the country against aggressors who were continuously attempting to capture its riches and threatening its independence: according to them, Russia was always a peace-loving power and had not once started a war. The Soviet Government used the same cliché to justify its actions in Ukraine and Belorussia, claiming that it had extended a brotherly hand to save them from being enslaved by the German capitalist forces. Most of us fell for all of this.

Two and a half months later, the Soviet Union was engaged in another conflict. Finland, whose entire population was the same size as Leningrad's, was denounced as an aggressor threatening the security of that city. Strategists predicted that the action would be wrapped up within a couple of weeks, but tiny Finland put up a desperate fight, and the campaign continued all winter. Large numbers of Red Army officers and men lost their lives in the Finnish forests and marshes, on the battlefields and in the severe frosts. The Soviet Government was forced to mobilise civilians to fight at the front. It was only in March 1940, once the frosts were over, that the Red Army finally achieved victory. Finland was forced to hand over half of the territory of Karelia with its principal city, Vyborg.

The Soviet Union announced to the whole world that it could have captured the entire territory of Finland, but had decided not to: it was simply taking the territory necessary to guarantee the security of Leningrad, while allowing its northern neighbour to retain its independence. But what the war really showed was that the Soviet armed forces and the country's leadership were not ready for a large-scale conflict. Even this minor one was enough to cause a noticeable deterioration in the standard of living: at the start of 1940, food and other goods disappeared from the country's shops overnight.

Among the projects started in preparation for war was the construction in our district of a major road, 1,500 kilometres long. Its starting point was to be the town of Ust-Kamenogorsk; it was then to pass through the villages of Georgievka and Kokpekty as far as Lake Zaisan, before continuing through the Samara, Bolshenarymsk and Bukhtaminsk regions back to Ust-Kamenogorsk. As it was to pass through the territory of the two districts of Eastern Kazakhstan and Semipalatinsk, it became known as 'The Eastern Ring'.

The road, like other major construction projects, relied heavily on the manpower and resources of the two districts' collective farms. Work got underway in the summer of 1940, between sowing and harvesting. The road was to pass through stony marshlands and arid semi-deserts, and the workers had to do heavy manual labour in atrocious conditions exacerbated by swarms of mosquitoes and midges, insufficient supplies of fresh drinking water and lack of basic comforts. Using picks, spades, wooden stretchers, manual rollers and oxen-drawn carts, they needed tremendous muscle power to get the work done: in the scorching July heat they hacked through rocks, dug the rocky ground with their spades, and carried piles of earth and road metal about on stretchers. My Uncle Kozhakhmet was among them, and articles constantly appeared in the local press about his trail-blazing work.

The road-builders worked through all the hours of daylight. Their equipment kept falling apart, the tyres of the few trucks at their disposal were always getting punctures, and their oxen sometimes collapsed with exhaustion; but they managed to put up with everything and keep going. Once we had broken up for the school holidays, my classmates and I did what we could to help, inspired by the adults' amazing example.

Meanwhile, across the country there was a fall in the output of consumer goods as the production of arms and military equipment increased. The army's overall strength was increased many times over by a three-year reduction in call-up age, and by the conscription of people previously exempt, such as students, teachers and specialists in certain branches of the economy.

In my secondary school there was only one teacher left with a higher education, and she taught chemistry. The Government was forced to take trainee teachers and send them to work in schools before they were anything like qualified, with predictable results. The pupils – who in some cases were almost as old as their teachers – took every opportunity to catch them out. This is not to say, though, that there was anarchy in village schools: most of the teachers were older men who knew how to command respect, and the children were too well disciplined to indulge in what is known nowadays as 'challenging behaviour'.

In 1941 my peer group, born in 1921-22, became eligible to be called up. I was nineteen. It didn't cross our minds to try to avoid conscription – we had been indoctrinated into a pan-Soviet allegiance. But one thing troubled me: if I was called up that year, my schooling would be interrupted – and I really wanted to complete my secondary education. How would I manage to go back to it after serving in the army for three years? It was unclear whether I would get a chance to or not.

As always, I sought the advice of my mentor Semion Akimovich, who suggested that I approach the Ust-Kamenogorsk teachers' training college about doing a correspondence course. Not long after sending off an enquiry, I received a reply informing me that I could sit the examinations for the ninth and tenth years of secondary school at the college that summer, and then at some later date take four further examinations for a teacher's certificate of education. So I started studying on my own for the summer exams. When the time came, I was warmly welcomed at the college: it turned out that I was the only external student it had, and everything was tailored to my needs.

Meanwhile, in April 1941, I and those of my contemporaries who had been passed fit for military service were given our enlistment papers, indicating the forces we were to serve in when the call-up came. I had been selected to serve in the cavalry.

For all of us, the idea of serving in the Red Army was an extremely attractive one. This was largely to do with patriotism, but not entirely. Conscripts were given rousing send-offs – there were parties with singing and dancing in their honour – and demobilised troops were welcomed home like heroes. During their time on active service, young men used to change beyond recognition, returning home older-looking, handsome and smart in their well-fitting army uniforms.

The propaganda machine was also hard at work, asserting that the people's Red Army was the invincible and legendary defender of the Fatherland, unequalled throughout the world. There is no doubt that its status increased after its victory over the Japanese at Lake Hasan and the River Halkin-gol, and its triumphant campaigns to annex the western parts of the Ukraine, Belorussia and Bessarabia, and the Baltic States. All these 'triumphs' encouraged young people to join up, and I too dreamed of army life, and returning home looking like all the dashing demobilised troops I had seen.

ii

One Sunday, two months later, a small group of us young lads attending the teachers' training college walked around town and then dropped in at the market before getting back to the hostel, slightly jaded and sticky from the heat, and flopping onto our beds for a rest. We were woken up by a terrible commotion as our friends came rushing in, yelling excitedly, 'War! War!' They all looked anxious and flustered. I only had a vague idea then of the scale of the conflict with Germany that had just broken out and the danger it posed to our country, and I reacted calmly to the news. Besides, I was totally convinced that the Red Army was going to smash the Fascist troops within a couple of weeks on German soil. Nevertheless, I suddenly became aware of an entirely new feeling as a chill ran through my body and shivers ran up my spine.

On 3 July, the twelfth day after the outbreak of war, our leader Stalin made the following radio announcement: 'Only now are the main forces of the Red Army joining battle. Soon the enemy will feel the full might of our valiant army.' After hearing these words, I felt even more confident about us winning a speedy victory. Most of my compatriots felt the same. Our faith in the genius of our leader and the indomitable might of the Workers' and Peasants' Red Army was enormous.

The very next day, people began lining up at the local recruiting office, asking to be sent to the front. When a group of us student teachers went along, we had to queue for half a day just to get inside. There were so many volunteers that the office simply could not cope with them all. Quite a few had to return home without registering. They were all told to keep working at their jobs, and if the need arose they would be called up.

Increasing numbers of recruits started arriving at the district centre to be sent off to the front. But soon views on the war began to change. The news from the front during the first few weeks – that the glorious Soviet Army was retreating eastwards, abandoning our territory to the enemy – bewildered and alarmed people. Why was it happening? Had the enemy really got the better of us? Or was the Red Army command deliberately luring the Fascists into a trap? Questions like these were on everyone's lips.

iii

After six weeks of exams at the teachers' training college, I received the secondary education certificate I was longing for, and returned home. The war continued and the daily announcements on the military operations at the front caused concern and alarm. Our army was still retreating. Troops, vehicles, horses, carts and other equipment needed at the front continued to be mobilised. The collective farms began experiencing a shortage of manpower and transport, and the haymaking and harvesting took longer than usual.

Mobilisation increased, but the military registration offices took a long time to contact the young people next in line to be called up, and it was early October by the time we heard from them. There were 80 young lads, including myself, summoned for duty from our region.

As I was getting ready to leave, Uncle Mukatai came to see us. When he started asking Mother the usual questions about her daily life, she replied, 'Remember that old folk-tale about the two-headed serpent that conquered a kingdom and forced the people to provide it with a goat and a young girl every month by way of a tax? It threatened to kill off everyone if they didn't say yes, so the people agreed to pay. The families would take it in turns to deliver the victims to the serpent; it would gobble them up straightaway and then sleep peacefully for the rest of the month. But as soon as it woke up, it would demand more food. There was another bit in the story about how the parents used to suffer the night before they had to give their daughter up to be sacrificed. Well, now I'm just like a mother in that tale, getting my son ready for that two-headed serpent we call war.'

Uncle tried to console her by saying that everything, to his mind, happened for the best, but she went on crying just as bitterly.

When I and the other recruits arrived at the district office, we were told that our military service started right there. We were then made to walk twenty or so kilometres in formation to a village on the Irtysh from where we going to continue our journey by steamer; those of us with our own means of transport were told that we were not permitted to use it. By contrast, the older men were allowed to make their own way there, and on arrival to stroll through the village whenever they liked and call in to see relatives; the ones who lived in the village simply went home to their families. We youngsters were billeted in the local clubhouse and strictly forbidden from going anywhere.

After waiting 24 hours for the steamer to arrive, we were just about to embark when the regional military commissar arrived. He stood in front of our formation and shouted out, 'The men whose names I read out, take five steps forward, the rest – stand still!'

Then he handed a sheet of paper to an officer and instructed him to read it out. The officer began reading, 'Ivanov, Petrov...' and so on, right through the list.

All the conscripts who stepped forward were Russian, except for one Tartar, and only us Kazakhs were left standing in the formation. This basically meant we had been split into two ranks according to our nationality. We could not believe it – and neither could all of our parents, relatives and friends who had gathered to see us off. We did not have long to think it over because the military commissar immediately announced, 'Conscripts whose names have been read out are to go to the quay and board the steamer and set off for the army. The rest are to go home.'

There was absolute silence for several seconds. Then the protests from the young Kazakhs started:

'Comrade commander! May I ask a question?'

'Why are you only discharging Kazakhs from immediate military service?'

'Why have you only selected Russians to serve in the army?'

'What's going on? Please explain!'

To which the commissar replied, 'An order has been issued to leave you Kazakhs until further notice.'

These words caused an uproar. Questions, explanations, accusations and calls for common sense were all shouted at once, so that none of them could be heard properly.

'What do you mean, "until further notice"?' demanded the mothers of the Russian conscripts. 'The Soviet authorities need everyone. Why should only Russians defend the country and die for it? It's not fair! Kazakhs should go to the front, too! Why should our children have to go to the war and risk their lives while the Kazakhs stay at home and take things easy? Send the Kazakhs to the war as well!'

The Russian recruits and their fathers, on the other hand, didn't say a word: they fully understood what we must have been feeling.

We went on kicking up a fuss and demanding a proper explanation. This time some of the Kazakh mothers intervened.

'Oh, stop it!' one of them said. 'Whoever heard of anyone pleading to join the army?'

'Stop arguing with the commissar! He's promising to call you up later on, isn't he? He will, then. Calm down!' begged another.

Once he realised that nobody was listening to his explanations and the commotion might go on for some time, the commissar led the Russian recruits over to the quay, leaving us behind to continue our noisy discussions. After deciding that our protest was futile, we started dispersing

The next day this incident gave rise to all sorts of speculation. Some people concluded that Kazakhs were considered incapable of fighting at the front without surrendering or going over to the enemy's side. Other far-fetched theories spread fast, offending our sense of national pride and sowing seeds of distrust among people of other nationalities towards us. In the end, however, these petered out.

There was a riverside quay in the village of Kamyshenka where my family was then living, which was like a window through which the region could receive goods and communicate with the outside world: people in the region used to refer to it as 'our local Leningrad'. All the mobilised new recruits from the Markakol and Kumashinko regions set off on steamers from it, and anyone seeing them off would walk or drive over to our village with them. Watching their goodbyes was terribly upsetting: mothers crying as they clung to their sons on parting; wives pressed against their husbands' chests, wailing; a little girl with her arms locked round her father's neck, having to be forcibly parted from him. Some people said that too many tears before a long journey were a bad omen, and it certainly seemed to be the case that few of the soldiers who were given excessively emotional send-offs returned from the front.

iv

As for me and my Kazakh comrades, the real reason for the deferment of our military service became known two months later. It turned out that the USSR State Defence Committee had passed a secret resolution recommending that units be formed on the basis of nationality, and at the beginning of December we were duly called up. We were supplied with uniforms – even including handkerchiefs – and given provisions for the journey to our posting and for the first two weeks of service in our unit. We were also, as cavalry, provided with horses, *britzkas* and harnesses.

After a grand send-off, our detachment rode horses harnessed to sledges all the way to Ust-Kamenogorsk, staying overnight at the mining settlements of Retivy, Taiynty and Targyn, and in the village of Leninka. We were given official receptions everywhere we stopped – all splendid, friendly occasions. Once all the recruits like us from all the different regions had been gathered together in the district centre, we were dispatched in a single party by train to the capital, Alma Ata, on 21 December. It was pouring with rain when we arrived in our sheepskin coats and felt boots, and we got drenched in no time at all as we traipsed through the city's streets. Our boots became soggy, and our coats sagged till their hems nearly touched the ground. We spent the rest of that day and the following night staying in an unheated cinema in soaking wet clothes. A few of us, naturally, caught colds, and I went down with a fever, with the result that five of us were sent us back home. It turned out that the division we were supposed to be joining still did not have barracks, let alone a medical unit.

The policy of organising units by nationality did not last long. The idea – opposed from the very outset by the front-line army command – had apparently been to use feelings of national pride and honour to boost the troops' morale while so many setbacks were being experienced at the front. However, it was then realised that problems might arise in co-ordinating their operations with those of the other forces, and indeed in commanding them all. Within a year they were merged with other formations in the Red Army.

At the end of 1941, and during the first three months of 1942, there was an intensive recruiting drive. Even key workers who had previously been passed over were now mobilised. After my return from Alma Ata there were only four out of fifteen male teachers left at my old school, where I now started working, and a month later I was the only one left.

I felt constantly guilty about my fellow recruits, as though I had deceived them by being sent home instead of sharing the dangers they faced, and I was lonely without my male colleagues, relatives and friends. I also felt deeply sorry for the grieving women who had been left without their husbands and were having to deal with all the vicissitudes of life themselves. They fretted constantly about the fate of their loved ones at the front, their family responsibilities, and the new jobs they were now having to perform; but as time went by, they proved able to run the collective farms and other State organisations just as well – for the most part – as men.

Chapter Twenty-Five

In the Red Army

My dull and lonely life was interrupted on 17 February, 1942 when I received another call-up notice to the army. I had just turned 20. This time I was to travel with other recruits older than me to a reserve infantry regiment in Semipalatinsk. And so the next day, early on a frosty morning, our relatives – my mother among them – tearfully said goodbye to us, and stood on the edge of the village watching us go off to the military enlistment office.

At the regional centre we were split into detachments. When we were just about to set off on the next leg of our journey, who should suddenly appear at the office gates but my mother. She had walked twenty kilometres in the freezing cold.

I rushed up to her saying, 'We've already said goodbye, why have you walked here in this frost? We're leaving at any moment. You could easily have missed us.'

'How could I sit at home when you were going off on such a long, dangerous journey? I wanted to kiss you again and so here I am,' Mother sobbed, wiping away her tears.

A short while later she regretted acting so impetuously, because once our detachment had moved off, she was left all alone with no means of transport in an unfamiliar village. With awful irony, my detachment stopped in our village that night, so I ended up spending it at home but without Mother.

This time there were one hundred or so new recruits aged between twenty and forty-five travelling in a caravan of more than twenty carts. It took us five days to get to Zhangiz-Tobe station. This trip was very different from the one to Ust-Kamenogorsk after my first call-up: nobody greeted us or offered us hospitality. We were billeted overnight in private homes and had to put up with very cramped conditions, because there were no public buildings in the aul and villages we stopped at.

Upon our arrival at Zhangiz-Tobe station, we boarded a train and arrived in Semipalatinsk that night. We spent a week in quarantine, all crowded together in one room, and were then split up into units of the reserve regiment stationed in Semipalatinsk.

At one parade a senior officer came out in front and addressed us as follows: 'Who wants to join the artillery? All those who want to, forward!'

Nobody volunteered. Then one of my village friends, Vasily Morozov, who had served in the artillery before the war and happened to be standing next to me, grabbed hold of my arm and stepped forward, dragging me with him.

When I tried to resist, he whispered, 'Shut up, I'll explain later. You won't regret it.'

It is quite astonishing how sometimes in life your destiny depends on someone else's good (or not-so-good) intentions. Morozov's intervention shaped my time in the army, and in many ways the rest of my life.

New recruits always feel very insecure, so they try to stick with others from the same part of the world: for this reason, a whole group of recruits from our village followed Morozov's example. However, over half the detachment of young Kazakh recruits from our region remained standing in line, not daring to stick their necks out. When I signalled to some of them to join us, only one man – who had no idea what the word 'artillery' meant – stepped forward to join us. What no one apart from Morozov knew at the time was that life was easier in the artillery than in the infantry, and there were significantly fewer casualties.

So we were enrolled as gunners in the regimental battery of 45-millimetre guns.

I still remember my first night at the barracks. Stepping inside the cheerless building, I found myself in a chilly, virtually bare room with two tiers of roughly-hewn benches running along three of its walls. There were large sacks of fresh straw lying on top of them which were supposed to serve as mattresses. When I lay down on one, the straw inside crackled and clouds of dust puffed into the air. I felt so uncomfortable and strange lying there that I did not sleep a wink all night: it was like lying in a pile of straw on the floor of a livestock pen. But after a couple of days of intensive training, the straw mattress felt as though it was stuffed with down, and a while later I was day-dreaming fondly about it as somewhere idyllic to sleep.

Our battery formed part of an artillery regiment and operated as a battalion. It may have been less stressful than serving in the infantry but it was not all that easy. All day long, from six in the morning until eleven at night, we drilled and fought mock battles. The actual drills were not particularly difficult, but they were terribly tedious to repeat day in, day out, as we dismantled and re-assembled rifles and learnt how to handle grenades.

Then there were exercises with our one and only 45-millimetre gun. We used to dig a pit in a field to conceal it in, and practise firing at dummy tanks; several times a day we had to change our firing position by rolling the gun somewhere else and digging another pit to conceal it in and a trench for ourselves. We were also taught how to launch an assault on a town, rolling the camouflaged gun out into the street and pulling it all the way to the allotments behind some houses, where we concealed it and set it up. Then we had to fill up all the pits and trenches we had dug and smooth them over. By the end of the day we were worn out, but as soon as we were asleep, the alarm would be raised and we would be sent off on a ten-to-twenty-kilometre sprint or march. As we were not on nourishing rations, we used to get completely drained. When we did get a chance to sleep, we were expected to share a mattress and a blanket; for a long time we did not even have sheets.

Some of the new recruits found the discipline hard to get used to, especially when orders were issued in language peppered with expletives, and there were occasional flare-ups caused by junior officers' unreasonable and frequently offensive conduct. Many of them had only been to school for a couple of years and were semi-literate, with no idea how to behave towards other people. Intoxicated by power, they conducted themselves like officers in the old tsarist army: all they were concerned about was getting us to carry out their pedantic and frequently pointless orders unquestioningly. It was this attitude – widespread in the Red Army's rear units at the time – that caused the strained relations between junior officers and men; as a result, some of the recruits looked of ways of getting their own back, and treated even the battle training with contempt. This was bound to have repercussions when they finally reached the front.

The same was true of the dire shortage of equipment: instead of real rifles, we had to make do with wooden models for bayonet practice, while for target practice we were only given three cartridges each during our entire training. Similarly, the only instruction we received on firing our gun was when our battery commander demonstrated by firing it three times in front of us.

There were over one hundred men in the three sections of our regimental battery. The single gun had six horses to pull it, with another two horses for the regimental britzka. The battery staff consisted of nine section commanding officers, three unit commanding officers, their assistants, a sergeant-major, an assistant political officer, a junior lieutenant and a Communist Party political officer.

None of the men in charge of the battery had ever been regular officers: indeed, they were all reservists. The commander of our third unit was a former mine-surveyor, who fortunately was a highly cultured, conscientious and reasonable man. He was good at getting on the same wavelength as his men, and at giving fatherly advice, so the men respected him and tried not to cause him problems. Similarly, the battery commander – a lieutenant aged 24 – was exacting but always fair. In the evenings he used to call in to the barracks and chat to us about our lives and families, and when we had free time he would get everyone singing and dancing to keep their spirits up.

Two months after I arrived at the battery, I was appointed its clerk. From a physical point of view, life immediately became less stressful. There was routine office work to do, with reports to make to the regimental command in the mornings and various telephone messages to record. I also had to make sure that regimental orders were relayed to the battery, and draw up weekly timetables of the military drills and political instruction given to personnel.

During our time at Semipalatinsk, there was an incident involving a middle-aged Russian recruit which had tragic consequences. The man was working in the regimental stables when, by his account, he accidentally chopped off four of the fingers of his left hand with an axe. However, a medical commission of inquiry concluded that he had cut off his fingers deliberately, and his case was referred to a military tribunal which sentenced him to be shot.

ii

There were a great many conscripts from Eastern Kazakhstan in our regiment, and very occasionally men would receive visits from their parents, wives and other relatives. One day a soldier's wife turned up from a remote aul in the Kumashinko region to visit her husband. All she had by way of an address was the number of his military unit and the town it was stationed in. She kept showing this to passers-by and asking them to tell her the way; but the locals had no idea which military units were positioned where in the town. Someone advised her to ask at our barracks, so she arrived at the gates early one morning and hovered by them for several hours, calling out her husband's name to the occasional people going in and out. Unfortunately, most of the personnel were out on exercises, so there was nobody about who knew her husband; nor did anyone advise her to go to regimental headquarters, where someone could have given out her husband's address. The poor woman became totally flustered, and had no idea what to do next.

It so happened that I was summoned that day from my barracks to regimental headquarters on some clerical errand. I had just passed through the gates when the woman came rushing up to me and started pleading with me, '*Dzhigit*, young man, I do not know if we're related at all but you're a Kazakh for sure, so please wait a minute. Listen to me. I've travelled a long way to see my husband Ziyada Baipakbayev. He's serving here. Maybe you know him? Please tell him I'm here and get him to come out to me.'

By chance, I did know her husband. Before he was called up, he had worked as an inspector in our regional education department, and I had seen him only recently at a Young Communist League meeting. He was serving in the ranks of the third battalion.

When I told her all this, she was overjoyed, and begged me to take her to him; so I walked with her all the way to the eastern outskirts of the town, where Baipakbayev's battalion was stationed. Unfortunately, he turned out to be at a Party meeting at regimental headquarters, so we had to go there instead – in a rush, since the working day was now drawing to a close. The woman trailed after me wearily, but still full of resolve. She didn't ask me anything about myself.

As soon as we arrived, I left her by the gates, assuring her that she would soon see her husband, and I was just about to go off to do my work when she called out, 'You don't by any chance know a young lad from Kamyshenka who's serving here in Semipalatinsk? He's related to...' – and she gave the name of Aiken's wife.

I asked her to repeat what she had just said. Sure enough, I had heard her correctly the first time. The person she was asking about was me.

It turned out that she had spent several days waiting in Kamyshenka for a steamer to Semipalatinsk, and had stayed with my family. Of course, Mother and Aiken's wife used the happy coincidence to send me greetings and a small food parcel by her – but the woman had become so distraught searching for her husband that everything she knew about me, apart from Nurlygain's name, had gone completely out of her head. However, she had remained true to her word and started looking for me as soon as she had tracked down her husband. Her surprise was as great as mine.

iii

One day when our battery and the battalion who shared our yard were on military exercises outside the town, I spotted someone I recognised sitting on his own in our unit's yard. It was Kusain Shafigulin, who had given us lectures on Darwinism at the Ust-Kamenogorsk teachers' training college. Everyone has a natural sense of gratitude to a teacher who has taught him a lot of useful things, so I was delighted to see him, and went over to ask how he was and how long he had been in those parts. It turned out that he had only just been called up and was serving in the infantry battalion next door. He had been released from military exercises for health reasons, and that was how he came to be sitting on his own in the deserted yard.

As soon as he found out what my duties were, he said, 'I've been here for a fortnight, but I still haven't been able even to get a note to some relatives of mine who live in the town, because I'm not allowed beyond the gates. Help me get over to visit them and tell them how I am; I can do it in the couple of hours before the officers get back from their exercises.'

I explained to him that men were not allowed to be absent from their billets: the senior commanding officer only gave his permission in exceptional cases. According to martial law at the time, any soldier who left his unit without leave of absence for more than two hours faced the death penalty.

However, my ex-teacher kept asking me to help. He swore he would not let me down and, if anything were to go wrong, nobody would ever find out I had anything to do with it. Because I felt sorry for him and trusted him, I wrote out a pass entitling him to a two-hour visit to town (from 10:00 to 12:00) and put his name on it. Of course, I had broken the official rules, but two hours were not long enough for anybody to notice his absence.

As ill luck would have it, I was summoned just then on a routine official matter to regimental headquarters, where I remained until the evening. Meanwhile, instead of spending his two hours' leave visiting relatives, Shafigulin went off to a beer stall.

After enjoying a few drinks, he managed to get back to his unit's billet in time. But a short while later he decided that he had not had enough to drink, and set off to look for me and get another pass. Somehow or other he managed to get past the sentries and into our office. Noticing on a desk the pass I had used that morning to go to headquarters, he changed the time from 12:00 to 14:00 and sent off to town again. Later that day, an army patrol came across him in a drunken stupor, carrying the pass in my name.

An inquiry was launched. Terrified at the prospect of the death penalty, Shafigulin forgot his promise and claimed that I had given him the second pass.

The matter came to the attention of the regimental commander, Colonel Varlamov, who gave instructions for the matter to be passed over to a military tribunal. Later the same day, however, at the suggestion of the chief staff officer, Captain Grotsman, he changed his order. Instead, Shafigulin and I were enrolled in a company of reinforcements who were about to leave for the front.

To this day I feel a debt of gratitude to Captain Grotsman. He knew me well, and we used to meet on a regular basis, as I dealt with regimental staff matters in the course of my clerical work. Had it not been for his support, my teacher would have definitely got ten years in prison while I would have probably got between three and five years. I reckoned we had been let off lightly, since it was an honour to be going to the front and we were supposed to be leaving for it soon anyway.

As a result of this incident, I made up my mind that if I stayed alive, I would never do anyone else a good turn. Of course, I forgot this promise, but I could never forgive Shafigulin. What made me feel even more resentful was the fact that my teacher got lucky, as far as he was concerned, and ended up not going to the front at all because of some medical problem with his legs. He set off home without even saying goodbye to me.

Later on, fate brought us together twice. It never even occurred to me to seek revenge, although I easily could have done; but I never forgot how he had betrayed me, and I did my best to avoid seeing him.

iv

We joined a company of reinforcements so large that it took up an entire troop train. It turned out to consist entirely of Kazakh troops, all from the Aksuat region of the Semipalatinsk district, and between 35 and 45 years of age. The regimental command had decided to send them to the front even though they had not yet completed their full military training programme. These men from remote auls did not speak Russian, and so during their two months of training they had had neither the time nor the ability to master even the elementary skills required of frontline soldiers. What's more, none of their commanding officers were Kazakh-speaking.

To deal with the language problem at least, the regimental command appointed half a dozen young Russian-speakers, including myself, as section commanding officers. Nobody was concerned about what sort of leaders we would make or what we could teach the men: we were just glorified interpreters.

Our troop train moved west on the evening of 7 July 1942. The Germans had already started their advance through the south-west of the country, and it seems to me now, over sixty years on, that it should have been an absolute priority for all the troop trains heading for the front to reach their destination in the shortest time possible. But in actual fact, there was no sense of urgency at all. Our train stood for days in stations either because of line closures or because of the shortage of steam engines. We only reached the Western front – the Smolensk district, to be more precise – twenty days later.

One of the things that happened during the journey was that men kept getting left behind. You see, nobody ever knew how long the train was going to stand in a station for: the men used to wander off in search of food and drink, and then an engine would suddenly be found and the train would move off again, leaving the stragglers. On one occasion we were having a meal in the canteen at Tambov station when local railway officials hitched the empty carriages of our train onto a locomotive and sent it off without anyone on board. It took a whole day to rectify the mistake.

Sometimes men would get left behind deliberately: they were usually those who had already sustained injuries at the front and had now been passed fit again. The overwhelming majority of them were from Russia and had relatives in the towns the train was passing through. The military commandant's office used to gather all the stragglers together in a group and put them on any troop train bound for the front.

There is another thing I still cannot get over: when the Germans had captured the Don and were speeding towards the Volga, it was quite obvious that our troop train should have changed direction at Tambov and tried to reach Stalingrad ahead of the enemy; but the order only came through fifteen days later, when we had already arrived near Smolensk. However, as subsequent events were to show, it was already too late.

So, after many pointless stops, our troop train finally approached the front line. Our commanding officer informed us that we were to disembark later that evening and march through the night to our final destination.

It was nearly dusk by that time. Black rainclouds were gathering in the west, exactly where we were heading, and a thunderstorm with occasional flashes of lightning rumbled far away beyond the horizon.

'We're going to get caught in the rain,' remarked one of the soldiers in exasperation.

But one of the veterans replied, 'Those aren't rainclouds, and all that booming and flashing isn't thunder and lightning. It's the smoke and roar of an artillery cannonade from the front line.'

Realising how near they were now to the battle, some of my comrades cheered up, while others looked glum. But the noise and flashes alarmed all of us. I remember prayers being said.

As we had been promised, we got out of our train as darkness fell and then marched all night long in a column westwards. By dawn we were very close to the front, and lay down in a wood.

Chapter Twenty-Six

At the Front

The process of assigning us new recruits to our various units got underway at once. First, a junior lieutenant and sergeant-major began walking round our ranks shouting out, 'Does anyone want to join Reconnaissance? Who wants to become a scout?'

Five of us section commanders had become close friends during our month-long journey to the front, and had always stuck together in our own little group away from our middle-aged charges. Now we found ourselves taken by the idea of becoming Reconnaissance men.

'Look, lads, what's the point in us being officers?' I argued. 'What do we know about giving orders except basic ones like "Forward!" "Right!" "Left!"? When the battle starts tomorrow, we could end up getting men killed unnecessarily.'

So the five of us made up our minds to volunteer.

None of the other reinforcement troops wanted to join reconnaissance. The older men in our company begged us not to leave them.

'Why are you giving up on us?' they said. 'What are we going to do in battle tomorrow without you when we can't understand the

Russian officers' orders? When they order us to lie flat, we'll do the opposite and stand up. We'll be lost without you!'

Afraid that we might change our minds, the commanding officer led us away quickly. We said our goodbyes to our fellow countrymen and set off into the unknown.

Our recruiting officers turned out to be a platoon commander and a sergeant-major from the 656th regiment of the 116th infantry division. There were around twenty men in the scout platoon when we joined them, at a separate location from the regiment's other front-line units.

Some of them had surprised and curious expressions as they greeted us, while others treated us with ironic disdain, obviously considering us not good enough to be reconnaissance men. You see, they were all Europeans, and many of them had never set eyes on Asiatic Kazakhs before. On the commanding officer's orders, one of the experienced men was put in charge of each of us, to brief us on our duties and the rules of Reconnaissance at the front. They scared us by telling us that enemy fighting positions were close by and we could easily stumble across German scouts; they also explained the secret system of signals the platoon used and the different rules we were expected to observe on night- and day-time reconnaissance. We gradually absorbed all this new information as we began our front-line duties.

The man in charge of instructing me, who was called Ivanov, turned out to come from the same area as I did. He was 27 and looked after me like an older brother. We slept in the same tent and went on all our reconnaissance sorties together. He never let me out of his sight, and did all he could to help me and offer me advice. He was a courageous and determined young man with a wonderful sense of humour – though something unexpected happened to him later on that ruined his, and the entire platoon's, reputation.

The day we arrived, our division was resting in the second echelon of the front line. The reconnaissance men were more or less off-duty, and we reinforcements were given the first five days off to have a complete rest. We were in the middle of a beautiful, dense forest with waist-high grass and wonderful fresh air; we were amply fed and had comfortable uniforms and boots. All we needed was something to take our minds off the fighting.

On one of those first few days off-duty, the five of us new scouts were out on a walk when we spotted a rusty old German mine. It was the first time we had ever seen a real one. We had a good look at it, and then started arguing about why mines sometimes did not explode and wondering if this old one might still do so. We decided that it would if it was thrown into a fire, and thought we would have a go. So we set to and made a pile of brushwood in a clearing, put the mine on the top, and stuck a match. As soon as the fire had flared up, we ran further away and lay flat. The fire started blazing fiercely, but the mine still did not explode. Every now and then we lifted our heads and looked at the blaze.

Just then, an officer we had not seen before appeared out of nowhere and asked us why we were hiding and why there was a fire burning.

'Comrade Lieutenant,' we replied, 'lie down quick! There's a mine in the fire and it's going to go off any minute now.'

The officer turned the air blue with expletives and ordered us to get up and run after him. Then he dashed off.

He sounded so terrified when he gave the order that we tore headlong after him. Once he considered we were out of danger, he ordered us to lie flat. A few seconds later there was a shattering blast. The officer then made us go back to the spot where we had been sheltering from the explosion when he found us. There were mine splinters all over the ground. His chance appearance had saved us.

During the same few days, we underwent another chilling experience. Without any explanation, as though acting on secret orders, our commander drew the platoon up and gave the order to advance. A short while later we came to a large meadow. The battalions drew up, one after the other, until the whole regiment was assembled in formation. Directly in front of us was a mound of freshly-dug earth on top of which a serviceman was sitting, bareheaded, in a loose army shirt and boots without puttees – the uniform of a rank-and-file serviceman under military arrest. Men began whispering in the formation: 'He's been sentenced to death by a military tribunal and now he's going to be shot! That's why the whole regiment's been brought here.'

The prisoner was ordered to stand up facing the formation. It turned out that the poor man had run away from the front line and hidden in the woods for several days. The commander gave an address in which he spoke of the crime committed by the prisoner as a betrayal of his comrades and his people and high treason. Then the military tribunal's sentence was read out: 'For cowardice in leaving his fighting position in battle, fleeing the front line, desertion and high treason, the prisoner is to be shot.'

As I watched this scene, my blood ran cold, and I could not take my eyes off the condemned man. I longed with all my heart for him to escape this terrible punishment. Some of the men in the formation were convinced it was all a show, and instead of being executed, the prisoner would be sent off to the front in a penal company. However, as soon as the sentence had been read out, a sergeant-major barked: 'Permission to carry out the sentence!'

Then he turned to face the condemned man and ordered, 'About turn!'

The man turned round and took one step forward. As he was doing so, the sergeant-major took his revolver out of his holster and shot the man in the back of his head. Instantly, the man fell flat on his back without a sound. The sergeant-major then went up to the body and fired another shot, this time aiming straight in the man's face. The man's head jolted.

As I had never seen blood spilt before, even in a fights, I was so shocked that I did not hear the order 'About turn!' given. So when the formation turned 180 degrees, I was the only one facing the other way, as though rooted to the ground.

I found this tragic incident so devastating that I developed a high fever and was unable to sleep. Several other men had a similar reaction to the brutal act we had witnessed. Even the hardened front-line veterans kept discussing it. Of course war is, to paraphrase Tolstoy, the epitome of all that is cruel, barbaric, murderous and contrary to the spirit of man: anything can happen in it. However, the public execution we had witnessed, no matter how heinous the crime, seemed utterly appalling. The military authorities obviously thought that it would act as a deterrent to the rest of us; but the truth is that it caused nothing but indignation among the rank and file.

ii

The German and Soviet armies differed in their procedures for those times when some sectors of the front line were quiet. Unlike the Red Army, the Germans did not keep all their men and commanding officers in the first line of trenches: instead, they would leave sentries on duty while most of the troops withdrew to dug-outs several hundred metres back, enabling them to rest and recover their strength. There was one dug-out for every squad, and a group of dug-outs for every company, arranged in a circle for all-round defence.

Although our division was resting, the reconnaissance platoon received the following order: 'Cross the enemy defence line at night and throw hand grenades into the dug-outs in which enemy soldiers are asleep.'

It was my first combat mission, and according to my more experienced comrades, it was going to be a difficult and dangerous one. They had long discussions and arguments while drawing up a plan. The most complex part, they considered, was not destroying the dug-outs but getting across to the enemy line of trenches and safely back again.

The plan brief read as follows: 'A group of twelve men is to be given the task of destroying the enemy dug-outs with hand grenades: one man per dug-out and two soldiers to provide back-up. Another five men are to secure a safe passage across the enemy line of trenches for the first group. A third group of five men is to secure the main group's retreat. Under cover of darkness it is to take up positions to the side, near the place were the main group is to cross, and wait for its return. Should the need arise, it is to draw enemy fire on itself, distracting the enemy from the main group'.

All the groups started out on the mission at the same time of night. When we got near the German trenches, we lay flat, and the first five men went on to clear the approach for the main group. Soon the signal 'Way clear' was given. Our comrades had successfully taken out the sentries on duty in the enemy trenches on the advanced line. We crossed them and reached the dug-outs, unnoticed and without a hitch. It all seemed to be going so smoothly that, to begin with, I felt that my service in reconnaissance was going to be quite easy.

Still, I could not say that I was not scared: in fact, I was very jittery. But when I saw how calm the experienced men looked, I relaxed a little and tried not to show my anxiety. It was only when we had reached the enemy dug-outs and Ivanov and I were about to throw the grenades that I began to really panic: after all, there were people in there – Fascists maybe, but still people – and I was about to kill them.

At a prearranged signal, each man crept up to his allotted dug-out and then, at another signal, we all hurled our grenades at the same moment. Ivanov and I threw ours at the dug-out doors and then started running like the others. As soon as the grenades began exploding inside, all hell was let loose: there was shouting, screaming, and the sound of bullets whistling all around. It was then I realised what reconnaissance missions in the enemy rear were all about.

We were saved by the fact that it was pitch dark and the Germans, caught unawares, started firing at random. They could not see who was firing at them or where from, or tell us apart from their own men. The group of men responsible for covering our retreat also distracted them by drawing fire on themselves.

The way back presented less of a danger to us. The platoon had accomplished its mission, though nobody knew for sure what results had been achieved. Everyone, from the division and regimental commands down to the platoon itself, were astonished that all twelve of us had returned alive and unharmed: people kept saying, half-jokingly and half-seriously, that we must have been under divine protection. Such was my baptism of fire as a scout.

iii

The day after our mission, an order suddenly came through for the division to set out in an easterly direction. Our reconnaissance platoon was instructed to lead the column. Three hours were set aside for the entire division to muster.

After waiting for cover of darkness, we set out in full marching order along the road we had already travelled on our way to the front.

An unexplained order always sparks off rumours. All sorts of far-fetched ideas were bandied about the column:

'We're going to become a division of Guards,' somebody claimed. 'Our Supreme Commander, Comrade Stalin, has expressed a wish to confer this honorary title on the division himself. As Comrade Stalin has too many commitments to come to the Western front himself, he has ordered our division to be transferred to Moscow.'

'Oh, come off it!' said someone else. 'As if Stalin needs our division! Stop telling lies! What have we done to deserve to become Guards? The Germans must have decided to attack Moscow from the south. The General Staff have guessed what they're up to, and are simply calling our division to defend the capital.'

'You're way off the mark!' said yet another. 'The division has been in the front line ever since last winter and has suffered heavy losses. With my own ears I heard a commanding officer saying that we were being sent to the Volga area to have a rest, and picking up reinforcements at the same time.'

The arguments continued all night. At dawn the weary column turned into a wood at dawn and made a halt.

At the front, things change in a flash. We had only just got ready to have a kip and shut our eyes when someone sounded the alarm. All thought of sleep instantly vanished and the whole regiment leapt to their feet. As we came out of the wood and onto the road, we saw a line of waiting vehicles. Our regiment was loaded into trucks and driven off in an unknown direction. It was really strange for us infantrymen, who were used to marching everywhere, to be travelling in vehicles. Something unexpected must have happened – but what exactly?

We only found out the truth that afternoon, when we reached the town of Kozelsk after bumping along the pot-holed roads of the Russian Chermozem area, which had become a sea of mud after a night's rain.

The Germans had apparently broken through our troops' line of defence and were heading towards Kozelsk, which we had been hurriedly sent to defend. Fortunately, other front-line units had succeeded in repelling them. Only after the situation had been rectified was the chain of events explained to us: we had been heading for Kozelsk anyway as part of a move to defend Stalingrad, but in view of the sudden danger to the town, it had been necessary to get us there more quickly. From Kozelsk the division was to travel to Stalingrad by train.

It seems likely that the German command found out about our arrival in Kozelsk, because they managed to prevent us from boarding the train for several days. No sooner had a train been made up at the station and the order given to embark than German aircraft began bombarding us like mad. It went on like this for a whole week: only on 22 August did we finally begin our journey.

We were already on board when we heard the terrible news that an advancing German unit had broken through to the Volga to the north of Stalingrad, enabling enemy troops to encircle the city from the west and north. It was now in real danger, for the enemy forces outnumbered ours. But despite the desperate nature of the situation, our journey was again poorly organised and subject to serious delays. Several divisions took a week to complete the final stretch of the journey from Kozelsk, instead of the one and a half to two days that they should have.

We got off the train in the steppe at night, some distance from the front line, and had to cover the rest of the way on foot over three nights. As a result of further bad organisation, the vehicles carrying food supplies went off in the wrong direction and got lost, and we were left without food for two days. That, in turn, resulted in the columns being tired and hungry and moving more slowly. Our advance was held up for two days while the missing vehicles were tracked down, and as a result, our division so urgently transferred from the Western front took eighteen days to reach Stalingrad.

The day that our column was supposed to join battle, we marched towards the front line at dawn after a night on the move. Without camouflage, we were soon spotted by the Germans and came under fire from their long-range artillery. We scattered in all directions and dropped flat on an empty field nearby stretching along both sides of the road. The Germans then bombarded our field so heavily that we were unable to move for a whole day. So we lost even more vital time to the enemy.

Chapter Twenty-Seven

Stalingrad

We joined battle on the night of 3 September. Tired after the long march and hungry after several days without much food, we went straight into the attack. But despite out most determined efforts, we failed to break through the encirclement.

Part of the problem was that the other major reinforcements heading towards Stalingrad from the north-west had still not arrived by the time we went into battle. Worse, we only had enough reserves of men and equipment for two days of fierce fighting; and the new units who joined battle on 5 September had enough for a week at the most.

To the north-west of the city, the German forces were fighting on two fronts: the inner line of the encirclement, from which they were trying to storm Stalingrad, and the outer line, where they kept repulsing the Red Army's attempts to break the siege. The battles on both lines were persistent and fierce, with heavy casualties being suffered by German and Soviet troops alike. Quite often the same sector of the battlefield changed hands several times a day; the fighting positions also kept moving. In sectors such as these the bodies of the dead on both sides were strewn horribly across the ground: you couldn't take a step without stumbling over mutilated, bloated corpses. But because of the constant battles, there was no opportunity for quite some time to collect and bury the dead.

The wrecks of Soviet and German tanks were also jumbled together on the battlefield. As someone from the countryside, they reminded me of towering haycocks in the meadows at harvest time.

After considerable effort and the loss of a large number of men, our troops to the north-west still failed to break through the enemy's outer encirclement and join with those defending the city from within. The noose around Stalingrad was tightening.

But our constant attacks on the outer line did achieve one thing. They tied up considerable numbers of enemy soldiers, and forced the German command to withdraw some of the troops who were trying to capture the city and redirect them to ward off our offensive. As Field Marshal Zhukov wrote in his memoirs, 'At the beginning of September 1942, the fate of Stalingrad hung by a thread: under the onslaught of enemy forces who were numerically superior several times over, there was a substantial threat of the city falling. During the period from 5 to 13 September 1942, our forces' fierce assaults from the north-west of Stalingrad on enemy positions saved the city.'

Nevertheless, after these fierce battles in the first half of September, the ranks of the infantry regiments were so depleted that it became increasingly difficult to hold the outer line. New units had to be formed from the auxiliary services, including maintenance personnel and bandsmen, and sent into battle.

As a member of the reconnaissance platoon, I did not always take a direct part in the assaults. However, I would not be exaggerating if I said that, along with the other scouts, I crawled the length and breadth of the regiment's fighting positions and no man's land. This gave me a much better idea than most of what was going on.

The steppes around Stalingrad where our division fought were flat and empty open spaces without any ground cover. It was far more dangerous fighting in them than in woods or mountains. The

Germans had every single man in their sights, and regularly shelled the approaches to our front line. Hot food was delivered only once a day, and always under cover of darkness. The Germans kept up their machine-gun fire even at night, because they were afraid of nocturnal assaults by our troops and wary of our scouts. Soldiers who walked along the trenches to visit others during the lull between battles were often killed by stray bullets.

Nor did the steppes have anything that could be used as a reference-point. You only had to move a short distance from your trench at night and you would have a real job finding your way back. If you lost your bearings, the only way you would get back was to call out to someone in a trench nearby. They would then return your call and you would walk in the direction their voice was coming from. The Germans, of course, used such exchanges to direct their fire, and these added to the number of casualties.

If a wounded soldier was not able to move on his own, and was not quickly found by his comrades, he stood very little chance of surviving. During the twenty days I spent at the Stalingrad front I remember witnessing several terrible episodes when seriously wounded men had lain unnoticed on the battlefield for several days. I myself, quite by chance, came across a seriously wounded man who had been lying there for two days, and carried him over to a medical team in no man's land.

I also remember another episode with a tragic outcome. One evening, as the whole platoon was about to set off on a reconnaissance mission, we came across a soldier who had been wounded so badly in the hip two days earlier that he could not even stir. He was a countryman of ours, from the Aksuat Semipalatinsk district, who had travelled to the front in the same troop train as us from Semipalatinsk. Seeing how seriously wounded he was, we decided to carry him at least from the battle zone to somewhere he could be treated. However, because our mission was so urgent, our commanding officer refused to let us stay there any longer, promising that we would help the unfortunate man on our return the next morning. We marked the spot where he was lying to make it easier for us to find him again and assured him that we would be back. He was so grateful that he thanked us warmly in advance: 'God's sent you to me. It means I'm going to stay alive! Thank you, lads!'

We kept our word and went back for him, only to find that he had died during the night.

ii

During periods of intense fighting, we scouts got less rest than anyone, since it was all the more important for headquarters to know what the enemy was up to. One of our main sources of information was German soldiers whom we took prisoner in order to interrogate them.

Kidnapping an armed man alive from a battlefield is a complex business. The prospective prisoner has to be followed for a long time and tracked down like a wild animal. No wonder scouts are sometimes likened to wolves.

When wolves go out hunting, they track and pick out a weak victim that has either got separated from its herd or strayed out of its leader's line of vision. In exactly the same way, scouts go after sentries who are off their guard or soldiers who have become separated from their comrades.

As soon as our division reached the Stalingrad front, we received an order from headquarters to take a prisoner for interrogation.

On our first sortie we failed to find a suitable target. The same went for our second and third attempts. So the search dragged on. Reconnoitring becomes much more complex during a fierce battle: both sides intensify vigilance which is already strong. During night operations we would come under machine-gun fire in almost any direction we went in, because there were so many gun emplacements on the enemy line. Regrettably, there were cases when our reconnaissance men had to leave behind wounded comrades to be captured by the enemy.

As our platoon had so far failed to take a prisoner, it had to keep going out on missions every night. After each failure our commander would report back to headquarters, have to listen to their reprimands, and be given yet another mission, before returning to us in a foul mood. You could tell what he had just been through without him needing to say anything. The whole platoon's reputation was tarnished every time it returned empty-handed.

We finally struck lucky on the seventh night. Our *modus operandi* was to split into three groups of five, with one responsible for taking the prisoner and the other two supporting the first. After accomplishing their mission, the first group and the prisoner would go slightly ahead, while the two others followed on either side as back-up.

So it was this time. Under cover of darkness we crept right up to enemy positions, assessed the situation, and lay down to await our opportunity. About twenty metres behind the enemy front line we singled out an isolated trench from which a German soldier was sporadically firing flares, lighting up the surrounding area. Random but fairly regular bursts of machine-gunfire were coming from the trenches slightly further back, as the sentries kept close guard over the men asleep in the trenches.

Our platoon commander was leading the first group, 'Best target is the flare man,' he whispered. 'We've got no other option and we won't get another either. Every time he launches a flare, he stands still afterwards and doesn't look round: we'll use this to our advantage.'

The problem was that with our target's flares lighting up the bare, flat strip of steppe in front of him, we could only move in the brief interval of darkness between each of them being fired. On top of that, we had to wait for the nearest sentry to turn and start marching in the other direction.

That night the platoon commander included me in his assault group of five. Among the others was my countryman from the Ulansk region of the Eastern Kazakhstan district, Kabyl Turarov. We must have been picked because of our thin, small frames made it easier for us to crawl swiftly and unnoticed across the empty steppe. Our commander now ordered us to make our way over to the two back-up groups and inform them that we were going to take the flare man, so that they could move close enough to be able to make to the main group out in the dark. Then, if the alarm was raised, they could pin the enemy down with cross fire from either side, enabling the main group to get away with its prisoner.

After we had made it across to the other groups and back again in the brief intervals of darkness between the flashes of light from the flares, our commander ordered us to cover him and the two lads with him. Then they darted forward. We could only just see them jump down into the flare man's trench. There was silence. Not a sound. We stared into the darkness and waited. Time seemed to stop. Eventually the three captors and their prisoner crawled past us. It all happened so quickly that the Germans did not even notice the longer than usual interval between flares. The prisoner had been taken noiselessly, without a weapon being fired.

We had, according to the experienced men in our platoon, had a fairly easy time of it, and got off lightly in taking a prisoner without casualties.

But during fierce battles, the situation at the front changes not just daily but hourly, and we had hardly taken our first prisoner for interrogation when the enemy sent its reserves into operation and changed its numerical strength and its troops' positions. Our headquarters then needed information about all these changes, and another order came through for a prisoner to be taken.

We usually received orders of this kind in the second half of the day. Then the essential equipment would be got ready, and the group selected to execute the operation would sit down to discuss their plan.

'We're going to get knackered again tracking one down,' somebody would say.

'Well, they're not going to dangle one on a piece of string for us, are they? Damn them! There'll be holes in our trousers and our shirts from all the crawling we'll have to do!' another scout would reply.

'God knows how many of our own prisoners we'll give away in exchange for one of theirs.'

'Stop being so daft. If you're in reconnaissance, that means you have to take prisoners. If you don't like it, you can ask to be moved to the gunners on the front line.'

At this point the wrangling usually ended and the men started good-humouredly recalling previous missions. The banter went on until it was time to set off: it was a good way of trying to keep people's minds off what lay ahead. One scout was teased because he had to go rushing off to relieve himself whenever the order came through to take a prisoner; so was anyone who automatically ducked his head every time they heard a bullet whistle overhead. Those who had been at the front for a long time never did so: they knew that the bullet had already missed them by the time they heard it.

You can get used to anything, even being constantly in mortal danger. Sometimes during night-time reconnaissance missions, when the Germans suspected we were somewhere nearby, they would literally spray the area in front of their trenches with bullets. There was only one thing to do in a situation like that, and that was lie prone or stand stock still; and it was not unknown, while we lay there conscious that the slightest movement could give away our position, for somebody to fall fast asleep and start snoring. Fatigue could pose a real threat to people's lives

After clarifying all the details of the operation and having a good laugh as usual, our reconnaissance group set off on its new mission. We had been crawling through no man's land for some time when we noticed the outline of a man walking towards us from the enemy positions.

'It's either a spy or an enemy soldier who's lost his way. Let's take him,' ordered our commander.

We quickly formed a semi-circle round the man without him noticing and moved towards him. When he was surrounded, the commander called out, 'Hande hoch!' ('Hands up!').

The man started slightly and halted: he was so startled that he did not even raise his arms. He turned out to be a young officer who had got disoriented in the dark.

He spoke good Russian, and told us that he was a true Aryan

and Nazi Party activist, and a strong supporter of Fascism. While we were walking back to headquarters that long autumn night, stopping every now and then, we asked him about the Germans' reasons for attacking our country, and their intentions.

He fired back replies to all our questions: 'You're going to kill me, but your days are numbered. Very soon the German Army will take Stalingrad. Then it will be Moscow's turn to fall. Germany will be victorious, whatever happens.'

Of course, I knew that he was an enemy and I hated him just as I hated Fascism, but I couldn't help being impressed by his loyalty to his ideals. Still, the information that our headquarters got from him must have been highly valuable, because our commander was specially congratulated for capturing him.

One night my friend Ivanov and another man from our platoon, originally from Odessa, failed to return from reconnaissance. The other men accompanying them were not sure when they had lost contact with them; they also confirmed that there had been no exchange of fire with the enemy. They had spent a long time lying near the enemy front line, reconnoitring their weapon emplacements, and then returned safely to base, only to discover that these two were missing. A search party organised at once, but failed to find them; and though we kept on waiting for them to return, they never turned up.

Their disappearance caused a lot of speculation. Some of the original group came to the conclusion that the men had hidden themselves, waited for their comrades to go back, and then hurried over to enemy lines and given themselves up. The division's security section carried out a lengthy inquiry into the case, and the platoon commander also got into trouble over it. As Ivanov's trainee, I was questioned by security officers on several occasions.

'What was Ivanov like as a person?' I was asked, 'What did he say about the enemy and the war? Who was he friendly with? Did he say anything about surrendering to the German Fascists?'

The inquiry's conclusion was that the two men from the platoon had given themselves up; and there is no point hiding the fact that while millions of true patriots shed blood for their country and people, there were a certain number of soldiers who committed high treason.

Our platoon commander, Junior Lieutenant Smirnov, was the same age as me. He had only just finished secondary school when the German army occupied the district around Smolensk that he was living in, whereupon he joined a partisan brigade and went on fighting the occupying forces until February 1942, when the Red Army recaptured that part of the country and he was able to join the regular army. He lived, slept and ate together with his men and was always an inspirational leader, while the experience he had gained as a partisan obviously stood him in good stead. When, as a commanding officer, he was occasionally given a packet of cigarettes, he would share them with his men and take a roll-up made from really rough tobacco off one of them in exchange. We respected him deeply.

Unfortunately, we lost him as our commander when – because of the desperate shortage of men to defend the front line – he was put in charge of an infantry company. Two-thirds of our reconnaissance platoon were transferred with him, including my four countrymen who had travelled with me to the front from Semipalatinsk. Reluctant to part with them, I asked Lieutenant Smirnov to take me to the front line as well.

'Oh, Shayakhmetov!' he retorted. 'And I took you for a clever lad! How long do you reckon you'll be with your countrymen at the front line? A couple of days at most. If not today, then tomorrow, someone is sure to get hit by an enemy bullet. If they're lucky, they'll be wounded and sent off to hospital; if they're not, they get killed and taken off by the burial brigade.'

I discovered how right Smirnov was the very next evening, when I heard that one of my countryman who had been transferred to the infantry company the previous day had already been wounded. The next day another countryman, Bigalii Tokburin, arrived at our platoon's position with a leg wound so bad that I could not believe he had managed to walk the three kilometres or so to our platoon from the front line. I carried him to the medical battalion and handed him over to the doctors there. We were never to see each other again.

Not long afterwards, headquarters decided to send a group of scouts into the enemy rear to establish their position and numerical strength, and also to measure the height and angle of the railway embankment to the west of Stalingrad. As a preliminary, a thorough reconnaissance was needed of the sector where our team was going to cross the enemy line of defence. A week was set aside for the task, with round-the-clock observation to establish the least dangerous crossing point. I and a Siberian from Chita, by the name of Kostya Nikulin, were put in charge both of the reconnaissance and of the group carrying out the mission.

We settled down in a pillbox on our regiment's front line and began observing the enemy. We were to mark all our observations on a map: the enemy's machine-gun and anti-artillery emplacements, military equipment, the positioning of the trenches and pillboxes, any movement of troops and transport, and so on.

One day our platoon, now reduced to only a dozen men, received orders to carry out reconnaissance in force. Our small group was to create the impression of a massed offensive. Under cover of darkness, we were to spread out as far as possible along the front line, firing and making a commotion and doing everything possible to give the impression of a serious offensive with impressive forces. The object was to get the enemy to respond and give itself away by engaging all its units.

Unfortunately, there were so few of us on this mission that we found it impossible to make a lot of noise or create a realistic impression of a large battle. We not only failed to reveal the enemy's numerical strength, but also lost half our platoon in the attempt.

At war, of course, you are constantly in danger, but there are moments when you can consider yourself particularly fortunate to have stayed alive. I had four such moments at the front.

The first happened as follows. One day I went to fetch some water from the one and only spring in the area, about three kilometres from our line of trenches. There was a large group of men there when I arrived. I was in a hurry, and so I quickly filled up all my containers before anyone else and set off again. No sooner was I a safe distance away, than the German guns opened up and all the men still at the spring were killed.

Another time my guardian angel saved me was during a night mission to capture a prisoner for interrogation. All of a sudden one of our lads gave our position away with a careless movement, and the enemy started firing on us. We scattered at once, but the fire was so concentrated that we had to fall flat on our faces and lie still. German bullets kept raining upon us within centimetres of our heads and splattering earth all over our faces – but miraculously, not one of us was hit.

The third time was when some German shells exploded very nearby and a splinter flew into the deep trench my comrade and I were hiding in. Flying past my forehead like a hot wind, it made a hole in the helmet lying next to me. I had escaped death by millimetres.

My fourth lucky escape, oddly enough, was when I was wounded by a sniper's bullet.

iii

On the night of 26 September, with a short, sharp attack, our regiment succeeded in pushing back the enemy some 80 to 100 metres and capturing the floor of a deep gully. Unfortunately, our forward troops then found themselves cut off from our own trenches. The Germans maintained such heavy fire that no one could get through to deliver ammunition or food.

The following morning, towards noon, the captain in charge of reconnaissance arrived at our observation post on what had been the front line the day before, and ordered us to try and find an inconspicuous, safe route to the gully. Three of us were sent on the mission. Between 200 and 300 metres from our trenches there was a large mound of earth in no man's land that had been churned up by a bomb. One by one, the three of us managed to get over to it and began trying to identify a possible route through, but without success.

Just then, we spotted one of our men, wounded and lying hidden in long steppe grass. He was so weak that he was unable to move himself, but he managed to catch our attention by waving his forage cap on the end of his bayonet so we could just see it in the grass. We decided that the best way to rescue him was to put him on a groundsheet and drag him back to our lines; but he proved to be too badly wounded to cope with such treatment, so we had to stand up and carry him at a run. Much to the amazement of everyone on our side, the Germans did not fire at us at all.

The head of reconnaissance, after reprimanding us for this rash behaviour, then ordered us to attempt our mission again. This time we had to crawl all the way over to the right flank. First, we had to make it to a crippled German tank in no man's land. On past occasions we had been able to run to it at full height, get underneath or inside it, and observe the enemy from there; but this time, mindful of the captain's warning, we crawled to it.

The three of us crawled over in single file with Kostya Nikulin in front. A German sniper must have spotted him at once, because he started firing at him. The bullets flew so close to him that clods of earth kept flying up and spraying him like rain. I was terribly anxious about him: I genuinely thought he was not going to make it.

All of a sudden I felt as though someone had struck me an agonising blow across the spine with a thick club. I turned my head and looked over my shoulder. There was nobody there. Then I felt something trickling down my back and realised I had been hit by an enemy sniper's bullet.

A wounded man is always likely to be fired at again by a sniper. I knew I had to lie quite still or get out of his sights as fast as possible. I decided to rush to the nearest trench – but my legs had gone numb. I tried to drag myself along by clutching onto a few sparse stems of wormwood, but this meant lifting my face toward the sniper and giving him a chance to hit me in the forehead. So I froze to the spot instead.

The third man in our group, who had managed to jump into one of the nearest trenches, carefully stretched his rifle towards me, not daring to show himself. I just managed to seize hold of the end of his rifle and let him pull me into the trench. My mates rushed over to me and bandaged my wound. It was only then that it sunk in exactly what had happened and how. The German sniper had spotted Nikulin and taken aim at him; he had not seen me crawling after Nikulin, but unfortunately a glint of sunlight had reflected off the lenses of the binoculars attached to my belt, and he had fired at that. The bullet passed right through me, from left to right, just below my binoculars, ripping my leather belt as it flew out.

When I had been bandaged up, I glanced at my watch and saw that the hands showed 15:00 hours exactly. I was officially categorised as a casualty from that moment on.

Just then some of my friends from the platoon who were about to go out reconnoitring came running up, put me on a groundsheet, and started carrying me to safety. Another exchange of fire started, and they were forced to put me down several times and take shelter from the enemy bullets.

There was no need for them to risk their lives for me: there were orderlies specially detailed to pick up the wounded and take them to the medical battalion. But my comrades did not have much faith in them, and decided to do the job themselves.

The news of my injury spread fast, and when they heard about it, my countrymen in other companies came over to say their goodbyes to me. My loyal friend Nikulin found a horse and cart at the front line and drove me the four or five kilometres to the medical battalion in the rear. Knowing how many wounded men had lain for long periods of time on the battlefield without anyone to help them, I was immensely thankful to the comrades who saved me, and this sense of gratitude lives on in the heart of the soldier Shayakhmetov to this day.

Chapter Twenty-Eight

Casualty

For any soldier injured at the front, treatment involved a long, hard journey from the front line to a military hospital in the back of army trucks or goods wagons lined with straw. Only someone who has experienced it himself can fully appreciate what I am talking about.

First, casualties were examined and their wounds dressed by middle-ranking medical staff. They were then issued with a so-called 'injury card', with their name and a printed list of all the different types of possible injuries, on which the relevant details underlined. Mine read: 'Lacerated, through bullet wound in lumbar region with stomach injury.' According to this diagnosis, the bullet had done quite a lot of damage to my internal organs before it flew out the other side of my body. Front-line soldiers considered stomach wounds to be among the most severe, and particularly feared them.

Such an injury required urgent surgical intervention: most casualties survived a couple of days at most, and never made it to hospital. However, even though I was aware of the danger I was in, for some reason or other I did not feel in the least anxious, and just accepted the way things were. A military ambulance arrived at around ten in the evening and I was dispatched to the rear. I could not tell how long the journey took or where we travelled to, because my temperature shot up and I lost consciousness. Then I became delirious, and was brought round every now and then by the sound of my own voice. I only remember hearing someone moan every now and then. A full moon kept flickering outside the ambulance's window.

It turned out that there were two of us on board. We eventually arrived somewhere during the night and were carried into a large canvas tent, and put down on tables in front of people dressed in white; then we had our uniforms removed. Without saying a word to me, the people in the white overalls began examining my wound and conferring with each other. One of them started trimming the lacerated skin around my wound with surgical scissors. I must have lost consciousness from the pain. I was brought to my senses by someone exclaiming in a loud and angry voice, 'Why haven't you put a shirt on him – he's fainted!'

Then I was carried off to a nearby ward full of other wounded men, also on stretchers. We were in the divisional field hospital.

Next morning we were fed and then loaded onto a truck towards midday. Most of the floor space was taken up with those of us on stretchers; the walking wounded occupied the gaps in between.

It is impossible to describe what people suffered on this journey. There were men with shattered bones and broken limbs in splints but no plaster casts; men with bandaged heads, cracked skulls and broken jaws. For anyone with injuries like these, even the slightest tremor caused agonising pain – and here we were in the back of a truck, being jolted about and shaken up and down over bumps and ruts. The weakest and most seriously injured among us simply lost consciousness, while the rest kept moaning and calling out, swearing and cursing the driver as if he was to blame for the war, their wounds, the bad road and everything else.

'Do you reckon you're carrying logs, you bloody idiot?' someone snapped – and this was mild compared to other comments.

We finally arrived at the military hospital, which was located in a small village. Here we were unloaded into an open field where a doctor quickly looked at our injury cards, graded us by them, and said where we were to be taken to. When he came to me he said without hesitation, 'Take him to the school!'

Two orderlies picked up my stretcher and carried me over to a small building. It took a while to find a space for me in the two rooms inside. All the other men there were serious casualties and quite a few were delirious. The building echoed with groans, sighs and screams. All night long people kept muttering deliriously and calling out for their loved ones or shouting orders such as, 'Attack! Follow me!' 'For the Motherland!' 'For Stalin!'

At dawn it became quieter as people lost consciousness. In the morning the orderlies carried out five or six corpses. There was more space inside then.

By about nine o'clock I needed to go to the toilet. It was the first time in the three days since I had been wounded. A nurse came up with a vessel and helped me.

Shortly afterwards a military doctor came to the school, walked round the depleted rows of men and eventually came up to me. The nurse said, 'This man has just passed motion,' to which the doctor replied, 'Take him out of here and put him with the general group.'

This group consisted of two long rows of seriously injured men lying on stretchers in the open air. I was put down among them. It was only now I understood that the doctor who had sent me to the school the evening before had decided that I was a goner and would not last the night, for the school was where the mortally injured were sent. The fact that I had been able to relieve myself meant that my alimentary canal and bowels were unharmed, which was why I had now been put with those who might just be lucky enough to pull through. Although the sniper's bullet had certainly done a lot of damage to my insides, it had at least not killed me outright. The fact that it had passed through my body like that was, to my mind, my fourth lucky break at the front.

We lay on our stretchers in the open air for the whole day of 29 September. By the evening we were feeling really cold. The field hospital's management ordered straw to be brought over and packed around us for warmth. It was thanks to this that we made it through the night.

Next morning after breakfast we were loaded onto a truck again and made to endure another agonising journey to a nearby village.

We again spent the rest of the day in the open air on our stretchers and in the evening were put on a goods train. All the seriously injured were lowered onto the wagons' straw-lined floors. The men who could walk acted as orderlies, handing round water and fetching the one and only nurse on board.

The train moved incredibly slowly and kept stopping in stations or in open countryside to let troop trains heading for the front pass, or to wait for shelled sections of the track to be repaired. We all had to put up with stifling heat during the day and cold at night, not to mention watching our comrades with inflamed or infected wounds writhing in pain. Some wounds became infected with maggots; quite a few men had no bowel control. There was an almost overpowering stench from the infected wounds, excrement, sweat and unwashed bodies. We were thirsty, too, and to make matters even worse, every so often we came under enemy fire.

Everyone at the front knew who was on board the trains going back to the rear. Even so, the Germans persistently shelled our train, trying to finish off our injured men. One night there was a particularly terrifying enemy air raid. Recognising our train by the colour of its steam engine, enemy pilots began targeting us. Amidst the commotion, a rumour spread through the dark wagons that the train driver had got off the train and run away. What he had actually done was uncouple the engine and set off in it to draw fire onto himself and save the injured in the wagons. However, the Germans still had us in their sights and went on shelling us. Fortunately, all the shells narrowly missed, but the train shook so violently from the blasts that it was very nearly overturned. All we could do was wrap our coats around our heads and wait. Thank God we were spared.

I was surprised and intrigued by the reception we got in the villages and stations we passed through during those two days. Sometimes we had only just drawn into a station when local people, mostly women and children, started peering through the open wagon doors. Some of them were looking merely out of curiosity; others offered us bundles of food and buckets full of tomatoes and cucumbers, murmuring apologetically, 'Here you are, my dears, eat this. Forgive us, we haven't got anything else.'

A third, less scrupulous group, knowing that we would not have any money on us, offered to take our clothing in exchange for food. Men sold their coats, shirts, boots and even the underwear they had on them; some heartless profiteers would even buy single boots from men who had lost one of their legs at the front.

ii

The journey in the straw-lined wagon seemed never-ending. Eventually, however, on the morning of 1 October, we pulled into the town of Balashov. We were immediately carried to vehicles and driven to a school that had been turned into a military hospital. There were so many of us non-walking injured that the huge schoolyard was entirely taken up with our stretchers. After being taken off the train at nine in the morning, I did not reach the operating theatre until midnight, and some other seriously injured did not get seen until two in the morning.

I cannot express what it felt like to spend that cold autumn day in the open air, injured and exhausted. It was no easier for the hospital's medical teams carrying out complex, tiring operations, one after the other, for eighteen hours non-stop. I still marvel at the tremendous patience and courage shown by soldiers and doctors alike.

After living in cold, damp trenches, it felt amazingly good to be washed in warm water, dressed in clean underwear and put in a soft bed. I slept deeply for what felt like days on end.

The Balashov hospital was a kind of half-way house. After a short course of treatment, patients were graded according to the type and extent of injuries they had suffered and sent off to appropriate hospitals. This was done as quickly as possible to vacate their beds for the next group of casualties from the front.

I was categorised as seriously injured. On 11 October, I set off on an eastbound hospital train that had specially been laid on for troops with wounds like mine. Although I was considered to have serious injuries, I was in far better shape than, say, others with amputated or shattered limbs or chest injuries. Although the sniper's bullet had not splintered any of my bones as it flew from left to right through the small of my back, it had left me unable to walk unaided. Every time a doctor examined my injury, he or she would comment on the lucky escape I had had. They all said that had the bullet passed just half a centimetre higher, it would have hit my spinal cord, and I would have been permanently paralysed from the waist downwards. Half a centimetre lower, and it would have hit my guts, which in front-line conditions would have meant death in a couple of days. A centimetre higher, and both my kidneys would have been hit, and I would never have made it to hospital.

iii

The hospital train was made up of ordinary passenger carriages. Conditions on board were more or less bearable: the berths were equipped with bedding and there was a nurse to every carriage. The non-walking patients were allocated the first and second berths, while those who could get about independently were given the top ones. It took ten days for the train to travel from the banks of the Volga to Novosibirsk; but when we got there, the hospital had no beds for us. So then we were taken even further into Siberia. Twenty-four hours later we arrived at the town of Stalinsk (today's Novokuznetsk).

We were greeted by deep frost and snow. The staff of the town's base hospital took charge of us in a manner we had never encountered before. While still on board the train, we had all our clothes taken off us and were wrapped in specially designed warm, quilted dressing gowns; we were carried out of the carriages in the orderlies' arms, driven to the hospital, washed, dressed in clean underwear, and only then taken to the wards. The staff took away the clothes we had been travelling in to prevent the spread of infections and epidemics, fearing first and foremost that we might bring lice into the hospital.

Soviet military hospitals had an impressive record of nursing the wounded back to health: it is estimated that 70 per cent of patients were able to return to active service, greatly contributing to the outcome of the war. During the two months our group of patients was in the hospital, I cannot remember anyone complaining about the treatment we received.

Every day we discussed the situation at the front. After yet another setback for our troops, we would all go around with glum expressions and after every victory, no matter how small, we used to celebrate wildly like children. We were indescribably happy when the news came through that the German troops had been encircled at Stalingrad: we kept congratulating one another, hugging and kissing and shouting, 'Hurrah!' We recalled the promise Stalin had made two weeks before: 'There will be a party in our street, too.' It was a wonderful cause for celebration.

The second most popular topic of conversation was the future and what it had in store for us. How long were our injuries going to take to heal? Would we ever feel completely back to normal? Where would we go after hospital – home or back to the army? We talked, too, about our families back home, and would celebrate good news together, particularly that from girlfriends, fiancées and wives. But once in a while a man would hear that his fiancée had broken off their engagement or his wife had found someone else, and then the rest of us would do all we could to cheer him up.

There were some patients who were longing to get any news whatsoever from their homes. All of them were from the west of the Russian Federation – Ukraine, Belorussia and other territories occupied by the Germans. 'If only I could get a couple of words from home!' they would sigh. 'Just anything, to know someone there is still alive!' – and anyone listening would understand how they felt, and say nothing for a long while.

iv

By the time I reached Stalinsk, the wound at the bullet's entry point in my left side had already healed over, but the wound at the exit point in my right side was still open. Thanks to all the efforts of the hospital doctors, it gradually began to heal over. My injured back was still causing me problems, though, when I moved about: I could not bend over, straighten up properly or turn sideways. But the hospital's medical commission declared me fit enough for non-combatant service, so I was sent for three months to a paramilitary detachment in charge of security at the Kuznetsk metallurgical works, which had been converted into a munitions factory.

The detachment was run along army lines, but included civilians who could do as they pleased outside working hours. The work was badly paid, however, which was why recovering soldiers were needed to make up the numbers.

The conditions for convalescents like me were really tough. We had sixteen hours of watch duty, on a four-hour roster, followed by 24 hours off. We found the Siberian winters almost unbearable – the biting frost used to go straight through our light army overcoats and hospital-issued puttees and boots – and we also had to put up with the severely limited food rations allocated to the civilian population. Some of us began wistfully remembering life at the front, even though, of course, it was far worse there.

One of the first gigantic Soviet projects of its kind, the works we were guarding occupied an area nearly half the size of the town that had grown up around it. Many different types of arms were manufactured on its vast shop floors including bombs, shells, mines, cartridges and rifles. The entire place was classified as top-secret and under martial law. A special pass system operated throughout, even between sections sharing the same shop floor, and workers were not meant to know about the production of departments other than their own. Such stringent working conditions were essential, since there had been more than one break-in attempt, probably by foreign spies.

Apart from the harsh conditions, what I remember most about those three months 'recuperating' was the cultural side of life. After sixteen hours of tiring military service every day in a reserve regiment, and then round-the-clock front-line service under enemy fire when you never even had a minute to yourself, I at last managed to make up for lost time during my stay in Stalinsk. The libraries at the hospital and in the town and metallurgical works were much better than the ones back home, and I tried to read as much as possible. The hospital librarian had drawn my attention to the considerable number of books by local Siberian writers; I was amazed to discover that not all publishing houses were based in Moscow and that a local one in Novosibirsk produced books by superb local authors who nobody in other parts of the country had even heard of. From these I learnt a lot about the history of Siberia and its people's daily lives. It was also at this time that I had my first opportunity to hear live opera, and attend theatre productions by first-rate troupes of actors, evacuated from Leningrad and Moscow.

v

My period of recuperation came to an end in March 1943, when another medical commission passed me fit for combatant service. A detachment was being organised at the time of men like myself and local conscripts, and we soon found ourselves travelling by train back to Novosibirsk. There we were met by a military doctor's assistant and a sergeant-major, who introduced themselves in a relaxed, informal sort of way as border-troop representatives. They had, apparently, been waiting for our detachment from Novosibirsk for several days and would be taking us to Tadjikistan. They spoke enthusiastically about the advantages of being posted there and the importance of 'the second front in the country's rear'.

On our journey from Siberia to the heart of Central Asia, we discovered just how much life had changed for civilians since the outbreak of war. The lack of trains frequently caused congestion at railway stations, where crowds of passengers would gather and wait for several days. To control such massive build-ups of people, or simply to get rid of them, the management at the larger stations sometimes used to lay on extra trains with different types of carriages, which for some reason they always called 'train number five-o-one'. It was a type of train which became popularly known as 'number five-o-fun': it never appeared on any timetable, and if there was no steam engine available or congestion on the line, it would stand at a station for hours, if not days. It was on such a 'fun' train that our detachment ended up travelling. After leaving Novosibirsk on 20 March bound for Stalinabad (now Dushanbe), the capital of Tadjikistan, we travelled in such unimaginably overcrowded conditions that we reached Tashkent in Uzbekistan only on 3 April, nearly fifteen days late.

Our newly-formed detachment – known, for no apparent reason, as the 45th – travelled in the same carriage as civilians, most of whom were women with incredibly large, bulging bundles. They kept haggling and bartering with each other, trying to sell whatever they had – the reason being that the cost of living had rocketed, money was losing its value, and most of them were penniless. There was bustling trade during the stops at stations; then, once the train got underway again, passengers would go on bartering among themselves. The new recruits in our detachments also got enticed into this lively trading.

Every soldier was provided with a daily food allowance in the form of a dry ration or a hot three-course meal in the military canteens at the larger stations, but this was naturally not enough to fill the stomach of a healthy adult male. The men in troop trains heading for the front were forced to put up with these conditions, as they had nothing to barter or sell; we, however, had been told that when we were enrolled as border guards we would receive new uniforms, and soon men started stripping off and selling off their army clothing. There were plenty of buyers, for most civilians' clothes were by then worn out or very threadbare. A soldier usually exchanged his army overcoat for a shabby old jumper and his army boots for old railwaymen's boots, as well as a mutually agreed sum of money which, if he was sensible, he would spend on food. However, some of the older soldiers were heavy drinkers and gamblers, and that is where their money went. It had been known for some men to arrive at their final destination in their underwear and bare feet.

'We're going somewhere warm,' they argued. 'We won't need winter clothing there;' or, 'Who needs bloodstained army clothing from a hospital? Even if we get punished, we can't get sent anywhere worse than the front.'

Of course, not everyone behaved like this, but I remember how upset the military doctor's assistant in charge of our detachment was when he saw the state some of his men were in.

'How am I going to take you to the division half-dressed like that?' he exclaimed. 'How am I going to get you across the whole of town with people looking at you?'

Luckily for him, the train arrived in Stalinabad in the middle of the night, so he was able to get his division taken straight to a steam bathhouse without anyone seeing us.

There was something else new about passenger trains during the war. Before they drew into their final destination, all the passengers on board were required to wash themselves and all the train carriages were disinfected. On ours, the passengers in each carriage took it in turns to take showers while their clothes were put in a disinfection chamber and all their belongings were sprayed with some sort of fluid. It took ten hours for everyone on board to undergo the treatment; only after it had all been completed, was the train allowed to enter the city.

Passengers' state of health was also closely monitored at stations. If someone was found to be sick and there was any doubt over the nature of his illness, the carriage he was in was uncoupled from the train until a final diagnosis was made, thus delaying all the passengers with him. If the sickness turned out to be infectious, they were kept there until the necessary measures had been taken to contain it. Something like this happened with our carriage between Tashkent and Stalinabad: when a passenger fell ill, it was uncoupled from the train in Bukhara and stood there for 24 hours until the next train arrived, although the illness was later diagnosed as non-infectious.

Our visit to the bathhouse on arrival at Stalinabad was also, I believe, a precaution of this kind. Before we went into it, all our remaining clothes were taken off us, put in a pile in the courtyard outside, and set alight with kerosene. Then we were then given our new uniforms.

Chapter Twenty-Nine

On the Border

We were now enrolled as border guards in the 45th Cavalry Regiment, and it finally dawned on us that this was why our detachment had been given its enigmatic number.

The regiment turned out to be nowhere near full strength, so desperate was the need for men at the front line. Half the bunks in the regimental barracks were empty, and there was only one horse for every three cavalrymen. Our training was conducted in the usual routine way, and along with all the young recruits, we experienced combatants were taught ceremonial steps, and made to study the components of a rifle. The instruction given on horses was also laughable: men who had spent their entire lives working with them had to listen to lectures on the structure of a horse and be taught the names of different parts of its body. The practical training sessions consisted only of leading the animals to drink water, cleaning them and mucking out their stalls twice a day. None of the men actually got on a horse. We spent about two weeks being trained in this way, while no mention at all was made of what border guards were supposed to do.

One day, our regimental command received an order from above concerning a band of locals who had allegedly fled to the Pamir Mountains on the border with Afghanistan to avoid being called up to the army. The order was that these 'deserters' were to be eliminated. Since unquestioning obedience was the order of the day in the army, a detachment of 40 men was hurriedly put together and sent in two trucks to the mountains.

Once we got out of the town, beautiful southern countryside in spring bloom opened up before us in a kaleidoscope of flowers. One mountain would be covered in red tulips, another nearby in yellow ones. It all seemed quite wondrous.

Our journey took us through a series of *kishlaks* (villages) and the towns of Komsomolobad, Ordjonikidzebad, Kurgan-Tiube and Kulyab. Our enjoyment of the view was soon spoiled by the extreme discomfort of travelling along terrible roads. About 150 kilometres from Stalinabad the road gradually petered out; and when we started to climb up into the mountains, we were driving along donkey tracks. There were quite a few treacherous spots along the way: steep precipices and inclines, and a slippery road covered with ice from the melted mountain snow. The road was often so dangerous that we had to get out and walk. The driver would go on ahead of us shouting, 'If I'm still alive, I'll wait for you on the other side of the mountain. If something happens to me, remember me well!' It took us over twenty hours to cover less than 300 kilometres.

Our orders were to keep the mission secret from the local population. After saying goodbye to our transport, we marched into the mountains under cover of night, and spent the next two days checking a large area without coming across a single living soul. We did not find any trace whatsoever of the 'deserters' in the places they were likely to have gathered. It looked as of the reports about them had been wrong, but no one in command had dared take any chances – as a result of which we found ourselves stuck in the middle of nowhere.

We then had to walk to the nearest border post, located in a small *kishlak* that turned out to be the regional centre of the

Shurobad (Soviet) region of the Kulyab district. They apparently had been told to expect us, and although it was not strictly time for us to eat, they invited us to have a meal.

We old hands who were used to all our food being strictly rationed, and receiving 200 grams of bread per meal and a portion of porridge, simply could not believe our eyes when we saw the piles of sliced bread waiting for us on the army canteen's table. When the chef offered us seconds of both courses, some of us were so surprised we could not speak. Then, coming to his senses, someone exclaimed, 'Now this is what I call Communism!' We had got used to the idea that only front-line troops could expect a genuinely filling meal; but it seemed that border guards didn't do badly either.

ii

The terrible state of the roads and extreme shortage of vehicles evidently made it impractical to transport our 40-strong detachment over 300 kilometres back to base. There was also a serious shortage of guards on the border, so our regimental command decided to leave us there, divide us up and send us to the five different posts. I ended up at post Number Two, known as Bagarak, in the same Surobad region of the Kulyab district. Incidentally, these names figured repeatedly in the reports on the armed conflicts in Tadjikistan in the 1990s.

So there I was, a totally green border guard with no idea of the regulations and procedures involved. Luckily, it turned out to be much easier than other types of army service. It was a relief not to have to march in formation any more or be woken in the morning by the reveille and have to scramble to our feet; nor were there any mock battle alarms during the night. The unrationed food also cheered us up immensely.

All this did not mean, however, that life was relaxed. We had a strict daily schedule with every hour accounted for. We were responsible for maintaining, servicing and repairing all the equipment, and looking after the horses we had each been allocated. Between all these duties we were also finally given special training as border personnel. And then on top of that, there was our main work of guard duty for eight hours every day.

Guarding the border in a secret detail was considered the most difficult duty at the post. In the evenings, under cover of darkness, a pair of us in camouflage would go to a designated place on the border and have to lie low there for at least six hours. It was really hard not to fall asleep, especially just before sunrise. We were not allowed even to doze, in case an intruder crossed over – or, indeed, took us unawares and captured or killed us. And then there was the law to think about: if you did fall asleep at the border, you could be hauled up before a court martial.

The horses took as much looking after as small children. Our commanding officer would run his white handkerchief over their coats to check how clean they were, and it always had to remain spotless. The two-hour training sessions in which we were taught cavalry combat techniques were really tough – much more exhausting than a whole day of infantry exercises. They were particularly hard going for the complete novices. By May the border guards from Siberia, the Altai region and the European part of the USSR were already struggling with the tremendous heat.

During our service in 1943-44, relations between Afghanistan and the USSR were neighbourly. The governments of the two countries had come to an agreement whereby disputes were dealt with on the spot by border officials. Most incidents involved the local residents' livestock accidentally wandering across and sometimes roaming deep inside the other country. Stallions and bulls were particularly troublesome. As good neighbours, each side would return the livestock at the other's request. Because there were no telecommunications to link us, a white flag was raised to signal a request for a meeting. The other side would then show its agreement by raising another white flag. Then the officials initiating the meeting would have the right to cross the border in the place where the flag belonging to the other side had been raised.

I particularly remember one such meeting. During a visit to our post, the Afghan negotiators would usually leave their entourage with us while our senior officers took them down to the *kishlak* for official talks followed by a meal; the rank and file were supposed to stay put under our supervision. But on this occasion, when it was time for us to feed our guests, we discovered that one of the Afghan soldiers had vanished. Our sentry was completely baffled and had no idea what had happened to the man. The disappearance of any member of a delegation, however junior, was enough to cause a serious international row, so the post was put on alert and a search began for the missing man. He was found almost at once in a deep gully nearby, rummaging through a rubbish dump: he had already picked out some old horseshoes, lengths of wire and rusty old nails. In reply to our men's astonished questions, he explained that they did not have any iron in his country and there was such a lot of it lying there in the dump. His booty was confiscated and he was taken back to sit with the others until their superiors returned from the talks.

Relations between the two countries may have been on a peaceful footing, but the intelligence services on both sides continued to carry out operations. The Soviet spies were particularly active. We ourselves had nothing directly to do with these operations, but whoever happened to be on night duty would be warned by the commanding officer that 'our man' would be crossing the border in their zone, so that they did not raise the alarm when they saw him.

During my three years of army service, the longest time I spent in one place was at this border post. One of the benefits was that I was able to communicate regularly with my family and friends back home, and my comrades at the front, whereas in the past I had always sent news of myself without receiving replies.

Our duties included keeping an eye on people living within 40 kilometres of the border zone. This meant visiting the *kishlak* and talking with locals and getting to know about their lives. The Tadjik villagers were simple, trusting, generous and hospitable people; in those days they were very religious and observed the canons of the Islamic faith in a strict but non-militant manner. The Pamir villagers we got to know lived in remote areas miles from what was then thought of as civilisation and were mostly illiterate.

Sometimes there was not a single person in a *kishlak* who spoke a word of Russian, which made things difficult, because although we were all obliged to know a hundred Tadjik words, they all had to do with our everyday work and were no good for ordinary conversations. Once in a while, you would come across an ex-soldier who knew a few military terms in Russian, but those did not enable him to express himself freely either. There were, however, a few Russian girls living in the *kishlak*, working mostly as doctor's assistants or schoolteachers, who had been sent there before the war and then found that it was too dangerous to return home: they now spoke fluent Tadjik. The only other Russians I came across were in the regional centre, Shurabad: they were top regional officials, and agriculturalists, medical specialists and teaching staff.

The Tadjiks all belonged to the same ethnic group; there were no representatives of other nations among them except for a very small number of Uzbek families. Like everyone else in the country, the local population lived in poverty and suffered much hardship during the war; they did not go hungry, but their standard of living fell sharply. There were not enough draught animals on the collective farms, so everything had to be done manually or with very primitive equipment: for instance, they used wooden ploughs to till the land and ordinary strips of wattle fence as harrows. Instead of using rollers to thresh the wheat, they used to drive horses across a threshing floor covered with a layer of cut corn. You can imagine what the crop yields were like and how little wheat was left for the collective farmers after the standard amount was turned over to the State.

The people went around in patched, tattered clothing; even the women, who kept their faces, arms and legs covered at all times, walked around in torn dresses and coats through which you could catch glimpses of their flesh. I heard it said that some women and girls had to stay at home during the day because they did not have any decent clothes to wear outside. The situation must have become fairly critical, as the Tadjik Government set up a special commission to study the poverty levels and come up with a solution. It was headed by a man called Kurbatov who came to the district and visited various *kishlaks*.

I was one the men chosen to escort him and the local officials accompanying him. We spent nearly a whole day with them, and I was impressed by the way in which they came up with solutions to complex problems. At the end of his tour Kurbatov asked, 'How much cotton do you need to dress an adult? To make a dress, trousers and jacket by hand?' After working out some figures in their heads, the officials agreed that four kilograms of pure cotton was needed. Sitting astride his horse, Kurbatov did some mental arithmetic and replied almost at once, 'So, in order to dress everyone, your district needs...' and he named the number of kilograms of cotton. 'Get it delivered to the district centre and transported to all the *kishlak*, and then distributed to people so that they've got clothes to wear by the spring.' Then he said his goodbyes and left. A few months later the villagers were newly dressed in homespun dresses, trousers and jackets.

My service at the post was going quite smoothly. I had the reputation of being a disciplined and hard-working soldier, and my commanding officer, Junior Lieutenant Migulya, treated me in a very decent manner. He was humane in all his dealings with his men, never raising his voice at subordinates, and showed particular respect for those who had been wounded at the front; he did not, however, tolerate slovenliness or familiarity. When he told me how he had served as a border guard in the Katon-Karagai region of Eastern Kazakhstan, I felt a special bond with him.

One day, Migulya went off to the commandant's office; by nightfall he still had not returned, although he should have done. I was on duty at the post until the next morning. Taking advantage of their officer's absence, the guards on duty started telephoning from a neighbouring post and messing around because they were feeling bored. They kept ringing at short intervals all through the night, claiming to be various commanding officers, including our own, and demanding a report on the situation in the border zone. I got so fed up of their frequent calls that I told them I would complain to the commandant's office if they rang once more.

After midnight the calls began again. The same voice, claiming to be Migulya, demanded a report on the situation at the post. I replied, 'Stop pretending to be who you're not and hang up!'

Then came the reply, 'It's me, Migulya. My horse has run off. Send me another.'

I said, 'It doesn't matter, you can walk back!'

The person on the end of the line then retorted in exasperation, 'Shayakhmetov! Have you gone mad? It's me, Migulya. Why are you being insolent? If you don't recognise my voice, call my wife to the telephone. And that's an order!'

Then I, too, got angry. 'Listen to him – he's got a wife! You've got to become a commanding officer before you can marry – then I'll call your wife. I've got to send off the duty details now. Stop messing me about and stop calling!'

After that I hung up. It was time to send off another detail on border duty, but they could only be given their orders by the commanding officer or his number two; so I went and woke Migulya's deputy. When I eventually got back to the office, he was speaking on the telephone. After he had finished, he gave me an odd look and said, 'Why did you refuse to obey the commander? And, what's more, you were rude to him on the telephone. He has ordered me to take you off duty at once. When he gets back, he'll send you to the guardhouse.'

I woke up the following morning to the sound of raucous laughter outside the barracks. I listened carefully and I could hear Migulya recounting our telephone conversation. The men around him were splitting their sides with laughter. Everyone thought it a huge joke, which was lucky because it meant I escaped detention.

In the summer of 1943, a number of places at the Moscow Institute of Foreign Languages were offered to border guards. My name was on the list of recommended candidates. The terms of admission were that I should learn Afghan and then return to the border as an interpreter.

There are times in life when lucky breaks suddenly come your way and you turn them down through a lack of understanding or sheer stupidity or God alone knows why else. I would have definitely gone to Moscow if I could have studied Chinese, because China was next to my native region; I would not have minded studying Arabic either, as there are a great many Kazakh words borrowed from Arabic. But I had no desire to learn Afghan or, indeed, spend the rest of my life in the Pamir Mountains. A Georgian comrade of mine kept trying to persuade me to go with him, telling me that once we were enrolled we could ask to be transferred to the Arabic faculty; but I refused to listen to him. Sure enough, he was allowed to study the language of his choice, while I missed a golden opportunity to go to Moscow – something I regretted for a long time afterwards.

iii

In May 1944 the joints in my arms and legs started aching. I tried to ignore the pain and kept going until the middle of summer, but my joints became swollen and increasingly painful, and I was running a constant high temperature, so in the end I had to go to the hospital attached to the commandant's office. I spent a whole month there, but the doctors failed to come up with a diagnosis. So I was transferred to the Stalinabad district hospital, where I arrived just in time, since the pain had become so excruciatingly painful that I was confined to bed and not allowed to get up for two months. It turned out that I was suffering from an acute from of brucellosis; when I was at last able to move around again with the aid of crutches, I was declared unfit for military service, and discharged from the army.

I was so delighted that I at once sent a telegram home; but the following day I realised I had been too hasty. It turned out that a border guard could only receive his dismissal documents at the border post where he was currently serving – so I ended up having to travel the 300 kilometres back to my post. It would have been hard enough even for a healthy person to hang about for a lift in vehicle going that way – of which there were very few – and then rattle about in the back of a lorry along terrible roads for over 250 kilometres, before travelling the last fifty kilometres on horseback along narrow paths through the Pamir Mountains; and since I was still on crutches, the idea filled me with horror. I applied without success to military district headquarters, asking them to waive the regulations in view of the severity of my condition, but nobody was willing to take responsibility for doing so.

Wartime laws and procedures are harsh. The 300 kilometres I had to travel seemed further to me then than a Hadj for Muslims to Mecca and Medina. After being discharged from hospital, I stayed in Stalinabad waiting for a lift for exactly a month, until 25 November. By then there had already been falls of snow in nearly all the mountain passes – and I was still in the light army shirt I had on when I arrived at hospital in the summer. The drivers of the scarce army vehicles in the border district kept refusing to give me a lift because they were afraid I might freeze on the way.

Eventually I got lucky and hitched a ride with an officer who was travelling to the post with his family to start his service at the commandant's office. He took pity on me and gave me some warm clothing, but I still caught a chill on the way and ended up once again in the hospital attached to the commandant's office for nearly a month.

When I was discharged, I found myself trapped again by lack of transport, until some district commissioners decided to visit to our commandant's office and horses had to be sent to the town of Kulyab to collect them. I decided to take one of these, even if it meant riding through thick mountain snow all the way to Kulyab. So, after saying my goodbye to all my comrades, I tied my crutches to the saddle of my horse and set off. I was lucky again in Kulyab and caught a lift to Stalinabad. Exactly fifty days after being officially dismissed from service, I arrived there bruised, frozen and exhausted.

However, all these adventures seemed trivial compared to the agonising ordeals that began the moment I set foot on home territory at Zhangiz-Tobe station. It took me fifteen days to travel the 200 kilometres home, and I want to describe this terrible journey in detail so that my grandchildren can fully appreciate the hardships our aul and villages had to put up with during the war, and how difficult it was for crippled soldiers to make their way home. I am quite certain that nearly all my wounded comrades had similar experiences.

Chapter Thirty

The Journey Home

It is easy to imagine the feelings of any soldier on his way home after a long time away, and especially after being hospitalised. He longs to see his loved ones so much that the slightest delay seems like an eternity.

After arriving in Tashkent from Stalinabad, I spent 24 hours waiting for the next train to Novosibirsk. As soon as I stepped into my carriage, I noticed a young Kazakh soldier on a crutch and walking stick and a young Russian lad walking unaided and without any noticeable injuries. We introduced ourselves, and discovered we were all travelling a long way in the same direction – so we agreed to stick together, and though the two others were only going as far as Zhangiz-Tobe, I decided to get off with them there, instead of going on to Ust-Kamenogorsk.

During the journey our travelling companions kept changing as people got on and off the train. Every new passenger who started talking to us wanted to know our names, where our families lived, where we had been stationed, and all about the battles we had fought in and our injuries. Elderly Kazakhs particularly liked asking all sorts of questions: they even wanted to know who was waiting for us at home and whether our parents were still alive. We patiently answered every question we were asked and all the conversations ended the same way with the people saying, 'How happy your mothers are going to be! God has obviously answered their prayers. And you lads can't have done anything to anger the Almighty either, as you are returning home alive from such a terrible war.'

One of the people we spoke to, a middle-aged Kazakh who found out that we were getting off at the same station, invited us to spend the night with him at his sister's house in Zhangiz-Tobe. But by the time we got there it was one o'clock in the morning, and we were reluctant to trouble his sister. We thanked him but declined his kind offer.

'It is not long till morning now,' we said. 'We'll sit in the station.'

'Forget it,' he said. 'The station hasn't been heated for three years. And nobody in town will let you in to stay the night, especially not this late. Not so long ago an injured soldier like you three froze to death here in the snow.'

So we allowed ourselves to be persuaded.

The next morning we realised how right he had been. During the three years we had been away at war, the station had changed beyond all recognition, and the people had changed a lot as well. Instead of having open houses in the old traditional way, the residents of towns next to railway stations, and of auls and villages on the main roads, were now charging money to put people up for the night. That is why penniless soldiers could find nowhere to stay.

We spent the whole day trying to find transport without coming across a single vehicle or cart. In the late afternoon we started looking for a place to stay near the centre, but people did not even open their doors to us. Instead, they shouted through the crack in their door:

'We've got guests!'

'My husband's not at home!'

'I'm a single woman!'

'I can't and that's that!'

I cannot remember now how many houses we called at on our crutches, but we ended up feeling exhausted, frozen and terribly hungry. It was now dark and we knocked on another door without any hope at all. It opened onto a wide corridor where we could see a few elderly men sitting together. We started complaining about the residents of the aul and asking the men to let us stay the night.

'You cannot sleep here,' said the woman of the house emphatically. 'We are in mourning. It is the seventh day, and people are coming here to mourn this evening.'

But we were desperate, so we started wrangling with her. 'How can you call yourselves Kazakhs?' We said. 'We've been round the whole aul, and no one has let us in. You are practising Muslims: you must know the teachings of the Prophet – that it is a good omen for needy people to be present at gatherings to remember the deceased. You should be inviting us to share your meal, not chasing us away. Have we survived at the front only to freeze to death here in your aul? We're going to spend the night here. Try and make us leave!'

Luckily, one of the elders came up with a solution.

'There's no need to get all worked up, lads,' he said. 'Come with me. I've got somewhere you can sleep.'

It turned out that his only son was away at the front. We stayed with him that night and the following day and were treated as honoured guests. His family talked constantly about their only son who, like us, was having a tough time somewhere.

We spent two days searching for transport. There were plenty of horses and carts bringing grain to the railway station from collective farms and going back empty, but nobody would give us a lift.

'Look, dear lads, it's not the sledge and horses I'm worried about, it's you,' the drivers would say. 'You won't make it in the light clothes you've got on! You'll freeze before you get to Georgievka [the next village].'

It was true that our soldiers' overcoats and boots with puttees were not suitable for such journeys in bitter December frosts with remorseless, penetrating winds. We only struck lucky on our third day, when a farmer from Georgievka finally took pity on us: 'If you reckon you can put up with the frost and wind,' he said, 'get in.'

Thanks be to Allah, we had come across a compassionate man. He did not spare his horses and drove fast, turning off the road and dropping in at the Akzhal mine to give us a chance to warm up. Once we had thawed out, he drove us to his home in the late afternoon. His son of our age was away at the front, and we were well looked after by his wife, who kept saying every now and then, 'My Vanya's also on the move somewhere, like you. Eat up, lads, don't be shy.'

After our freezing cold journey, we began to relax in the warmth, feeling pleasantly full. We slept well and got our strength back. In the morning our host gave us some useful advice:

'The state you're in, lads, you shouldn't be hitching lifts in carts. As soon as you arrive in any village, go straight to the village council. If there isn't one, then go to the collective farm office and see the chairman. It's up to them to find you transport and get you to the next village, or look after you until they do. It's the law.'

So, to help us on our way, he took us to the Georgievka village council. It turned out that we were too late that day, as a group of ex-soldiers had already been dispatched to the next village: we would have to wait until tomorrow. The council chairman took charge of finding us somewhere to stay the night, and I ended up with an elderly couple. The chairman simply said to them, 'This lad's going to be with you until tomorrow morning.' They too had a son at the front, and showed genuine concern for me in a parental sort of way, though in those days having an extra mouth to feed was really difficult for people.

Next morning we and four other ex-soldiers were put in a sledge drawn by a pair of horses that was going to take us to the next village, Terentievka. We were still on our way out of Georgievka when two large trucks drove up behind us – a rare sight so far from the front. Our four companions, who were all walking wounded, flagged them down and arranged a lift; but the three of us were nowhere near fit enough to ride in the back of a truck, and though our companions tried very hard to persuade us to go with them, we decided to stay put in the sledge.

Not long afterwards we caught up with the two trucks again, stuck in the snow. Our former companions were helping the drivers to dig the wheels out. It was now our turn to try and persuade them to continue their journey with us in the sledge: 'Better late than never, lads!' we said.

'Not a chance!' they replied. 'We'll free the wheels any minute now and then we'll get to the next village in less than half an hour. But with those nags, it'll take you all day!'

Our driver headed on, and not long afterwards we turned off the road.

At Terentievka, a kilometre off the road between Georgievka and Kokpekty, we were immediately found somewhere to stay, because a strong snowstorm had blown up and it was impossible for us to go any further that day. The blizzard raged all night long, but we were quite comfortable in our lodgings. Our hostess told us that her collective farm had put her in charge of welcoming ex-servicemen, and once they had left she could claim the food she had given them back so that she was ready to receive her next lot of guests, who might turn up at any time. She assured us that all the collective farms had received similar instructions.

When we woke up the next morning, the gale and snowstorm had completely blown over and it was a brilliantly sunny day with sparkling, squeaky snow. How beautiful it looked!

We were fitted out with sheepskin coats in the collective farm's office, and helped into the sledge, where our legs were carefully covered with a felt rug. Then a fast pair of horses pulled our sledge swiftly to the next village, Nikolayevka, twelve kilometres away.

When we reached the village council, its chairman was just about to set off somewhere. 'A terrible thing has happened!' he told us. 'Two ex-soldiers got caught out on the road last night and froze to death. There were four of them: the other two got frostbite, but they managed to walk here. One of the men who died got as far as the village gate and that's where we found him. You couldn't even go outside, the storm was so bad all last night. The poor lads' bodies have already been taken to the regional centre and the two who survived have been sent to hospital. I'm just about to take some soldiers to the next village, Kalinin: they've been waiting here since yesterday. There are no horses left and won't be any until tomorrow now. So you'd better get in your sledge and follow me to the next aul.'

There could be no doubt about it: the men who got caught in the snow had been our travelling companions. We felt terribly sad for them, meeting such an end after surviving in the front line of a terrible war. They had been so desperate to get home, but had only succeeded in precipitating their own deaths.

ii

Our onward journey from Nikolayevka was marred by a small incident caused by our own hurry. The three of us accepted the chairman's proposal that we follow his sledge carrying the other ex-soldiers who had arrived before us. However, our driver then insisted that our horses needed to rest if they were to cope with the long journey to the next village. So we waited; then, when we were finally ready to leave, he said petulantly, 'I'm not taking you any further. The collective farm chairman told me to take you only as far as Nikolayevka.'

He was an insolent, wilful sort of lad. We tried to explain things to him:

'Didn't you hear what the village council chairman told you? You've got to take us to the next village.'

However, he simply dug his heels in. We tried frightening him by saying we would take his horses without him; but when we started pretending to carry out our threat, and got in the sledge and drove out of the yard and onto the road, he just went on standing there and watching us. So we 'stole' his horses.

It certainly turned out to be a long and difficult journey. It grew dark and we got caught in the infamous *baibura*, cold blizzards that sweep along the ground covering the road with snow. The horses moved slowly and the cold wind went straight through the felt rug covering our canvass boots, turning our feet to ice. Young and foolish, we decided to warm our feet up by walking for a while on our crutches – but, because we were not putting our full weight on them, this only made them even colder. We ended up nearly getting them frost-bitten and only just making it to the Kalinin collective farm in the middle of the night.

As we were supposed to, we hunted for the chairman's house and asked him for somewhere to stay and some food, telling him what a terrible time we had had getting there. He called for someone and told him to look after our horses and us for the night. As we were walking away, it occurred to me that I should get a written note from the chairman acknowledging receipt of our horses, harness, sledge and so on, and he duly signed a piece of paper to that effect – which, as it turned out, saved my bacon later on.

We were put up for the night and fed well by some kind people with a son away at the front. The next morning we wandered over to the collective farm office and found a group of eight other ex-soldiers waiting to be dispatched. We were put in two sledges harnessed to camels and taken the twelve kilometres to the next aul, Dombai. It was lunchtime and we were split into two groups and taken off to have a meal. The six of us in our group, all injured men, were given a single bowl of fried wheat and a samovar of boiling water to share between us. Our hostess kept saying guiltily, 'Don't think badly of me, my dears. Everything I can offer you is on the table. Just now we're living on strictly rationed grain that's weighed out by the collective farm for us. Honest, we are. If I had something to treat you to, how could I not give it to you poor souls?'

You could tell from her voice she was telling the truth. She had several children, and hearing her describe in such a stark and grim manner how people on the home front were semi-starving made me feel anxious and alarmed.

Our departure from Dombai aul, which was by a section of the road with the worst snow drifts, revealed just how impoverished and rundown the collective farm was – and that it was not only the war that had ruined it.

Just as in other villages, the people in this aul were anxious to get rid of us by the evening and deliver us to the next village. But when the other ex-servicemen, and particularly the men from Russian villages, saw that the villagers had got a pair of sledges harnessed to bulls ready for us, they exclaimed angrily, 'This is an insult to men who shed blood for their country and are returning home as invalids! Why haven't you prepared horses for us? Give us horses!'

Then the farm management explained that they did not have any horses on the collective farm except for three half-starved nags that were unfit for work. When my comrades refused to believe them, one of the local leaders piped up, 'Go and take a look at them yourselves!'

They led us all to the so-called 'horse yard' to prove their innocence. Standing in front of us were three desperately skinny creatures bearing a vague resemblance to horses, suspended by two ropes under their bellies. They were so frail that they could not stand upright any more and if they lay down, they would not be able to get up again.

They had clearly not been draught animals on the farm. What was more likely was that the managers had used them as riding horses. If these men had not even been able to look after three horses, you could not help wondering how they organised work on the farm and how much concern they felt for the people of their aul. Clearly, farming standards were appallingly low, and it was hardly surprising that their subordinates were reduced to living a hand-to-mouth existence on strictly rationed grain.

While we were arguing about transport on that short December day, the sun began dipping towards the west. In the end we had to make do with the two bull-drawn sledges. With all eleven of us huddled together, we had travelled no more than two kilometres when one of the bulls got stuck in a snowdrift, fell over and lay there, unable to get to its feet. It was hard to tell whether the poor, half-starved animal was really exhausted or simply didn't want to go any further, but it would not get up, no matter how we tried. Then all the walking injured without leg injuries set off on foot. It was ten to twelve kilometres to the next aul. Only us three – the two of us on crutches and the third with an injured chest – stayed put in the sledge that was now being pulled by the other bull.

The temperature dropped and the frost began biting hard. The bull ambled slowly along, and kept stopping as though trying to decide whether to take another step. How was it to understand the critical situation we were in? We were afraid to make it go faster in case it too collapsed. The others had walked on far ahead. As we rode along, we imagined the blissfully warm lodgings and hot supper our companions would surely have prepared for us by the time we reached our destination.

But when, late at night, we finally arrived at Chiorny Kliuch aul, our companions were still out in the freezing cold street knocking on gates, doors and windows. Nobody had been willing to give them shelter in the middle of the night. So we joined them. At long last someone opened their door, took us inside, and showed us that his house was already full of travellers like us and there was no more room. To make up for it, he pointed out a large house belonging to the collective farm brigade leader, and told us only two people lived there and they had no guests staying with them that night. So the whole lot of us trudged over there. In reply to our request a female voice on the other side of the door called out, 'My husband's not at home. I'm alone. I'm afraid to let you into the house. Go to another house where the owner's in.'

'Where's your husband?' one of my companions asked, thinking that he might be away at the war.

'He's gone to fetch some hay. He'll be back tomorrow,' she replied, unconvincingly.

We had already been to all the houses in the vicinity and had nowhere else to go. And we were absolutely frozen. Those of us with injured legs were suffering particularly badly from the cold.

So we agreed among ourselves to break into the brigade leader's house and stay there overnight in the warm. Some of us began battering down the door. The woman opened it at once. We then swarmed into the far room and got the woman and a friend who was with her to move into the front room. It was cosy inside and we quickly warmed up.

We were all famished after being so badly fed in the last aul, so we asked the woman about getting supper; but all she produced was a bowl of fried wheat for the eleven of us to share, and plain boiling water with a dash of milk. When we started grumbling and hinting that we wanted something more substantial, she told us that life was no better there than at the previous aul. She added, however, that there had been an incident nearby not so long ago when thousands of imported sheep had frozen to death as they were being driven from China. A strong snowstorm had apparently caught the flock out on the steppe road and the snow had frozen to their fleeces and covered them all over, turning them into lumps of ice and killing them. The carcasses had been brought to a neighbouring yard and massive piles of them were lying there.

'If you were to go and ask,' she said, 'you might get a carcass. After all, you've been defending the country for us. And then you'll have some supper.'

So we made a plan. Three of us would go to ask for a carcass; one would stay outside, while the other two went in to discuss matters. If we got what we wanted, we would return immediately; if not, the 'delegation' would stay put and continue the talks, and while we were inside, our third 'delegate' would nip in and steal a carcass.

Off we went. The herdsmen refused point blank to give us any meat, saying they would get into trouble if they did. After sitting there for an adequate length of time, we went back to our lodgings to find a stolen sheep's carcass lying on a ledge by the stove. It looked just like a big lump of snow with legs sticking out of it. There was no way we could cut it up until it had defrosted, so we put it in the front room to thaw out.

A short while later, the herdsmen somehow discovered one of the carcasses had gone missing and came round to ask for it back. They sat there for a long time, explaining that they would be prosecuted under strict wartime regulations unless we returned it. But we kept saying no, until one of our men then decided that the carcass had probably thawed out enough and we should start cutting it up, even though the herdsmen were still there. Off he went to fetch it – only to discover that it had vanished. The herdsmen had played the same trick on us: while we were busy listening to them, another herdsman had tiptoed in and taken the carcass back. Served us right!

iii

On the morning of 31 December 1944, the eleven of us shared a kilogram of fried wheat for breakfast at the brigade leader's house and then got ready to leave. The aul council members were anxious to dispatch us as quickly as possible so that they would not have to feed us any more. We were driven in two sledges drawn by camels to Kokpekty village, the centre of the local region. As we did not have far to go, we arrived by midday and were taken to the regional collective farmers' 'clubhouse', or guesthouse as it really was.

We were hoping for a better reception, more comfortable lodgings and larger meals here than in the aul, since Kokpekty was a regional centre. For a start, we were hoping not to be given 'bird food' any more. Most of our group had acquaintances or relatives they could stay with; only one other man besides me had nobody to go to, so the two of us stayed by the gates of the guesthouse. It turned out to be locked. We hung around there for what seemed like ages. By the time the young girl in charge showed up, we were well and truly frozen.

The girl opened the doors, took us inside, handed us some bedding and showed us two iron beds. The house was freezing cold because it had not been heated since the beginning of winter. When we asked in astonishment how we were going to sleep there and if there was anywhere else more suitable, the girl replied, 'You can stay if you want to. If you don't want to, leave right now, and I'll lock it up again. I haven't got time to deal with you: today's Sunday and it's my day off!'

We had nowhere else to go, so we had to stay in the room that we immediately nicknamed 'The Iceberg'. My companion, Georgy Bogatov, was an old acquaintance of mine – he had been a colleague at the school I taught at. He had fought in the Finnish war and then come to our school as a junior lieutenant in the reserve in the autumn of 1940 to teach military affairs, a subject that was introduced to our schools at that time. He left for the war in the very first week, and now – after being wounded at the front and losing most of his sight in both eyes – he was returning home to our village as a senior lieutenant with several medals on his chest. We had, of course, been delighted to see each other again when we met as part of the group of eleven at Kalinin aul, and to Bogatov it was a godsend to have a companion he could rely on, since he now needed a guide all the time.

So there we were, two injured veterans, one lame and on two crutches, the other virtually blind, all alone like people who had got lost in the deserted *taiga* and stumbled across an empty hunting lodge where there was no firewood or anything to eat. That Sunday all the State offices and food outlets in the regional centre were closed; nor did anyone turn up to help us. Not only were we shivering with cold, but we had terrible hunger pains from not having eaten since the day before.

By the time that the last day of 1944 drew to a close, we were well and truly frozen. We started trying to work out how to warm the room up and save ourselves from dying of hypothermia. The guesthouse did, in fact, have a stove that was supposed to heat the two rooms, so as it was getting dark we went outside in search of firewood. The small yard had a wattle fence around it and that is what we decided to use. As I was on crutches, I could not carry anything, but Bogatov's arms and legs were in good shape, so I guided him towards the wattle fence and then put his hands on it. He quickly started pulling the rods and withies out of the fence until there was a whole pile of them. Then he picked up an armful of such wood and I guided him back inside. Back in the room, we stuffed it into the stove and lit it; but the stove had grown cold over the winter and its flues and chimney had stopped drawing, so all the smoke came pouring into the room. We started choking.

'Don't panic, it'll be all right. My ancestors always used to heat their huts like this,' said Bogatov, trying to laugh it off.

'We'll see how it goes for a while. There's a chimney, after all, and it should start drawing before too long,' I said reassuringly. However, things did not go according to plan: as soon as the smoke started rising up the chimney and the stove warmed up, the stove's walls started cracking and smoke seeped through into the room again. We managed to warm up slightly by midnight, but it was not the ideal way to see in what was to be the year of victory – just the two of us, famished and huddling by a stove in a miserable rundown house.

When we tried to turn in, we found it impossible, because all the bedding was so cold from being in an unheated room; we had to warm it up by putting the mattresses and pillows on the hot stove and holding the blankets up against the fire. This took even more of that dreadful night. We finally got to bed just before dawn, only to find ourselves devoured by lice and bedbugs.

Day brought even more derisive treatment from the people of Kokpekty. It was a public holiday and nobody was at work, so we were left fend for ourselves as though we were in a deserted village. We managed to warm up the house, but we could not get warm ourselves because we were feeling too hungry. We had hardly eaten anything for nearly three days except the tiny portions of fried wheat, and we had eaten nothing at all for the past 24 hours.

Bogatov suggested going to the local military registration office, as even on a public holiday someone was bound to be on duty there. He was right, but the officer we found told us emphatically that we were the local authority's responsibility and he had no funds to help us. He then started enquiring about the routes we had taken to Kokpekty, saying that he had received a telegram regarding the theft of a pair of horses from Terentievka by some ex-soldiers. The details and time of the theft tallied with our itinerary: fortunately, I was able to show him my receipt from the collective farm manager, and that put an end to his questions.

While we were there we tried telephoning a couple of high-ranking local party officials to ask for their help, but neither of them answered. By that time it was nearly midday. We came out of the office, perplexed and unsure what to do next. As we were walking down the street, lost in our own thoughts, Bogatov all of a sudden said in a decisive tone, 'Take me to the post office.'

'What are we going to do there? Who's going to give us anything? I bet the only people there today will be young telephone operators,' I said; but Bogatov insisted.

At the post office, Bogatov asked the telephone operator to give him the regional procurator's home number. At first, she refused point blank; but then Bogatov showed her his officer's shoulder straps, medals, identity card and medical injuries certificate, and the woman had pity on him and gave it to him. He then telephoned the procurator at home, and as soon as he was connected said:

'Comrade procurator, I am a senior lieutenant of the Soviet Army. I narrowly escaped being killed by the Fascists at the front. Because of my injuries I am now on my way home and I am dying of cold and hunger in your regional centre. I haven't eaten for two days and I am freezing to death in an unheated room. I haven't come across anyone in the village I can turn to. I need your help urgently. If you can't help me now, it is unlikely I will last another night. Remember, Comrade procurator, if anything happens to me tonight and they find my body in the morning, I will leave a note in my pocket blaming all the people of Kokpekty and you personally. I am saying all this in the presence of the telephone operators at the exchange and another hungry ex-soldier like me.'

When he had finished, he listened to the voice on the other end for a while; then he hung up and said, 'The procurator's invited us at one o'clock to the office of the Regional Consumers' Union. He said that he'd get all the officials who should be looking after us to go there – that is, if he can find anyone on a public holiday. They'll sort out about our food there.'

We waited for one o'clock with a sense of relief, though the remaining 90 minutes seemed to drag on and on as if the hands of the clock and the sun were standing still.

Such was the difficulty of feeding two strangers in those straitened times that when we arrived at the office, we found a whole committee there, including the procurator himself and the top managers from the regional consumers' union and the local village stores. It was agreed that once a day the village stores would provide us with the daily ration for two people of meat, butter and grain from the reserves. In our presence they summoned the local canteen chef and the food storeman, and arranged for the chef to make a hot supper for us and serve it to us by five o'clock. It never occurred to any of them that after three days of hunger we might find it difficult to keep going until the evening; but we were still pleased with the way things had worked out.

Our joy, however, was short-lived. When we turned up at the canteen for our private supper at the agreed time, already savouring the taste of meat broth and gruel with a knob of butter in it, the chef came out with bowls of bland watery soup made from frozen cabbage and two small, half-rotten salted *chebak* (freshwater fish) each. When we kicked up a fuss, the chef insisted that these were the only products he had been given by the storeman. Nobody knew why this was so, but maybe he would deliver the other products the next morning. It was dusk by this time. Where would we go to complain in the dark, and to whom? Cursing the storeman, we went back to our guesthouse and set to work again, doing somebody else's job of lighting the stove and heating up our room.

Next morning, the breakfast waiting for us was the same as supper the evening before. How could he do such a thing to us! At that moment we felt as though all the troubles in the world – the war, its disastrous consequences, the grave situation in the country, the shortage of food, absolutely everything – was the fault of this arch-enemy of ours, the storeman. Beside ourselves with rage, we furiously cursed him, or rather the chef who happened to be standing there at the time.

We went back to the consumers' union office to complain. Seated opposite each other in the small, cramped office were the two people supposed to be supervising our food provisions: the chairman of the regional consumers' association and, perched on the only spare stool, the chairman of the general stores. Obviously taken aback, they started hurriedly trying to sort things out. The main culprit, the storeman, was sent for. The two of us stood by the office doorway waiting for him to turn up. Nobody offered either me, leaning on my crutches, or Bogatov a seat: but then, what would you expect of such people?

Bogatov whispered in my ear, 'Tug my sleeve as soon as the storeman comes in.'

At long last, the man who was to blame for all our troubles appeared. Unfortunately for him, he stopped right by my incensed companion. As soon as I tugged on his sleeve, Bogatov turned round, swung his fist, and thumped the storeman really hard on the head. The man got such a shock that he leapt over the chairman's desk and tried to hide behind his back. Bogatov lunged forward as he did so and knocked over the stool the other chairman was sitting on, sending him crashing to the floor, where he lay sprawled out and blinking in astonishment. But Bogatov kept trying to grab his victim across the small desk, shouting in a frenzied rage, 'For ridiculing us the way you have these past two days, you Fascist, I'm going to finish you off right now in front of everyone here!'

In the end, Bogatov calmed down and our modest demands were met. It was decided we would be given above-average quotas of dry rations from the storehouse for the past two days and additional grain for our journey later that day, as well as a hot meal before we left (we made it clear that we wanted meat dishes for the first and second courses). Still, what a palaver it was! Meat, for instance, could only be added to a dish with the permission of the regional consumers' union; as for bread, they did not have a single loaf in their store. When we indignantly asked what we were going to do on our journey with no bread and only uncooked grain, the chairman sent his assistant to borrow a small loaf from the orphanage in the regional centre – but the orphanage's director refused to give him one. In the end, the chairman – the region's top official in charge of food distribution – had to go and get it in person. Such were the consequences of the long, devastating war on the home front.

So we had our first normal meal of the New Year, and then set off straightaway to the village council, where we found a horse harnessed to a sledge and a driver waiting for us with a spare sheepskin coat, all ready to leave. My companion had a warm army coat and felt boots on, so he did not need anything extra for the journey, but I knew that my injured feet would need better protection than my thin canvas boots in such cold weather, so I asked for another sheepskin coat or a felt rug; but the local officials made out that they could find neither.

The short winter day was drawing to a close, and the local village council chairman, who had lost an arm at the front, started urging us to leave: 'Listen, friend, there's a dairy farm about twelve kilometres from here along the way. It'll only take you an hour to get there and your feet won't freeze in that time. You can drop by the farm and warm your legs up. And then it's only another thirteen kilometres to Bolshaya Bukon and if you travel fast again, your legs won't have time to freeze. Off you go now, there's a good lad. I had to travel just the same as you back from the front. If you hang about and don't leave now, you'll have to stay here until tomorrow.'

After hesitating for a while, I talked things over with my companion and we decided it was better to leave than stay in such an inhospitable place as Kokpekty any longer.

iv

The frost at once started biting fiercely and penetrating all the seams in my sheepskin coat, particularly at the back. My feet began freezing. After three or four kilometres the horse slowed down: we were obviously going to take longer than planned. There was still a long way to go to the warm dairy farm, but my feet were already numb with cold. I began to worry they might get further injured with frostbite, and regretted that I had agreed to leave as I was; my companion tried to cover my boots with the folds of his coat, but it did not help. We began wondering if we should turn back before we had gone too far.

The winter sun was already sinking towards the horizon, and a bitterly cold mist was now reducing visibility. I could feel the temperature dropping. We had just made up our minds to turn back when all of a sudden we heard the high-pitched swishing sound of sledge runners behind us; so we decided to stop and wait for the sledge to catch us up, and ask for help.

The young teenager who was driving us was not encouraging. 'Sounds like one of the regional officials or collective farm chairmen,' he said. 'They're the only ones with well-fed horses these days. They don't usually give anyone a lift: in fact, they always try to go past carts and people on foot as fast as they can. This one's not going to stop either. You can tell from the sound of the sledge – he's going too fast.'

How could we make him stop? We decided to block the road by turning our old horse and sledge sideways. But what if he was to get round the side of us and gallop on?

Bogatov had an idea: 'Where do you reckon he'll pass us? Lead me there. I'll be able to make out the horse's outline. I'll grab hold of the reins and make him stop.'

But while we were discussing things, the sledge drew up, with a pair of fine-looking horses that started impatiently prancing on the spot. A big, thickset man said to us, 'What are you doing, lads? Why have you blocked the road?'

I explained the predicament we were in and asked him to give us a lift.

'My dear lads, why of course I will! Get in! You shouldn't have to ask favours! What a nag they've given you, God damn them! The vile devils, they've got no compassion even for invalids who've been defending the people!'

He went on cursing and tutting while he helped me get into his sledge. It was lined with soft, wispy hay and had backrests. A heifer calf, six months old or so, was lying in the back with its feet tied together. The pair of horses set off at a lively trot again, pulling their heavy load with alacrity. But my feet still felt unbearably cold and numb.

'Agai [Uncle],' I said to our kind driver, 'please don't spare your horses. My feet are so frozen, I'm afraid I might lose them. Let's get to the farm as quickly as possible. We'll call in and I'll warm my feet up.'

'Right, lad, turn around. Now tuck your feet between the calf's back legs. They'll warm up in no time. We won't even need to call in at the farm. I'll get you to Bolshaya Bukon in a flash. Come on, sweethearts, giddy-up!' He urged the horses on.

I sat there for a while as the man had suggested, and the animal's groin was so warm, it felt like I was sitting by a stove.

I cheered up and started chatting to our rescuer. He was apparently on his way back from the regional centre, where he had taken his chairman from the Karaganda-kul collective farm. I might no longer remember his name, but I have never forgotten how kind he was to us. If he had not come along, I would definitely have got my feet frost-bitten, and heaven alone knows how my return home might have ended.

He dropped us that night by the collective farm office of Bolshaya Bukon village. There was, of course, nobody waiting there for us, but we were simply delighted just to find the office open at such a late hour. The stoker, it turned out, had dropped in to see to the stove.

We decided to spend the night in the office because it was warm. We had the loaf of bread for our supper. Another man suddenly appeared, but he obviously guessed who we were at once, and tried to slip away. The stoker, however, quickly whispered to us, 'He's the collective farm's brigade leader in charge of injured soldiers.'

The brigade leader turned out to be a young Cossack, about 30 years old, or maybe less. We asked him to find us somewhere to spend the night: we did not mind going anywhere as long as we had access to boiling water. We had our own food with us and we would not be a burden to anyone.

The Cossack took us to one of the nearby houses, explained to the owner that we were injured ex-soldiers, and instructed him to put us up for the night. The man said nothing, but his wife started angrily berating the brigade leader: 'Why do you always come to us first? We took in another two of them only a few days ago. Take them to someone else or better still, to your own home.'

'Don't get upset, love,' we said. 'There's no need to take offence or be rude to us. Let us in for the night. Maybe you've got a son a long way from home, looking for somewhere to rest his head like us. We've got our own food. Just heat up some water for us, please – that's all we need.'

During my long journeys, I had learnt how to stir maternal instincts. Practically every household had seen a son, husband or brother off to the war, and half of them were waiting for news from the front. Even the dourest families of Red Army men lightened up when they remembered their loved ones. So it was with this woman, after the mention of her son.

'All right,' she said to the brigade leader, 'they can stay the night.'

As soon as he heard her say this, the Cossack hurriedly slipped out the door.

In the traditional Kazakh way, the couple then proceeded to ask us all sorts of questions about our clans and families at home, our time at the front and our journey. The woman warmed to us and, despite our objections, went off to boil some meat in our honour. After going without food and freezing for several days in a row, what more could we have wished for?

In the morning we walked over to the collective farm office to continue our journey. Believe it or not, there waiting for us was the collective farm chairman's own light sledge harnessed to a pair of spirited bays, and with two sheepskin coats ready for us. But after my experience the day before, I refused to leave until I had been brought a pair of felt boots or a sheepskin to cover my legs. In the end the chairman, who was a Russian like most of the people in the village, sent home for a pair of his own boots and handed me the felt ones he was wearing.

The bays covered the thirteen kilometres to the next aul at a cracking pace in less than an hour. Ornek turned out to be a small Kazakh collective farm consisting of twenty households. There were two girls sitting in the office, who told us that there were only three men left in the aul: the collective farm chairman, the farm manager and an old herdsman. None of them were around at the time. It was up to the chairman and manager to organise our transport, so we would have to wait for them.

We waited for ages. In the end, the girls decided to try and find the manager and spent a long time searching for him, but without success.

Somehow or other we needed to cover another fifteen kilometres to get to Shugylbai aul, where relations of mine lived and we would not have to worry about accommodation or food. In anticipation of this, we had left all our food from Kokpekty with our hospitable hosts the night before. Now we again had nothing to eat.

It was past midday and we were still waiting. We cautiously asked the girls about lunch.

'Nobody in our aul will be able to feed you as we're all on strictly weighed daily rations. There's only one house you'll find any food in – the chairman's. His wife is a "sister" of your comrade,' one of the girls said, referring to Bogatov's Russian nationality. 'Maybe she'll offer her "brother" a cup of tea.'

What a contrast in living standards there was between the Russian village we had just left, where people had sufficient food put by to feed unexpected guests such as us, and this Kazakh collective farm, only ten kilometres away! Of course the residents in Russian villages were also having a hard time – the war was a common cause and had disastrous consequences for everyone in the country; but there was no escaping the fact that the Kazakh communities we passed through were much worse off.

We had to wait nearly the whole day for the men. Eventually we began to worry that we would have to spend the night there, so we went and knocked on the door of the chairman's house. The door was opened by a friendly young Russian woman with fair hair and blue eyes. How she came to be in this small Kazakh aul, heaven alone knows. She immediately grasped the situation and invited us in.

'I haven't any food ready right now but I've made some pastry dough for *baursak*,' she said. 'If you don't mind waiting a little while longer, I'll put them in the oven and make some tea and then you can have them together.'

She started running about the house getting things ready; but we never got to eat them. The collective farm's one and only camel arrived to take us on the next leg of our journey, and as we did not have far to go and had reliable friends the other end, we said our goodbyes and set off without waiting for our tea.

The camel pulled us faster than a mythological animal searching for a promised land in the Kazakh steppe. Within an hour it had reached the village where some of my relatives lived.

v

Aunt Rabiga, whose house we were looking for in Shugylbai aul, had been married to my cousin Muksiin Nurmukhambetov, the owner of the holy yurt which had caused so much anxiety fifteen years before. After his death, Aunt Rabiga had lost three of her four young children to the famine, and dire circumstances had forced her to marry a much older man and go to live in his aul.

She had not seen me for a long time, but when I suddenly turned up on crutches at their door in the fading light, she recognised me at once. She embraced me and began crying and lamenting in the traditional Kazakh manner. Not having come across this custom before, Bogatov was rather startled at first. With a mix of sorrow and joy, she congratulated me on my return and thanked the Almighty for saving my life, cursed Hitler and remembered her dead relatives and acquaintances in the army, and told me about the hardships of her life on the home front.

People were so tired of waiting for their loved ones who had been away fighting at the front, and worried so much about what was happening to them, that whenever anyone's relatives returned home, the whole aul rejoiced with them as though with their own fathers, brothers and husbands. Aunt Rabiga's neighbours and relatives – people we had never set eyes on before – came joyfully rushing over to congratulate her and take a look at us.

'This lad is a brother of my Batken,' she said, referring to her 20-year-old daughter, as she introduced me to them all.

In honour of our arrival, Rabiga invited six neighbouring families round and organised a small party. The women sat around the modest meal laid out on the *dastarkhan*, chatting happily and enjoying themselves without a drop of alcohol in sight, partying until well after midnight. They sang lots of songs full of yearning for their loved ones fighting against the enemy thousands of kilometres away.

Next day we had a steam bath, slept and rested. After two weeks of having slept in our clothes, suffering from the bitter cold, and practically forgetting what real food tasted like, we at last felt human again.

It turned out that my cousin Batken was married and living with her husband's elderly parents. Her husband too was away in the army. She had the second best job after the collective farm chairman in terms of having access to food, as she was in charge of the storehouse. She was just as delighted as her mother that I had returned from the front alive, and took it upon herself to organise plenty of enjoyable things for us to do on our second day of rest.

Then she asked for a week's leave from work, borrowed a horse from the collective farm, and drove us the 40 or 50 kilometres back to our village. It was the most deserted section of the road, straddling two districts, and we travelled slowly because the horse had trouble pulling the sledge over the trackless snow. On the way we stopped for an hour to feed it and let it rest; and so it was that an elderly woman and young girl from our village came across us on our journey, and went running on ahead through the light, crumbly snow, trying to get to Kamyshenka first to spread the joyful news – not only to my family, but to all the other villagers as well – that after two years and ten months at war, I had finally come home.

EPILOGUE

MUKHAMET SHAYAKHMETOV realised his dream of becoming a teacher. The boy who had been expelled from school as a kulak's son rose to be head of his local education department, and headmaster of a secondary school in Ust-Kamenogorsk – a position which he held for 25 years, until his retirement in 1981.

In 1945 he married his sweetheart Nurkamal, who was a teacher in a neighbouring village. They have three sons and a daughter, as well as grandchildren and great-grandchildren.

GLOSSARY

Aul   A nomadic community of people belonging to the same clan or related through marriage. The term denotes both the extended family and the collection of yurts or temporary dwellings in which it lives.

Baursak   A dish consisting of fried pieces of pastry.

Belsendi   Political activists.

Britska   A pony trap.

Brother *etc*   Relationships are often metaphorically exaggerated to express respect and degrees of closeness. Thus a male cousin may be referred to as 'brother', an aunt as 'mother', and older man as 'uncle' or 'grandfather' *etc*.

Dastarkhan   A table or table-cloth, also meaning 'feast', 'abundance' or 'hospitality'.

Dzhigit   A youth or young warrior.

Kishlak   A village.

Kulak   A well-off peasant, identified as a 'class enemy'.

Region   An administrative area, smaller than a 'district'. A 'regional centre' is the village or town from which it is run.

Taiga   Coniferous sub-Arctic forests.

Talkan   A dish consisting of fried grains of wheat.

Yurt   A nomadic tent made up of wooden poles and withie-and-osier sections clad with felt matting.

Zhuz   A peaceable 'second-tier' system of allegiance – of which there are three – in Kazakh society, deriving from territorial presence, grazing practices and tribal allegiances.